AF333273

UNINTENDED AFFINITIES

Russian and East European Studies

Jonathan Harris, Editor

UNINTENDED AFFINITIES

Nineteenth-Century German and Polish Historians on the
Holy Roman Empire and Polish-Lithuanian Commonwealth

ADAM KOŻUCHOWSKI

University of Pittsburgh Press

Published by the University of Pittsburgh Press, Pittsburgh, Pa., 15260
Copyright © 2019, University of Pittsburgh Press
All rights reserved
Manufactured in the United States of America
Printed on acid-free paper
10 9 8 7 6 5 4 3 2 1

Cataloging-in-Publication data is available from the Library of Congress

ISBN 13: 978-0-8229-6571-8
ISBN 10: 0-8229-6571-2

Cover design: Alex Wolfe

To the memory of Jerzy Jedlicki (1930–2018)

CONTENTS

ACKNOWLEDGMENTS

This book was first published in Polish as *Powinowactwa mimo woli: Święte Cesarstwo Rzymskie Narodu Niemieckiego i Rzeczpospolita Obojga Narodów w niemieckiej i polskiej historiografii XIX wieku* in 2016 thanks to the support of the DEC-2013/11/D/HS3/02460 grant of the National Science Foundation and with the assistance of the staff of my home institution, the Institute of History at the Polish Academy of Sciences in Warsaw. While working on the book, I greatly profited from discussions with my colleagues: Anna Brus, Magdalena Micińska, Magdalena Gawin, Joanna Nalewajko-Kulikov, Andrzej Wierzbicki, Zbigniew Romek, Maciej Janowski, Maciej Górny, Mariusz Kulik, Aleksander Łupienko, Hans Petter, Krzysztof Niewiadomski, and Mikołaj Getka-Kenig. Patrice Dabrowski and Hans-Jürgen Bömelburg offered me their insightful and inspiring reviews of my work.

Although I initially wrote this work with the foreign reader in mind, I still felt that simply translating the book into English wouldn't be adequate for the American edition. While working on the English-language version, I was able to make use of the reviews provided by Violetta Julkowska, Rafał Stobiecki, and Jacek Wijaczka, as well as remarks by Piotr Biliński. I have added some fragments, removed others, and changed the structure of my narrative, profiting from the insightful suggestions of Peter Kracht from the University of Pittsburgh Press. While struggling against the nuances of English grammar and style, I received enormous help from Elena Rozbicka, James Hartzell, and Robin Krauze. I owe my gratitude to all of them.

A NOTE ON NAMES AND TRANSLATIONS

East European geographical names are always a problem in English-language texts, so I did my best to reduce their number to the necessary minimum. If possible, I employ existing English names (Warsaw, Cracow, Vistula, etc.); if not, I use their present names (Vilnius, Lviv, Poznań, etc.) in the narrative. However, in the bibliography original names have been preserved (and so Lviv becomes Lwów, and Varsovie stands for Warsaw as the place of publication of a book in French). All book titles are rendered in English in the main text but appear in their original language in the endnotes and bibliography. Per its acceptance in modern English-language scholarly literature, "the Commonwealth" refers to the union of Poland and Lithuania, also known as the Republic of Both Nations (I found the latter confusing, as it was, after all, a monarchy inhabited by many peoples). I avoid the German term *Reich* (designating a particular idea of statehood, epitomized by the Holy Empire itself), preferring "the Empire" instead, except for the few citations whose authors, I believe, had in mind more than the Empire. I employ the widely accepted term Rus (and Ruthenian) as the common name referring to the lands of Belarus, Ukraine, and Western Russia before their modern identities were formed. I use the term "Jagiellon dynasty," respecting the Polish tradition of privileging Jogaila (known as Jagiełło in Polish) over his grandfather Gediminas (the name-giver in the Lithuanian tradition). Following some convincing, if complicated, advice I once received from an experienced specialist in medieval history, I prefer the name "Staufen dynasty" over the regrettable form "Hohenstaufen," which, I am afraid, remains much more popular.

All translations, if not indicated otherwise, are mine, as is responsibility for all mistakes and omissions.

INTRODUCTION

This book is an exercise in historical imagination from an era before it became generally acknowledged that the only thing Germans and Poles had ever had in common was mutual antagonism. It examines the ways in which German and Polish historians of the nineteenth century regarded the Holy Roman Empire and the Polish-Lithuanian Commonwealth—two states that symbolized national unity as well as their independence. It is based on the assumption that the histories German and Polish authors narrated shared a number of common, or analogous traits; it attempts to identify them and to articulate the reasons for these parallels.

The Kingdom of Poland, the cornerstone of the Polish-Lithuanian Commonwealth after its union with the Grand Duchy of Lithuania in the sixteenth century, for more than eight hundred years existed alongside the Holy Roman Empire of the German Nation, commonly referred to as the German Reich. In addition to the two countries' common border, they shared at least two other traits. In the final phase of their existence, both countries were considered political anomalies in a Europe dominated by absolute monarchs, and their status as independent political entities was questionable. After the Peace of Westphalia (1648), the Empire was in fact a confederation of independent states whose central governing bodies were subject to consensus, something that proved increasingly difficult over time. From the second decade of the eighteenth century, with the exception of a few short intervals, the Commonwealth was a de facto Russian protectorate whose sovereignty was limited not only by the Russian military stationed on its soil but also by the paralysis of its central political institutions, which were dependent on a parliamentary consensus, achieved no more often than in the Holy Empire. The political similarities between the Empire and the Commonwealth were pointed out by some of the most prominent theoreticians of the era: Jean Bodin, Samuel von Pufendorf, and Gottfried Leibniz.[1]

They also shared a common fate. Between 1772 and 1806, as a result of the aggressive politics of their powerful neighbors, the two countries were wiped from the map of Europe. This double similarity was a topic of consideration for writers of such stature as Edmund Burke, Karl Marx, and Edmund Sorel.[2] On the eve of World War I, Antoine Guilland, in an essay (actually a polemic) on German historiography, put the fall of the Commonwealth and the Empire on a par with the French Revolution—as symptoms of the collapse "of the Middle Ages" and the triumph of the "modern state."[3] In short, they were considered anachronisms doomed to failure.

In more recent historiography, the similarities of the political-constitutional situation, as well as the fates of the Empire and the Commonwealth, have been taken on by Michael Müller, Hans Jürgen Bömelburg, Otto Hintze, Tadeusz Cegielski, and Klaus Zernack, who reach a variety of conclusions.[4] As a side note, it should be added that after nearly a century of decrying the Empire in German nationalist historiography as "at best meaningless and at worst as an obstacle on the road to progress and national unity," interest in the Empire has enjoyed a renaissance in world historiography since the second half of the twentieth century.[5]

This book, however, is not about whether the Empire and the Commonwealth, or German and Polish history in general, were actually similar. Its subject is the parallels in how nineteenth-century historians approached the Empire and the Commonwealth within the framework of national history in Germany and Poland. So at this point it is sufficient to realize that both early modern Germany and Poland took a path that was regarded as significantly different from the one considered to be the standard and desirable one: they did not build up centralized, absolute monarchies, like the British, the French, or the Spanish.

Now, let us for a moment consider what the Germans and Poles of the nineteenth century considered to be their national history. Polish historians of the period wrote of "national history," "the history of Poland" or "old Poland," by which they understood the history of a political community within the framework of both the state and the people. Such histories nearly without exception began in "prehistoric" times, relying more or less on legendary tales from medieval chronicles, with only few continuing to the times of the partitions. As a rule, the historians were not interested in the past of lands that did not fall within the borders of the Kingdom of Poland or the Polish-Lithuanian Commonwealth; the range of their interest changed with the redrawn political borders. Similarly, German historians writing *Deutsche Geschichte* (German history) as a matter of principle considered it to be the history of the lands organized in a "German" state—broadened, if need be, to include mentions of German settlements in adjacent countries, which did not, however, mean including the history of those countries in "German history." Obviously, this refers only to a general framework, to the boundaries of the topic. The emphases within a "national history" could be quite diverse; some authors concentrated strictly on political history, while others highlighted the significance of broader social processes. While one might argue that many Protestant German historians, notably from the so-called Prussian school, depicted the

Empire as "non-national" in the period after the Reformation and as representing a sort of obstacle to the proper development of the nation, this does not change the fact that *Deutsche Geschichte* encompassed the entire Empire within its official parameters, even if the imperial institutions were demonized, disregarded, or ignored in a certain period.

This lengthy caveat is essential in order to understand what will be compared in this book and the sort of unwitting affinity it describes. I do not intend to investigate whether the courses of Polish and German history up to the nineteenth century proceeded according to a common path or whether nineteenth-century historians perceived such parallels (though attempts were made, as discussed below). My focus is on the images of the past, the accuracy of which, in light of more recent research, is of secondary importance to me, as is the question of whether historians at the time noticed the very analogies I am seeking. The interpretation this book offers is "doubled," to use Michel de Certeau's term: I attribute to the texts I analyze meanings their authors did not necessarily recognize.[6] My intent is therefore to point out the analogies one finds in the narratives of German and Polish historians regarding their respective national histories, even if and especially when the authors claimed that these histories were unique and unmatched by any country in the past.

Without yet going into great detail, I acknowledge that this approach can raise general concerns of two sorts. First, it could be said that there is nothing surprising in the fact that the vision of a national past in a given era and in, to a large extent, a similar cultural-historical context would in its projection be similar to an analogous vision. It may seem a banality, demonstrating that historical writing operates within a specific, transnational paradigm, that the same research and writing methods in various countries yield similar results, and that historical imagination is fairly limited overall. Second, this approach can be discredited using the opposite argument: it is obvious that the histories of German and Poland followed completely divergent trajectories, that they revolve around fundamentally different issues, and that, because of this, any comparison would be unwise. Proof of this is that the nineteenth-century historians in these countries would never even have thought of it. German historians compared their history to that of England, France, or perhaps Italy; Polish historians saw their history in the context of Hungary or Bohemia—and one should stick with this scheme.

As for the first argument, I readily agree and even share it to a certain point. Historians of certain periods undoubtedly call on a rather limited set of concepts, methods, arguments, and metaphors—with only very few authors managing to demonstrate any real originality. But this is merely an intuitive assumption, which does not mean that we should not look into whether and to what extent it is true. Despite a number of elegant exceptions, research on the history of historiography, on its conceptual and rhetorical content, remains deeply determined by national divisions.[7] This book is an attempt to counter this tendency. Assuming that thinking and writing about the history of Europe in the nineteenth century were significantly determined by a number of common factors, that a Hegelian zeitgeist hovered over them, this book tries to show what these factors and ideas in fact were through a close examination of German and Polish narratives about their national past. It is possible that if a third country were added to this pair, the results would be markedly similar. To the best of my knowledge, no one has yet undertaken such a task.

As for the second concern, it is burdened with our knowledge of what later took place, after the unification of Germany in the Bismarck era and the festering German-Polish antagonism of the second half of the nineteenth century and the first half of the twentieth. However, even if we assume that this animosity was in fact older, doing so does not prevent us from finding similarities in the antagonists. Enmity is also a sort of bond, and not necessarily a weak one; it forces the relationship of "challenge and response." Also—and of key importance for the premise of this book—the situation looked quite different during the first half of the nineteenth century. Certainly there was much that divided the Germans and the Poles; nonetheless, one can say with considerable certainty that they shared a similar approach to their own histories.

This similarity is based on the fact that from the last partition of the Commonwealth (1795) and the dissolution of the Empire (1806) until the unification of Germany in 1871, neither the Germans nor the Poles had their own state. Naturally, one can say that Germans had their "own" countries, perhaps even too many: between 1815 and 1866, the German Confederation consisted of forty-three entities, among them the Austrian Empire, the Kingdoms of Prussia, Bavaria, Saxony, Hanover, and Württemberg, four free cities, and numerous other, often miniature, principalities. In the eyes of German patriots, however, none of them represented the fundamental German national interest, and the fragmentation itself was considered a painful anomaly. The disappearance of the Empire and the Commonwealth from the map of Europe was seen by many contemporary observers as equal to the end of their constituent nations, at least in the sense of their being political communities. Such, apparently, was the intention of Russia, Prussia, and Austria—the three powers that partitioned Poland-Lithuania between 1772 and 1795 and that agreed never to use the term "Poland" to name any of their newly acquired provinces. After all the turbulence of the Napoleonic Wars, the Congress of Vienna decided to establish the German Confederation (possessing even less power over its members than had the Holy Empire), and the Kingdom of Poland (under the Russian protectorate), encompassing roughly one-fifth of the former Polish-Lithuanian territory.

The German Confederation was widely considered a surrogate for German unity and a "substitute" for the former Empire (as Hans von Gagern put it in 1833). Of course, the notion of unity—symbolized by the Empire—was understood variously. For Catholic conservatives, the mediatized aristocracy, and the declassed political elites of the former free cities, the *Reich* meant the restoration of the old Empire. Liberal youth and intellectuals yearned for a state that would be able to overcome the influences of the conservative aristocracy, which ruled a majority of the German states and principalities. The Romantic national movement saw the Empire in almost mystical terms; Friedrich Ludwig Jahn believed that it should be a subject of prayer.[8] Talleyrand wickedly remarked that it was mainly the impoverished aristocracy and university professors who dreamed of a restoration of the Empire; the latter, however, were in a position to infect their students with their faith. The patriotic youth who had gathered at a convention in Wartburg in October 1817 declared, "Yearning for the Emperor and the Reich remains unshaken in the breast of every German man and youth."[9]

"Poles and Germans," writes Michael Müller, "as nations without national states, found themselves in a similar situation at the beginning of the nineteenth century. Proponents of the early national movements saw in this a commonality of goals. Their aspirations for political emancipation and nationally unified states— of founding a new republic, so to speak—joined Poles and Germans, in a certain sense."[10] In both countries, those who harbored patriotic feelings rued the lack of a united and independent state and saw it as an anomaly; it was simply assumed that Germans and Poles deserved political unity and independence, as they were no worse than the English or the French and as they had already had such states in the past. This popular assumption about German and Polish statehood now brings us to the historians' task.

Broadly speaking, one can say that when writing the histories of the Empire and the Commonwealth, historians faced a challenge dictated by their times (leaving aside, for the moment, the legitimate challenges of research and writing): that of portraying their past in all its glory, as national and patriotic sentiment demanded, while at the same time explaining the causes of their decline and fall. By recalling bygone grandeur and might, historians legitimized the current political aspirations of their compatriots; they designated a time in the past as a point of reference that was at the same time the "horizon of expectations" (according to Reinhart Koselleck's terminology). In this respect, the task German and Polish historians faced did not differ substantially from the patriotically inspired expectations that historians from other countries in that era encountered. If one is to believe Herbert Fisher, this had already been expressed in the German context by J. G. Herder, who nevertheless considered the Empire unworthy of being the exponent of German national aspirations.[11]

What made the German and Polish historians' job unique was the other side of the coin: the need to understand and explain why neither the Empire nor the Commonwealth had endured—a task as analytic from the professional aspect as it was therapeutic from the point of view of the national community. History understood as a social mission forced German and Polish historians into similar situations in a psychological sense: it was their responsibility to describe the "old republics" in the context of both nations' aspirations for their restoration or for the building of a new state for which the historical one would serve as a model or *memento*. They had to explain how it happened that they had once had their own state, which for centuries had seemed a mighty power, and now did not. Who or what was at fault? What lessons can be learned from the histories of the Empire and the Commonwealth?

Proportions and Directions

It seems difficult in many ways to compare the output of historians in Germany and Poland during the nineteenth century, especially when we look at the numbers. History as a separate discipline found its independence in Poland a generation or two later than in Germany and on an incomparably more modest organizational base, which the partitioning powers brutally curtailed. As a result, at the beginning of the twentieth century there were only fourteen chairs of history in Poland, while in Germany there were ninety-three (of these, sixty-four were at universities and twenty-nine constituted equivalent research positions).[12] Even taking into account that a significant amount of Polish research was conducted by amateurs as a sideline to their paid professions or at least outside the academic world, the proportions vary dramatically (Germany also had many amateur historians, many of them highly successful authors). We find a similar disproportion in their international standing in the history of historiography: Polish historians of the period are mentioned only marginally, if at all; German historians hold a respectable and sometimes even a central place. Niebuhr, Ranke, Savigny, Droysen, and Mommsen—to name only a few—are considered to have made original and significant contributions to the development of their discipline and to its methodology at the international level, at least since the publication of Lord Acton's article, "German Schools of History," in the first issue of the *English Historical Review*, in 1886.[13]

There is also little doubt that intellectual exchange between the two countries flowed overwhelmingly in one direction. Among the 220 people whom Andrzej F. Grabski counted and classified as researchers or authors who were engaged in history in Poland in the four decades prior to World War I, nearly 100 had studied in Germany or Austria. Despite the fierce ideological and political antipathy toward some trends in German historical scholarship that were predominant toward the end of the century, Polish scholars widely recognized its model status, as exemplified by the comment of Wincenty Zakrzewski, a historian who wrote in 1897 that German history "sets the scientific standard and separates the professionals from the dilettantes."[14]

While I do not dispute the disparity between the two historical cultures, I also do not think that one should be daunted by it. First, Polish (as well as Czech or Hungarian) historiography of the nineteenth century cannot be seen as merely a miniature (both literally and figuratively) version of its powerful German cousin. The dynamics of their development were simply different—Polish historians often followed the examples of the French and English rather than the Germans. Second, as I already mentioned, the subject of this book is how the two countries responded to the same basic question: What happened to our country and why do we not have our own national state? This will lead us to see how they evoke similar emotions, metaphors, ideology, and values and employ similar narrative solutions. Finally, it seems that national history as a paradigm or an intellectual field compelled these historians to entertain a set of themes and to respond to a number of questions in a specific way (such as which era, rulers, and events in the history of the nation bring us glory and which bring shame). As Monika Baár writes in her book on the Romantic historians of central Europe, "Expectations from a nation with an 'established position' included a glorious history, which was *ancient, continuous, unified and unique.* These leading themes appeared in countless variations, but on the whole, the core aspects were considered axiomatic and had to be articulated and justified through well-grounded historical arguments."[15]

Despite their obvious inclinations to "stretch" the historical narrative in the direction of the above-mentioned axioms, historians did have to work with the specific material that was at hand, and despite their best intentions, not everything could be stretched. In general, it would seem that nineteenth-century historians best demonstrated imagination and creativity in their recasting of antiquity and the uniqueness of their own national history and institutions—much attention was devoted to the alleged forebears of their peoples, such as the British Anglo-Saxons or the French Gauls.[16] In the case of the Germans, as we shall see, they reached back as far as the Aryans of India.

Nevertheless, substantial differences arose. Out of necessity, the unity of national history was less emphasized in Germany, as regional historiography stubbornly struggled to outpace the national. In the understanding of many historians, it was precisely these strong regional and traditional differences that determined the uniqueness of German history and were even, as Heinrich Leo put it, the source of its "depth."[17] Only a tiny minority of Polish historians underscored links between prehistoric Slavs and Polish national history, much to the detriment of its ancient history, for doing so would have been a risky political endeavor in the context of Russian pan-Slavism.

Speaking of politics, one must also remember that both historical cultures shared a mind-set because their situation at that time—being bereft of a national state—was perceived by both Poles and Germans (until 1871) as profoundly unsatisfactory. Affirming their national past, the historians of both countries were malcontents for whom the sense of national history remained unfulfilled. In this respect they differed substantially from such Western observers as the Whigs, who saw the British electoral reforms of 1832 as the crowning achievement of their country's exceptional path of development that had begun with the Glorious Revolution of 1688, or the French liberals, who wrote of the July Revolution of 1830 in a similar tone.[18] In 1764, the Polish Jesuit Szymon Majchrowicz could still claim in *The Fortunate Endurance of Kingdoms or Their Lamentable Downfall before the Eyes of a Free Nation* that the Commonwealth would forever enjoy God's special favor, thanks to its orthodox Catholicism, because he could not have imagined the partitions.[19] In Germany, it was only after 1871 that it was possible to consider the vision of a national history as being essentially fulfilled, an interpretation that soon became trivialized as national dogma. It is important to note that historians from the Prussian school (e.g., Sybel, Droysen, Häusser) enjoyed fame as coauthors of the new state, thanks in equal measure to their scholarly work, their journalistic activities, and their political involvement. Disputes about appraising the past, the patriotic historian Walter Goetz asserted in 1919 with satisfaction, had been silenced, in accordance with Heinrich von Sybel's postulate of mutual trust between the state and its citizens.[20]

Texts Analyzed and Their Contexts

The texts I have selected for analysis represent of course only a modest portion of the enormous number of works produced in the long nineteenth century, and they are, as is nearly always the case, the result of a selection process that is in part arbitrary. The task of identifying the most "representative" texts and authors within the entire historical legacy of the two countries represents a rather tricky endeavor. I have tried to consider the main trends and various "schools" of history as evenly as possible according to their significance and popularity, while giving voice to various points of view. Still, as we shall see on closer examination of these texts, such divisions should be treated with caution: sometimes they tell us more about what kind of history the given author had in mind than about what the author actually wrote.

I have focused on syntheses of national history, giving voice to a number of authors who are largely forgotten today. Yet, some highly influential historians never wrote such a synthesis, so I had to complement my selection with monographs covering particular periods of national history, along with a number of articles of crucial importance for the development of the debate about the Empire and the Commonwealth.

Let us begin with Poland. Chronologically, my choice of texts begins with the highly popular *Historic Songs* by Julian Ursyn Niemcewicz (1757–1841), probably the last work representative of Enlightenment ideas. The next stage is marked by the appearance of Joachim Lelewel (1786–1861), famous both for his Romantic interpretation of Polish history and for his personal engagement in politics, he being an adherent of republican democracy.[21] Given Lelewel's enormous body of work, I focus primarily on his most composite and comprehensive synthesis: *Considerations on the History of Poland and Her People*, first published in French in 1844. Another influential Romantic author whom I consider here is Karol Szajnocha (1818–68), who wrote extensively on the union of Poland with Lithuania. From among the many works that are more or less aptly considered imitations of Lelewel's writings, I have chosen to take a closer look at the most comprehensive and perhaps most serious of them: the four-volume *History of the Polish Nation from Ancient Times*, by the Lviv scholar Henryk Schmitt (1817–83), published as a series in the 1860s.[22] His contemporary ideological opponents are represented here by Karol Boromeusz Hoffman's (1798–1875) *History of Political Reforms in Old Poland*.

The so-called Cracovian school, dominating the scene in the third quarter of the nineteenth century and famous for its opposition to Romanticism, is represented here by the four-volume *History of Poland*, by Józef Szujski (1835–83); by the most famous and most controversial work of this cohort, *An Outline of Polish History*, by Michał Bobrzyński (1849–1935); as well as by excerpts from the writings of Stanisław Smolka (1854–1924), considered a rare example representing truly German-style historicism in Poland.[23] I have chosen *History of the Polish Nation* by Władysław Smoleński (1851–1926) and selected works by Tadeusz Korzon (1839–1918) to represent the so-called Varsovian school, which emerged in the 1880s as a politically idealistic and methodologically positivistic challenge to the Cracovian historians.[24] I also refer to the writings of other influential rivals from the University of Lviv: Ludwik Kubala (1838–1918), who was a specialist on the seventeenth century, and Oswald Balzer (1858–1933), a legal historian.

The last generation of Polish historians active before World War I, generally described as neo-Romantic, are represented by two syntheses of national history: one by Feliks Koneczny (1862–1949), better known for his later Toynbeean study *On the Plurality of Civilizations*, and one by a highly popular amateur, Antoni Chołoniewski (1872–1924). They are accompanied by a study on early modern Polish history by Adam Szelągowski (1873–1961), as well as the collective work of eight historians devoted to the causes of Poland-Lithuania's partition (*Causes of the Fall of Poland*), published at the symbolic end of this era, in 1918.

Germany represents a broader and much more complicated field. In particular, the image of German historical writing in the nineteenth century is dominated by the controversial paradigm of historicism as a specifically German philosophy of history, as a methodological approach, and, debatably, as an ideological tendency.[25] In practice, however, historicism accommodated a wide range of attitudes toward the past, often in conflict with one another, and thus it seems of little value as a criterion for the representative capacity of the texts to be analyzed. Therefore, I refer to generational divisions, which largely coincided with the ideological controversies of the time.

Most of the authors in my first group belonged to the broadly defined democratic liberal camp, which dominated the field in the first half of the century. They opposed absolutism, religious obscurantism, and the remnants of feudalism and still held a sentimental view of the Empire as the symbol of German unity. For representatives of this group, I look primarily at the writings of Wolfgang Menzel (1798–1873), Karl von Rotteck (1775–1840), and Friedrich von Raumer (1781–1873). Heinrich Leo (1799–1878) herein represents the Romantic-federalist opposition to the main trend. The achievements of these historians were often marginalized in professional literature on the subject due to criticism leveled by their more famous adversaries, representing the so-called Prussian school. These rivals accused the Romantic-federalist historians of ideological and methodological backwardness and labeled their version of patriotism as naïveté. After the unification of Germany, the Prussian historians emerged triumphant; still, the actual popularity of my first group of authors up to the last quarter of the nineteenth century should not be underestimated.[26] Besides, I shall refer to a number of writings by the era's most famous historian, Leopold von Ranke (1795–1886), whose professional career spanned more than six decades, who is widely considered the cofounder of historicism (and modern historical research methods), and whose political and ideological alignments remain problematic to this day.

My selection representing the Borussian historians (i.e., advocates of Hohenzollern Prussia and its historical mission) includes fragments of the works of Johann Gustav Droysen (1808–84), a leading theorist of historicism; Heinrich von Sybel (1817–95), founder of the *Historische Zeitschrift*; and Ludwig Häusser (1818–67). This generation is also represented herein by Wilhelm Giesebrecht (1814–89), author of the most impressive study on the medieval Empire, as well as some of the most influential ideological opponents of the Borussian historians: the highly popular Johannes Janssen (1829–91), Ignaz von Döllinger (1799–1890), Onno Klopp (1822–1903), and Julius von Ficker (1826–1902).

I have chosen Heinrich von Treitschke (1834–96), Karl Lamprecht (1856–1915), Hans Prutz (1843–1929), Eduard Heyck (1862–1941), Oskar Jäger (1830–1910), Ludwig Stacke (1817–1906), Felix Dahn (1834–1912), and Johannes Haller (1865–1947) as representatives of the next generation, active mainly after the unification of Germany in 1871, when the ideas of the first generation of Borussian historians, modified in one way or another, became widely accepted as the standard interpretation of German history.

Writing History in the Nineteenth Century

Historians emphasize two tendencies as characteristic of nineteenth-century historiography, although theoretically they are hardly reconcilable. First, history as a discipline changed enormously. University professors replaced amateurs as historians, and their field emancipated itself from the umbrella of moral philosophy and rhetoric and navigated toward the institutional and organizational structures of the sciences, becoming professionalized and establishing an impressive network of auxiliary entities such as museums, libraries, archives, bibliographies, societies, and academic journals.[27] Germany was the unquestionable leader of this process, whereas Poland was left in the rear guard because of the restrictions imposed by Russian and Prussian anti-Polish policies, as well as the country's poverty. However, Poles, like the majority of Europeans, were deeply impressed by the German model of doing history (and of the German education model in general) and dreamed of imitating it. Second, nineteenth-century historians are usually regarded as profoundly involved in contemporary political and ideological controversies, and it is commonly believed that their sweetest dream was to become statesmen's advisors. Seen from the latter perspective, nineteenth-century history writing may have a reduced cognitive value, except as evidence of the mentality and intellectual trends of its time. Nevertheless, despite their dissonance the two perspectives are scarcely separable, and the vast majority of then-contemporary historical production includes both the claim to reconstruct past developments as they appear in light of a careful and indisputable analysis of the sources, as well as an obvious ideological and political bias.

In this work I have tried to overcome this confusing discrepancy by avoiding the question of whether these historians were, in light of the most recent research, right or wrong in their interpretations. First, I believe this is not the most fascinating or even fair question one may ask of the historians of past generations, and, second, it would make this book a bibliographical essay composed of references relating particular passages from the nineteenth-century books to the later literature on the subject. Instead, I have focused on the rhetorical-interpretive aspect of the writings discussed, investigating what these authors wanted their readers to understand or, if you like, to believe with respect to their national histories, that is, which factors and processes determined them; what their turning points and key figures were; which moments they were supposed to be proud of; and which they should regard as shameful and ominous ones, never to be repeated. Obviously, this is not to say that historical writing may be reduced to a peculiar, and indeed quite intricate, rhetorical strategy of advocating contemporary political or ideological claims. The issue of a high-quality historical narrative is too complex to be reduced to this purpose exclusively, regardless of its author's intentions, be they conscious or not. I suppose that in the end, in the case of our historians, the word *reduced* is a misnomer, given their high ambitions, their sense of mission, and their actual political impact.

This had much to do with the literary standards of their historical production. In sharp contrast to our time, the nineteenth-century historians' most challenging rivals were not their fellow colleagues, flooding professional journals with papers and proposals on whatever subject they could imagine before they did so themselves, but rather fiction authors, who successfully shaped the image of the past in the minds of the public. There was an enormous interest, indeed appetite, for history among the educated public in nineteenth-century Europe, and over time a significant portion of the working classes adopted this appetite, which was mostly satisfied by historical novels. Approximately 750 such novels were published in Germany between 1850 and 1888. According to Jerzy Maternicki, at the turn of the twentieth century historical novels constituted a majority of all titles lent by public libraries in the working-class districts of Warsaw.[28] In short, the historical novel was the most powerful rival of academic historians in shaping popular images of the past. The nature of this rivalry, however, was more familial than antagonistic. Despite progress in the professionalization of historical research and the integration of the historians' craft into academia, history in that epoch was still viewed as closely related to literature (as testified to by the granting of the first Nobel Prize in literature to the German ancient historian Theodore Mommsen). A number of authors discussed in this book (e.g., Schiller, Dahn, Treitschke, Niemcewicz, Szujski, and Szajnocha) combined historical research with writing in other literary genres. The fact that some of them are remembered as historians, while others are recalled as poets and dramatists, partly obfuscates their own self-identifications and aspirations.

At the same time, politics was no less intimately related to history than literature, and a number of our historians—Droysen, Sybel, Raumer, Lelewel, Bobrzyński—temporarily abandoned their craft for political engagement, serving as parliamentary deputies, government officials, and revolutionary activists. Importantly, it was believed at that time the relationship between politics and history was bidirectional: on one hand history was supposed to inspire and instruct politicians, and on the other hand political involvement was viewed as extremely beneficial for historians. Ironically, German historians of that time, so admired abroad for their professionalism, felt disadvantaged in this respect: despite their massive involvement in the 1848 Frankfurt Parliament's activities, they were all university professors with no experience in decision-making politics, in contrast to their ancient predecessors and contemporary British and French counterparts.[29] Naturally, the ambition to make a political impact also resulted in an emphasis on the rhetorical component of their historical writing.

Therefore, this book represents an approach to history predominantly as a field of controversy and debate, one in which new ideas and interpretations matter particularly as arguments of rhetorical potential, whereas the old ones can easily be absorbed and employed to serve an authorial point of view. Moreover, one of this book's ambitions is polemical, going against the most popular interpretations of the development of history and historical thinking in nineteenth-century Germany and Poland, as well as the way historiography develops in general. This is an interpretation that stresses fragmentation over continuity. According to this view, the history of historical thinking and writing is determined by a number of spectacular turns. In Germany before 1848, liberalism dominates the picture, and it is then replaced by historicism and the Borussian school, which in turn is challenged by Lamprecht's positivism and the neo-Rankean school. In Poland, Romanticism dominates before the 1863 uprising, which paves the way for the preponderance of the Cracovian school, which is subsequently challenged by the Varsovian school, with its combination of idealism and positivism, and then by the neo-Romantic generation.

Some of these divisions are problematic. For example, Ranke's disciples (estimated to have numbered about sixty), who are supposed to remain influenced by the eminent historian, constituted nearly all of the elite ranks of German historians of the late nineteenth and early twentieth centuries. However, Georg Iggers reduces this number to only one historian of modern times—Heinrich von Sybel, who on a number of key issues held views that were fundamentally different from those of his master.[30] Moreover, ideological and methodological differences are being confused, just as they were in the eyes of our historians. For example, the Borussian, or the "lesser German," historians saw themselves as the golden mean between the cultivation of history detached from social life, with its "worship of sources," and history understood as an "ordinary servant to politics" (a jab at the liberals).[31] The "lesser German" label was contrived by Onno Klopp, a bitter opponent of this trend, in a series of polemical articles published under the title "Kleindeutsche Geschichtsbaumeister" in *Historisch-politischen Blättern* during 1861 and 1862.[32] In Poland, the historians who challenged the highly idealized image of the national past in the name of realism, arguing that the partitions of the Commonwealth were in part a result of its political and military impotence, were accused of pessimism by the next generation.[33] This division into pessimists and optimists (who believed that the Commonwealth had been partitioned by its greedy neighbors because they feared its potential might) dominated all interpretations of Polish historiography until Olgierd Górka questioned it in 1936, claiming that the idea of being an innocent victim of foreign aggression had little to do with optimism.[34]

Obviously it is not my intention to question these chronological and methodological classifications or to deny their importance. Even though a number of prominent historians—such as Ranke, Giesebrecht, and Szujski—escape these divisions, they certainly inform us about crucial ideological and methodological changes in historical thinking in both countries. Apparently they also correspond to a more or less universal principle of the conflict of generations: each in turn is certain that their predecessors were blinded, in one way or another, by prejudices or reservations in their search for the true image of the past, and in criticizing those predecessors they cultivate other prejudices and reservations, which in turn would again be passionately rejected by the next generation. It is also obvious that political shifts, such as the 1848–49 revolution, the unification of Germany, or the 1863 uprising in Poland, influenced the way national history was perceived. However, in the longer view, no historical school or tendency prevails, and none of them manages to dismiss permanently the achievements of its "opponents." Thus, in the minds of subsequent generations, their claims and interpretations typically become amalgamated, coexisting as two sides of the same coin.

Thus, I hope that the comparative approach this book adopts has managed to elucidate some continuities spanning the political, ideological, and methodological divisions among our historians and that it sheds some new light on what was common and permanent in their narratives. Of course, some of these elements were simply regarded as obvious and noncontroversial by our historians: they constituted a core of the standard interpretation of national history that no one questioned. Still, I believe that analyzing them was not a trivial pursuit, because nineteenth-century standards often seem quite exotic to us today, and it is precisely these standards that escape our attention if we focus on the controversies that inspired all the internal shifts and divisions within the historical fields in the two countries.

A Note on Some Fundamental Historical Concepts

P olish and German historians' could accomplish the task of narrating their respective national histories only by drawing from an arsenal of concepts and values rooted in a particular ideology that enabled them to explain the source of a political weakness that existed in both countries. This fact leads us to address determinants of a different kind: those to which previous historiography owed a debt.

The starting point for historians from both countries has been to look at the history of a state that had already left a legacy spanning several centuries, a legacy full of glory in times of old and one that had been transformed many times over, both politically and in terms of international standing, only to finally become dysfunctional, leaving each country vulnerable to aggressive neighbors. It was a unique situation in the particular context of countries that had each once had a functioning national state but in the nineteenth century—when national ideology was celebrating galloping successes—had found themselves, to put it colloquially, "on ice." In the context of Western historical thought, however, there was nothing exceptional in this problem: every high school graduate knew that there had been such states in the past, that their rise and fall constituted a normal pattern. Any historian or student would naturally be quick to point to ancient Greece and Rome as examples of this phenomenon.

The decline and passing of politically powerful states, together with the fall of states to rapacious invaders, has kept historians occupied for ages; one could even say that in the late eighteenth and early nineteenth century, the life cycle of states was one of the leading questions in Western historiography. As Alexander Demandt noted, in ancient times two interpretations of the problem were dominant.[1] Both in some way referred to, or rather registered, the idea—the remnants of which we can still find in the nineteenth century—that previous generations had been characterized by greater bravery, fortitude, virtue, and perhaps even reason. Demandt offers Homer as the progenitor of this view: the poet had suggested that contemporary Hellenes could not hold a candle to the generation of the Trojan expedition, and he added, in Nestor's words, that that generation in turn had yielded to the previous one—and so on, all the way back to the mythical heroes and gods of Olympus.

According to the first interpretation—what we would today call psychological-ly oriented but in the nineteenth century would have been considered morally in-flected—the fall is always the consequence of an illusory self-certainty, the result of a sense of security and a life of luxury. We already see this in Herodotus (who believed that luxury corrupts), Plato (who saw Athenians' fear of the Persians as a blessing), and Aristotle, who of course systematized it, pointing out that a sense of danger sparks vigilance and animation, while self-confidence has a tranquilizing and stupefying effect. Isocrates expounded on this at great length in 355 BC in a speech on the history of Athens, although he was of the opinion that intelligent people would be able to overcome these natural tendencies.

According to the opposing, yet essentially complementary point of view, the decline and fall of a state were part of a natural process, the equivalent of the aging and dying of living organisms. This view assumes a cyclical understanding of the nature of time that was characteristic of ancient cultures. Proceeding from this assumption, Ammianus Marcellinus, Seneca, and Florus had all prophesied the fall of Rome in spite of the myth of *Roma aeterna et perpetua*. Polybius instructed Scipio Africanus to ponder the fate of Troy on the ruins of Carthage and to expect a similar fate for his own homeland. This last historian was also the author of the most elaborate theory of the cyclical growth, decline, and fall of states, connect-ing the two interpretations. According to his theory, the natural cycle of growth, stagnation, and decadence had corresponding political mind-sets: the young state was characterized by vigor, discipline, and aggression; as a result of conquest and growing wealth, its elites would wallow in selfishness and luxury, neglecting the art of governing and defense; that situation eventually would lead to revolution-ary turmoil and invite aggressive and hungry neighbors to launch a predatory invasion.[2]

If one takes a broader look at the legacy of antiquity, this division will seem ar-tificial, since both interpretations were often similar in their moral and philosoph-ical reflections on transiency and the variations of fortune. Apologies for bygone virtues would be followed by condemnation of the arrogance (Greek: *hybris*) that arose from the good fortune those very virtues brought—followed invariably by the punishing intervention of Nemesis, whose attribute was a wheel. "Pride goeth before a fall" (*hybris-ate*) can be considered the moral of the works of Herodotus, as is evident in his biographies of Xerxes, Croesus, and Polycrates, as well as generally in his history of the Achaemenid Empire. The same can be said of Thucydides and the history of the power and the fall of Athens, as well as of the stories of the he-roes of Attic tragedy: Aeschylus's Agamemnon, Sophocles's Oedipus and Ajax, and Euripides's Pentheus.[3] In addition to the histories of classical antiquity, the Old

Testament also provided a powerful source of inspiration with its descriptions of the woes of "once populated cities" (Jeremiah, Isaiah) that had brought the wrath of God upon themselves for the sin of confidence in their own power. Last but not least, a basic historical-moral lesson that Christians drew from the Gospels was to dissociate themselves from the Jews, who were believed to have been fooled and deceived by their own success; trusting that their status as the chosen people had been given to them forever and always, they had failed to recognize the renewal of the covenant and the divinity of Jesus Christ.

The fate of Rome, for which the gods, if we are to believe the poet, had promised *imperium sine fine*, was a catastrophe that engrossed scholars during the subsequent centuries.[4] In early Christianity, these considerations were linked with the promise of the Second Coming—with religious reflection on the vanity of this world. Augustine and other Christian writers, however, used the word *degeneratio*—being the equivalent of aging. In the history of nations, as well as in human lives, *auxisis* (youth) was followed by *akmé* (maturity), which, in turn, was followed by *phtisis* (decrepitude). This was a view drawn from Stoic philosophy; the previously mentioned Lucius Annaeus Florus was the first to introduce this theme to historiography, in his *Epitome de Tito Livio*.[5] Petrarch would rhetorically ask centuries later which people and what state can expect to last when even Rome has passed into obscurity. Both nations and the whole world itself, the poet would add, have their own times and old age—and then pass on.[6] Orosius, however, in *Historiarum adversus paganos libri VII* (fifth century), interpreted the fall of Rome in the spirit of Polybius, attributing it to the overexpansion of the Empire.

Decadence, as such, was first taken on by writers of the Italian Renaissance: Leonardo Bruni, Flavio Biondo, and Luigi de la Porto (as Pierre Chaunu informs us, the phrase *tomber en décadence* appears in the French language as late as 1675 in *Remarques nouvelles sur la langue française*).[7] After them, authors of the stature of Machiavelli, Bacon, Le Roy, Vico, and Voltaire added their words to the topic, exhibiting ideas close to those of Polybius.[8] Machiavelli, in his *History of Florence and of the Affairs of Italy* (Book V, Chapter I), expressed it as follows: "It may be observed, that provinces amid the vicissitudes to which they are subject, pass from order into confusion, and afterward recur to a state of order again; for the nature of mundane affairs not allowing them to continue in an even course, when they have arrived at their greatest perfection, they soon begin to decline. . . . The reason is, that valor produces peace; peace, repose; repose, disorder; disorder, ruin."[9]

Even Gibbon was partially inclined toward a similar interpretation: "the decline of Rome was the natural and inevitable effect of immoderate greatness. Prosperity ripened the principle of decay."[10] He also stressed the loss of civic virtue, which would bring about a loss of political instinct. However, there was a subtle yet crucial difference: although modern authors generally shared the belief that Rome somehow collapsed under its own weight, that the political instincts of the Roman elites had been dulled by delusions of their own invincibility, and that luxury demoralized them, they gradually departed from the view that such a fate awaits every great power, as Polybius or Christian doctrine suggested. Enlightenment thought leaned toward empirical investigation and practical application—toward discovering what went wrong and what should be seen as a warning for leaders, thus leading to the formulation of a general theory more solidly based on empiricism than the earlier views, which had their bases in morality and metaphysics. An example from Montesquieu's *Considerations on the Causes of the Greatness of the Romans and Their Decline* follows in this spirit: "It is not chance that rules the world. Ask the Romans, who had a continuous sequence of successes when they were guided by a certain plan, and an uninterrupted sequence of reverses when they followed another. There are general causes, moral and physical, which act in every monarchy, elevating it, maintaining it, or hurling it to the ground."[11] The search for the factors that caused the fall of ancient Empires inevitably led to the stigmatization of such factors (hence the great debate over whether the spread of Christianity had been one of the reasons for the fall of Rome; Gibbon and Voltaire believed it had been, while Montesquieu doubted it).[12] Therefore, it is sometimes difficult to say what came first: cool analysis that led to the identification of critical factors or a moral judgment that demanded that destructive influences be found in phenomena deemed negative.

Adam Ferguson concluded his *Essay on the History of Civil Society* (1767) with the traditional condemnation of luxury as a source of both moral and political degeneration. However, in *The Ruins* (1791), Constantin-François Volney described injustice and selfish oppression as the most destructive elements: "Thus that very principle of self-love, which, when restrained within the limits of prudence, was a source of improvement and felicity, became transformed, in its blind and disordered state, into a contagious poison." In this spirit he explained the reasons for the collapse of the ancient states, denouncing the despotism of the rulers, the excesses of the elites, and the oppression of the people. At the same time, he argued that the "science" of morality is fundamentally similar to the natural sciences and that when this fact is widely recognized, people will understand that "to wish to enjoy at the expense of another is a false calculation of ignorance."[13] Here we see a significant shift in emphasis—especially when it comes to faith in the power of science—yet it was one with a long tradition: Bruni (*Historiarum Florentini populi libri XII*) had already suggested that the fall of Rome had begun with the collapse of civil liberties and the transition from the republic to Caesarism.[14]

Reflection on our topic, therefore, began at a time when moral views reaching as far back as ancient Greece and rooted in Christian ideology, trust in empirical investigation, and the belief that the social and political world must be governed by laws similar to those of nature (and that the role of the scholar was to discover them) all coexisted in a fragile state of equilibrium.

The two older competing views may be found in many of the texts analyzed in this book: on one hand, the view that pride goeth before a fall and that those blinded by pride fail to see the warnings and signs sent by Providence itself; on the other, that decadence is the result of a departure from the primeval virtues of the Fathers, a denial of one's own identity. The final verse in Shakespeare's *King John* offers evidence that the latter opinion was nothing new:

> This England never did, nor never shall,
> Lie at the proud foot of a conqueror,
> But when it first did help to wound itself.
> . . . Nought shall make us rue,
> If England to itself do rest but true.

Having been a tradition that had endured for centuries, the idea that the fall of a state is a natural occurrence—and that its previous success offers no guarantee of resilience but instead predicts its inevitable decay—did not disappear overnight; it still represented an important context for the issues that will be discussed in this book. It was also applied to other realms of life; for example, according to Hume (in his *Essays*, from 1742), the deterioration of the arts and sciences would be a natural consequence of their perfection, which would act as a disincentive for subsequent generations and thus desensitize the public to second-rate imitations.[15] In 1815 Joachim Lelewel, who was to become the most famous Polish historian of the first half of the nineteenth century, noted, "[The nation], indulging in its prosperity, will fall into laziness and sweet dreams, resulting in negligence, a growing laxness of manners, its wits languishing, and the nation, weakened as a whole, will be unfit to endure the adversities that will easily humiliate it."[16] Nevertheless, this idea posed one of the main intellectual challenges faced by nineteenth-century German and Polish authors, who had wanted to present the "old republic" as a source of legitimacy for the young national movements. The implications of such a view could seem deadly for their purposes. As a Polish Romantic poet explained, "I come upon the words: 'Our country had reached its zenith, it had to decline.' Away ideas of the devil!"[17]

Their efforts, as a matter of course, had to move toward a more modern approach to the problem, in the spirit of the above-cited Montesquieu statement: toward indicating the specific causes of the conditions afflicting the Empire and the Commonwealth. They approached the autopsy of the politically dead entity with the understanding that its death was premature and that—let us use a metaphor of our times—its cause did not have a genetic basis. It was rather a disease resulting from the lifestyle of the deceased, an ailment that they assumed could have, with a change in habits or more aggressive treatment, at least hypothetically been fought off.

The analytical aspect of this approach focuses on searching for the *causa effi-ciens*—the single factor that can be held responsible for the fall of the state, while the narrative aspect is marked by an attempt to reveal the *trope*—the culminating point, that is, when the breakdown occurred and defeat was irrevocable. In this respect, the histories of the Empire and the Commonwealth structurally resemble classical tragedy: the heroes struggle against their fate, long unaware—unlike the reader—of its inevitability. Their struggles against the inevitable demonstrate the tragedy and pathos of those efforts. If, however, one recognizes the nation as the real hero of the story, we may then see its struggle with the reversals of fate much like the Aristotelian *peripeteia*—climbing toward power and success, forgetting the same, and falling back into humiliation—all being a prelude to what one Polish historian would call a "rebirth in decline."

Meanwhile, a new, powerful player appeared on the intellectual battlefield: He-gel's philosophy of history, with its "court of judgment." In a nutshell, its relation to failed states boiled down to the conclusion that, so long as they fulfilled their historic mission, they would succeed, and if they fell on hard times, it was because their mission had been completed or the spirit of the time flowed in another direc-tion, for the judgments of history are always "rational."

Hegel articulated the justification for a cosmic plan in history in his *Elements of the Philosophy of Right* (1821): "World history falls outside these points of view; in it, that necessary moment of the Idea of the world spirit which constitutes its cur-rent stage attains its absolute right, and the nation [*Volk*] which lives at this point, and the deeds of that nation, achieve fulfilment, fortune, and fame."[18]

Despite the reserve and even reluctance of professional historians to adopt Hegel's approach, this notion of a semimystical relationship with the state took deep root in German historicism (for which it was later often criticized), thanks primarily to Leopold von Ranke.[19] Seeing the state as inherently different from all other social institutions and coming straight from God, this most famous Ger-man historian of the nineteenth century saw the judgment of Providence in the state's history and thus in its successes and defeats. Power, therefore, became a measure of historical justice.[20] It is clear that this approach would fail to satisfy pa-triots dreaming of reviving the "old republic" in some form or another; as we will see, however, it did have a major impact on the thinking of nineteenth-century historians. Even when they managed to avoid reaching an unequivocally Hegelian diagnosis concerning the history of the Empire or the Commonwealth, its spirit to a great degree still determined their detailed considerations.

On the other hand, the intellectual implications of the idea of a "spirit of the time" led the historians discussed here more than once to counterfactual deliberations. Knowledge of what actually happened, contrasted with the belief that the "spirit of the time" demanded other measures or solutions, posed a constant temptation to describe alternative scenarios. Moral convictions also begot those same temptations, especially those inherent in presumptions regarding political decadence: that it must be at least in some measure Providence's punishment for various sins—whether for the "willingness to exploit at another's expense," or *hybris*, fatal pride, and the sedating sense of one's own strength. This in turn collided with the idolatry of realpolitik, served in a more or less Hegelian sauce, with both laying claim to scientific and empirical authority. "They should have taken ruthless and brutal steps," some authors claimed, while others protested, declaring that such immoralism is shortsighted and always fails in the long run or that it is unwise and contrary to historical method to demand that one's forebears predict the long-term effects of their decisions or that they take actions that are in conflict with the mentality and intellectual horizon of their times.

The majority of German and Polish historians characteristically hoped to save at least part of the legacy of the "old republic" as an inspiration for their national movements and efforts to rebuild their nation-states, thus marking a departure from their historical approach to ancient Empires. Here, a tradition older even than that associated with the Roman Empire deserves mention: that of Troy. It is meaningful for our topic not only because it marked the birth of contemplations on the fall and passing of civilizations in Western culture but also and mainly because of its somewhat paradoxical optimism. It can be found in Virgil's story of Aeneas as the founder of Rome and in later legends referring back to it.[21] It can also be found in the story of his brother Francus, founder of France, of his cousin Brutus, who was to found the kingdom of England (according to Geoffrey of Monmouth) or to be the progenitor of the Lithuanian nobility (in the Sarmatian version of the legend). The popularity of the motif, as well as the fantastic cosmopolitanism in the expression of Aeneas's progeny, indicates its creative potential and ability to evoke a deep emotional resonance. As one can see, having origins in defeat can be ennobling. This founding myth can be seen as a secular substitute for the resurrection of Christ as a symbol of the untamed resilience of the nation.

Apparently, it involves a sort of reflexive backlash to the discouraging *hybris* of the Hegelian cult of historical judgment, as well as to the hope of reforging defeat into a lesson. As Reinhart Koselleck put it, "In defeat lies the comforting potential for a learning benefit."[22] The defeated learn something important about themselves that those who are intoxicated with success can never know. They also have a tendency to see themselves as better than their oppressors, whom they eagerly perceive as culturally backward barbarians, and to view their defeat itself as glorious, suffered against overwhelming forces who had likely resorted to foul play—the examples of Leonidas, the Maccabees, and Brutus come to mind. As Ernst Troeltsch wrote in *Traumland Zustand*, escaping into the realm of fantasy is a standard response of the defeated. According to Freud, frustration born of the inability to take revenge can bring on a collective "hysterical neurosis." Jung saw the feminization of national symbols that was prevalent in such cases (e.g., the cult of Queen Marie Louise of Prussia after 1806, or the renaissance of Joan of Arc's popularity in France after 1870) as a fantasy of returning to the womb—the symbol of a nation's immortality.[23] These are of course only a few of the themes that will surface in this analysis of nineteenth-century German and Polish historiography. At this point, there is no need to ponder the relevance of the interpretations signaled here; I only mention them to emphasize that we will be encountering a discourse as rooted in the traditions of the Western world as it is unique in its particular context.

Finally, one may ask whether the German and Polish historians discussed herein believed at all in the idea of progress in history. At this point, I would merely point out that a highly ambivalent attitude toward the notion of progress as encompassing and ordering all of history distinguished the German and Polish historians from their Western counterparts. This story begins in the times of the collapse of the so-called enlightened paradigm of history, which had been founded on faith in the progress of civilization, in the spirit of Voltaire. Meanwhile, many German and Polish historians of the nineteenth century more or less decisively distanced themselves from that belief. What they shared was, for example, a skeptical attitude toward Western civilization due to their own nations' "young age" relative to the Latin nations, an attitude that was usually, although sometimes with reservations, considered a strong asset—both in the moral sense and as a source of the specific vitality of a people uncontaminated by the decadence of their "corrupt elders." The other side of this coin was the conviction that the two nations were in some "miserable" way backward in relation to the Western model—for example, compared to France, with its centralized monarchy. Hidden behind this idea was faith, if not in progress, then at least in a progression leading from "feudalism" to "modernity."

Furthermore, many of the historians discussed herein succumbed to the temptation of a belief in timeless ideas whose carriers were to be nations or states—even if the simplistic, contrived designs of philosophers irked them. Such ideas—for example, freedom—were, in accordance with Herder's philosophy, to have specific meanings for individual nations; they would undergird their identity and be constructed over the course of history, being therefore subject to development in time. As we shall see, these ideas, considered both unique and decisive in determining the exceptionalism of the nation and viewed as representing the nation's contribution to the history of the world (that is, Europe), were often presented in a surprisingly similar fashion in the two countries.[24]

As Horst Walter Blanke has noted, the assumptions underlying the historiography of the Enlightenment—its cosmopolitanism and its belief in natural law and progress—were largely ignored rather than openly denied in nineteenth-century German historicism. The only German historian of the time who was considered a Romantic, Heinrich Leo, was also the only one to openly condemn the legacy of the Enlightenment as "satanic."[25] German historicism, as a philosophy of understanding history (with all the controversies regarding what features in fact constituted it) is generally seen as standing in opposition to the idea of progress, following Leopold von Ranke's thinking that all historical epochs "stand directly before God."[26] If one is to believe Ernst Schulin, Ranke's opposition to Schiller's tenet that history should be seen as a "genetic explanation of the present world" would have been a formative experience for the great historian.[27]

But it is also worth remembering the other side. Considering historic necessity to be "cheap wisdom" (Johann Gustav Droysen), the coryphaei of historicism and their followers saw the proper task of the historian to be the identification of the "leading trends of the era" (Georg Gottfried Gervinus) or, more precisely, those that bore fruit beyond their own time.[28] As Georg Iggers has pointed out, despite the declarations of Ranke and those of his younger colleagues, they did in fact believe in progress—at least in the sense that they considered their own times the culmination of all previous eras and Western civilization to be unquestionably superior to any other.[29] This belief manifested itself with redoubled force after Bismarck's unification of Germany, which patriotically enthusiastic German historians portrayed as the culmination of their national destiny, fulfilling the centuries-old mission of Prussia and the Hohenzollern dynasty in accordance with Gervinus's postulate, that of perceiving the historian as "an advocate of destiny [*Parteimann des Schicksals*], a natural champion of progress."[30] Karl Ferdinand Werner called this evolution, born under the sign of the historicism, the "grotesque contradiction of German historiography."[31] One explanation for this paradox may be the religiosity of the majority of German historians of the time. It was Protestantism that inspired the so-called Borussian historians to see the Reformation as Germany's most momentous contribution to the history of the world and "Prussia's German mission" as not only a national but also a religious calling. Thus, the first issue of *Historische Zeitschrift* in 1859 announced its struggle against dilettantism, backwardness, and ultramontanism. Protestantism was considered progressive by definition.

CHAPTER ONE

Nature and Nation

The early histories of Germany and Poland begin in the dark forests, viewed through the spectacles of a traveler from the sunny civilization of late ancient Europe, one who is well aware that none of his compatriots is capable of verifying his narrative about the forest's inhabitants. Nevertheless, like their colleagues from other parts of Europe, the German and Polish historians from the nineteenth century, having only scattered and dispersed evidence on the period, wrote extensively on their nations' early history, and with much self-confidence and passion. Moreover, this early period of their national past was apparently meant to be narrated according to principles of its own, principles considerably different from those relating to newer times. Still, in the last decades of the nineteenth century, historians quoted ancient authors who had commented on their countries at length (in the case of Germany, Tacitus's *Germania* was by far the most respected and popular), and drew far-reaching conclusions from their narratives. With reference to the ancient past, they extrapolated information and interpreted events that took place in later periods, and they drew colorful images of societies about which they knew very little. In short, in modern terms one might say their narratives were full of fantasies and reasoned hallucinations, based on premises no longer considered credible.

One may wonder why, having so little evidence at their disposal, they dove so deeply and eagerly into their national past. Obviously, the answer must be speculative. First, the nineteenth-century historians believed (as Hegel argued), that nations are living organisms.[1] They also believed that national history stretches as far back as one can trace any information concerning the ancestors of contemporary Germans and Poles or, for that matter, people of any other nation. This was only partly related to the so-called "national question," or the problem of national self-consciousness, which they investigated carefully and critically, albeit using a different methodological approach than that which dominates today's social sciences and historiography. The apparent obsession of the nineteenth-century historians with their nations' prehistory evokes associations with genealogy. The purpose of genealogy in feudal societies was not to satisfy curiosity or provide idle entertainment for a sentimental mind; its goal was prestige, and one's ancestry needed to be ancient and spectacular from the beginning. The same principle apparently applied to the history of nations; in order to establish and deserve a respectable position in the hierarchy of nations, that position must have been occupied from time immemorial. Perhaps this was the legacy of writing history to please the tastes of wealthy families and generous rulers, from Homer to the times of absolutism.

Second, if nations were organisms, then all their fundamental features had to have been present at their infancy. It was then that the national character was formed, and it was necessary to find out what factors influenced the development of that character in order to describe it and understand its nature. The most prominent philosophers of the Enlightenment—Kant, Montesquieu, Hegel—believed that the natural environment played the greatest role in shaping nations: the climate, the landscape, the soils and the foods they offered. Differences between peoples were natural, because they were products of natural conditions. This view was the origin of modern racism, which was first developed by German authors such as Johann Friedrich Blumenbach (*On the Natural Differences of Humankind*, 1798); Ernst Moritz Arndt, who first articulated the concept of the Caucasian race (*An Attempt at a Comparative History of Peoples*, 1843), and Carl Gustav Carus (*On the Unequal Talents of the Human Tribes*, 1849).[2]

With respect to the historians whose writings are analyzed in this book, the consequences of this view were twofold. First, they unanimously shared it. As Julian Niemcewicz, chronologically the first Polish historian whose work is presented herein, put it, "Our geographical location, the air we breathe, and the customs and laws of our past, have imprinted their mark on us, as they have with other nations."[3] Moreover, they believed that the national character was essentially unchangeable, and they attempted to trace its continuity from the most distant past until their own time. Second, they viewed national character as the decisive or at least the most important factor in each nation's history, and they also believed that the course of this history depended on whether the original national character and its virtues remained intact. One should not get distracted by the apparent inconsistency of this position: a nation could not abandon its natural character fully; it could only develop it and adapt to the given circumstances. If a detour from the natural line of development occurred, it was only temporary and inevitably resulted in a decline in the prevailing social and political conditions. Like a human being, a nation needed to behave according to its natural dispositions, and if it did not, a serious illness could be expected. Notably, this approach made the historians' position particularly elevated: they were the ones who were to define what the national character actually was and what behavior best suited it. This was the true purpose of history, and to fulfill this task the historian, like the psychoanalyst, needed to go back to the origins. Henryk Schmitt, a post-Romantic Polish historian, encapsulated this view in a straightforward fashion: "Any detour [from the path of national development that was determined by Providence] provoked numerous failures and disasters, which ought to be viewed as lessons for future generations . . . that the only way to recover from the misery is to resume the line of development that is appropriate for the nationality. And what is nationality, and what are the principles of its healthy development? This is what national history, if narrated properly, tells us in the most indisputable manner."[4]

As mentioned, nineteenth-century historians' opinions on their nations' early history were based largely—simply because of the lack of any other evidence—on the narratives of a few foreigners. In the German case, Roman authors occupied the most prominent position; Tacitus, Caesar, Ammianus Marcellinus, and Procopius were the most often quoted. In the Polish case, except for the famous passage on the Slavs in Ptolemy's *Geography*, some remarks of Byzantine authors and Paul the Deacon were available, next to the more extensive information provided by medieval chroniclers such as Thietmar of Merseburg and Adam of Bremen. Information provided by the first Polish history writers, Gallus Anonymous and Wincenty Kadłubek, as well as that included in the northern sagas, were considered with much criticism.

However, there were also newer sources of inspiration for our historians. One of the central ideas associated with the Germanic tribes of the late ancient and early medieval period, namely their alleged love of liberty, was perpetuated by numerous authors of the modern period, in particular those who opposed the rising monarchical absolutism of the Bourbons and the Habsburgs. They included supporters of the Fronde in France, Hugo Grotius in the Netherlands, and Hermann Corning, a publisher and commentator on Tacitus's *Germania*. Moreover, a number of Enlightenment authors, such as Montesquieu, Gibbon, and William Robertson, also praised the early Germanic tribes for the same reason.

As for the Slavs, Johann Gottfried Herder's characterization achieved the greatest popularity. In his view, expressed in his *Ideas upon Philosophy and the History of Mankind*, the Slavs were benign, hospitable, hard-working, and peaceful peasants. This bucolic image was full of sympathy, but the philosopher also stressed that Slavs had no inclination for politics or indeed any higher forms of social organization, and thus even if they were brave individuals, they easily fell victim to foreign invasions. As far as the Germans were concerned, he basically repeated what the ancient authors had claimed: he praised their physical beauty, strength, loyalty, and bravery, discreetly remaining silent about their intellectual or moral capacities.

Herder's opinion remained canonical until the end of the nineteenth century, when archaeology became an alternative source for discovering the history of the period, offering a different view of the national prehistory. German historians repeated Herder's assessment of the Germanic character with overt pride. In the epoch of Wilhelm II, when paganism ceased to be seen as a problematic legacy, the ancient Germans became one of the strongholds of German chauvinism, which was on the rise in both official propaganda and mass culture. In Poland, the "reputation" of the ancient Slavs (ancestors of the Poles) was more complicated. Romantic historians, and particularly Joachim Lelewel, the most respectable of them, idealized the ancient Slavs in the Herderian fashion, especially for their alleged love of liberty and their semimythical institutions of self-government. The next generation of historians, who rose in opposition to the Romantic school, took a more nuanced view: even though they believed that Herder was essentially right, they questioned the idea that prehistoric Slavic society was a perfect pattern to follow. In their opinion, the Slavs' alleged virtues were dangerously apolitical and made them easy targets for their neighbors' expansionism. Prehistory was considered a time of happy infancy for the Slavs, who were supposed to grow up in the school of history.

To summarize, one can observe two tendencies in the approach nineteenth-century German and Polish historians adopted for relating their nations' prehistory. The first approach seems obvious. Early national history was viewed as a distinct historical epoch, with its own dynamics and special features. While it could be viewed as particularly fascinating, since it stood at the beginning, partially hidden in time immemorial before "history," and as it determined future developments in a very special way, nevertheless it represented a very distant past. However, as professionals, the historians believed, and regularly reminded their readers, that no historical epoch entirely disappears, that all of them should be seen as a series of modifications and transformations of the problems originating in the past. As Kurt Breysig claimed in the conclusion to his 1,442-page introduction to the *Cultural History of Modern Times*, "It is impossible to speak about the social history of Europe without taking a glance at the earlier epochs."[5]

The other tendency of the historians was to view prehistoric society as the nucleus of the nation's history as a whole. The national character was supposed to have been formed during that early time, as well as to have determined all future transformations, simply adapting to changing circumstances. One could say that the nineteenth-century historians shared the ancient Roman authors' view of the Germanic peoples as "infants," an approach Europeans later employed to describe various "barbarians" and "savages." Like children, the ancient Germans and Slavs were supposed to have represented the basic traits of their character, which was deemed to have determined their entire future. For the historians to support this line of reasoning, the striking inconsistencies in national character, as related by the ancient authors, were actually convenient: this was the only way for them to serve as explanations for a number of contradictory developments and currents in their subsequent national histories.

Naturvolk, or the People Who Did Not Like Peace

We begin our survey of the ancient Germanic tribes with Karl Lamprecht's *German History*, in which a century of German national historiography culminated in an apologetic assessment of militaristic and communitarian values among those tribes. When the Germans first encountered the Romans, Lamprecht claimed, they formed a political community of armed men—the *Volksstaat*. "An armed slave became a free man," he explained. The formal leader of the community, the *Hauptling*, was also its main priest and augur, but his respectable function was also risky, as a false divination could easily cost him his position or even his life. As the Germanic people were constantly at war, actual power rested with the assembly of the free fighters—the *Thing*. This troop of armed men made its decisions by acclamation: shouting and raising their weapons. Most often these decisions concerned, as Lamprecht tells us, undertaking a military expedition, praising and rewarding heroes, or punishing cowards.[6] Naturally, what the community valued most was courage, persistence, and loyalty—considered to be a specifically Germanic virtue. Interestingly, this ancient community recognized private property only with respect to personal belongings—the land was owned and exploited by all members of the community together—and Lamprecht claims that remnants of this custom were still observable in the German countryside in his day. He also emphasizes that the social organization he describes became "a foundation of German public life," and he juxtaposes that social organization against the social realities of his time, which he obviously finds regrettable: "The prehistoric Germanic commune, which survived till our time, was not a community of owners of land or education; it was a national community of men of great hearts, bright heads, and arms ready for defense and attack, ready to respond to any insult."[7]

Felix Dahn explains that the Germans inherited their bellicosity from the Aryans and that their life on the steppes of Asia and in the forests of northern Europe improved the "roughness of their souls and bodies."[8] Other German historians emphasize the contrast between the healthy Germanic morality and their bodies versus the physically and morally degenerated Romans, who, however, taught the Germans how to drink wine and use money.[9] Lamprecht also informs us, with evident delight, that the ancient Germans did not have any consciousness other than as members of their tribe and family: as perfect warriors, they did not consider themselves as individuals, and they regarded women and children as their property. Paradoxically, he adds that women "were the only bearers of spiritual culture." This primordial condition of a perfectly unified society of warriors, which, the historian argues, made them seem supernatural to the Roman authors, was, however, ruined by their own military successes: the fortunes of war brought them in contact with other societies and poisoned the initial harmony of the community.[10]

Eduard Heyck also emphasizes that the absolute authority of men over women and children was a particularly Germanic trait. A German man might expel, kill, or sell any member of his family, especially when "the Roman reached for the blond women and blue-eyed children." What the Romans considered Germanic brutality and barbarism, he explains, was actually a symptom of their youthful vitality. Ultimately, according to him, they were "well spirited," and their family life was an idyll.[11] In Germanic societies, Ludwig Stacke informs us, former slaves frequently joined the ranks of free persons, and if they did not, their status was still "much closer to that of humans than it had been in the Greece of Homer." He also claims that the status of women in the Germanic world was much higher than it was among the Romans. What he apparently means is that Germans were not "frivolous and promiscuous" like the Romans, and so their women, although deprived of any rights, were still treated with respect. Another positive consequence of the ascetic sexual morality of the Germans was, in his view, that their society was free of feminine intrigues, which was one of the reasons for Roman decadence.[12] The rough Germans were not easy to seduce or manipulate.

Felix Dahn, who won popularity due to his best-selling novel *Struggle for Rome* (sixty editions between 1876 and 1912!), in his *German History* also claims that, although ancient Germans could have more than one wife, they had great respect for women, as they believed women had a special connection to supernatural powers.[13] However, in contrast to his colleagues, Dahn admits that Germanic morality was not very strict insofar as male sexual fidelity was concerned, especially during military expeditions. He also argues that initially the Germans had had no slaves, and when they became familiar with the institution of slavery from their contacts with the Romans, they treated their captives much better than was the case in Rome and Greece, even though their customs were in general quite harsh: they practiced cruel punishments and human sacrifices, and they murdered sick infants and old people.[14] Finally, Oskar Jäger informs us that according to Tacitus—to whom, apparently, we owe the entire debate on the status of women in Germanic societies—the German peoples believed in the divine nature of femininity.[15]

One should not be confused by the apparent contradictions in the German historians' narratives about their ancestors' family life and their attitudes toward women. In fact, they all referred to the same evidence—notably Tacitus's mysterious remark on Germanic women's special relationship with the divine.[16] The real reason for the complications and variances in their arguments arose from their different strategies of idealizing Germanic society. One strategy they all had in common was to juxtapose the healthy Germanic morality and lifestyle with Roman decadence, immorality, and perfidy. What troubled all of them was how to explain Germanic brutality and cruelty as virtues or at least not to discourage the modern reader. The most popular answer to this question was emphasizing the "youthful" character of the Germanic race, a strategy rejecting all possible criticism by placing its object, in a true, even if vulgarized, Nietzchean manner, beyond good and evil in their conventional modern sense.

A few authors did not share this apologetic approach. One of them was Heinrich Leo, a representative of the older generation for whom the Enlightenment ideals—Christianity and civilization—were still dear. In his view, the customs of the Germanic people were terrifying. They murdered sick or weak infants, and they even killed healthy ones when there was little food available or the omens were bad. They also killed old and handicapped people or left them alone in the woods to die, which, he comments, "we would find outrageous if we did not know that these people asked to be killed themselves." They were, he concludes, "somehow similar to Thor" and "knew no sentimentalism at all." The only excuse he can offer to justify their harsh and brutal morality is that they lived in constant danger and struggled against nature (such as dreadful beasts, including "a crocodile-like monster," the remains of which have been found), their poverty, and the miserable conditions of their lives—in short, that they were "born amid a tempest."[17]

Analogical controversies arose around the problem of the legendary political virtues of the Germanic people: their loyalty and faithfulness on the one hand and their individualism and love for liberty on the other. However, in this case the controversies were not purely rhetorical, as they involved some serious political criticism. Stacke, for example, argues that the loyalty of Germanic warriors to their leaders and comrades, incomparable as it was, actually hampered the development of German national consciousness. The legendary warriors simply knew no other loyalty and indeed no identity other than the one within their squad; thus, not only were they incapable of becoming patriotic members of a larger community but they were also eager to serve foreign masters, most often the Romans.[18] Dahn draws similar conclusions about the "unlimited individualism" of the Germanic warriors, clans, and tribes, which meshed with their "incomparable courage" but was of little help in constructing a larger political community.[19] Heyck argues that "Liberty has been the capitalized name of the Germans" and that liberty determined their history, like the *glorie et esprit* of the French. However, he also believes that German individualism was an obstacle on the road to the unification of the Germans, as well as a pillar of their regional and class particularism up to the nineteenth century.[20]

One can easily discern the dominant line in the German historians' reasoning: an attempt to explain German history in its entirety by referring to the national character as formed in the earliest period and as a factor that determined all future developments. From the modern point of view, this assumption seems bizarre, but even if we were willing to accept it the way it was employed, it may still raise some doubts.

First, it is astonishing that nineteenth-century historians avoided mentioning how little they actually knew about the Germanic peoples of the late Roman period, as well as how uncritical they were in assessing what evidence they did possess. In most cases, their analytical strategy was to accept the rhetoric of the Roman authors, who praised the Germanic virtues (implicitly bringing German historians face to face with the realities of their own society, which they disregarded), as indisputable fact or as the foundation for their own rhetorical speculations. The image that emerged from this operation, however, was quite often even more apologetic and panegyric than the original Latin version. Let us take a closer look at Felix Dahn's interpretation of Tacitus's *Germania*, for example. The historian quotes the Roman author's paean to the Germanic people at length, emphasizing their physical beauty, moral virtues, and other assets. He crowns his description with Tacitus's comparison of the Germanic people to the Persians, whom the ancient historian found to be the only barbarians who deserved a similar appraisal. Dahn then pauses and notes that Tacitus idealized the Germanic people. One should not credit him in this respect, however, as he immediately proposes to replace the Roman author's analogy with that of his own: the Greeks of the Homeric epoch. The reason for this is manifestly to draw an image of the Germanic people that would be even more enthusiastic and flattering for the national pride of the Germans. The Persians, whom Tacitus viewed so favorably, simply did not seem good enough for Dahn: after all, in the minds of the nineteenth-century German public, educated in the cult of the Greek legacy, the Persians might provoke associations with barbarism, despotism, fanaticism, and decadence. For Tacitus and Dahn alike, the Persians, whatever achievements they might have had, were still strange Easterners, in contrast to the Greeks. In other words, his remark that Tacitus idealized the Germanic people was a rhetorical trap, and its true sense is to make his readers distrustful about the Persian analogy, which, in order to support his own argument, he replaces with a Homeric analogy. To make sure that his trap works, Dahn points out that if one cannot see the striking similarities between the proto-Germans and the Homeric Greeks, it is only because the Greeks were "talented craftsmen" who managed to produce an impressive legacy in literature, sculpture, and architecture, which was possible only because of the more favorable climatic conditions in Greece. Thus, he leaves his readers with the alternatives of either considering Greek cultural achievements to be a minor difference, which in no way undermines his analogy, or to believe that the Germanic people would have certainly left a similar legacy if only had they lived in the sunshine of Greece.[21]

Copying from the ancient authors, the German historians rarely cared about the psychological probability of their accounts, or perhaps they just painted these accounts with the colors of their patriotic imagination. Let us consider one more example, to be found in C. A. Bonath's high-school textbook, which we may view as a typical Germanic variation of Jean-Jacques Rousseau's concept of the noble savage. First, the author discusses the legendary loyalty of the Germanic warriors, explaining that it was common for them to commit suicide if their commander perished in battle, as outliving him would be an intolerable disgrace. Second, he considers their other principal virtue: hospitality, which would go so far that "if a guest killed his host's father, he might feel safe as long as he stayed at his home." Finally, he suggests that their honesty made them completely unaware of the very idea of theft and forgery. As they liked playing dice and drinking, once they lost all they had, including their wives and children, they would play for their own freedom, and if they lost again, they peacefully accepted their newly acquired slave status and fully obeyed their new master.[22]

It is also astonishing to what degree the German historians ignored the contradictions within the image of Germanic society they created and perpetuated. According to the narratives analyzed herein, the ancestors of the Germans were supposed to have valued liberty and individualism above all and, at the same time, to have been the most obedient and loyal members of their clan or squad. The historians suggest that these German forebears knew only the "sense of order" (*Ordnungssinn*) and that they had no individual identity at all. They were supposed to have respected women more than did any other peoples of their time and yet not to have considered them humans at all. It is virtually impossible to find any attempt to explain these apparent inconsistencies in the historians' narratives. As noted, however, it seems that perhaps no such explanation was deemed necessary, as the image they constructed of the German national character in its earliest—and therefore clearest—form, was essential and served as an interpretive key to the entire national history that ensued. This was a post-Hegelian idea, that of a synthesis embracing opposite poles of radically different elements. A structure as complicated as a nation had to be profoundly inclusive, hence the need to combine both the individualistic and the communitarian elements: hatred of strangers paired with hospitality, love for liberty plus a desire for order. The historians did not bother explaining how it was possible that all these elements had coexisted and worked together, because their main goal was to present them as seeds from which the future German history was to grow. And finally, these elements had to have been present at the beginning of the national history in their original, naked, and pure form, as they were doomed to be polluted and abused in the future under the influence of strangers: the Romans and their civilization, the Catholic Church and its cosmopolitanism, and various dangerous and immoral foreigners, the French being the worst. If the German nation of the nineteenth century was divided and uncertain of its own character and ideals, it was because its original virtues had been forgotten. The historians' task was to reinvigorate them and rediscover what was pure and truly German in their imperfect contemporary world.

Like many others, Lamprecht argues that military conquests, which resulted in captives being settled in German lands, brought about a profound change in Germanic society. The Germanic tribes now lived in constant contact with the Roman and Celtic cultures, they learned to cultivate land the way foreigners did, and as they ended their practice of constant resettlement, landownership became an issue. A new social elite appeared, consuming the lion's share of the conquered territories and exploiting the labor of the captives. This elite of "little tyrants" soon became the foundation of the early feudal system, and these elites usurped for their own benefit the prerogatives of public administration, such as taxation and conscription of soldiers. The more "civilized" the Germanic people were, the more their original values, particularly their beloved "German liberty," suffered and fell into oblivion. Thus, according to Lamprecht, the original Germanic customs and values survived in their purest forms in the most eastern provinces of the country: Bavaria, Saxony, and Thuringia, "with positive consequences for the constitution of the Empire in the tenth century."[23]

The Roman influence eventually became one of the most problematic issues for the German historians, who alternated between respect and disregard for the Roman Empire. The aforementioned analogy with the Greeks, so dear to the national pride of the Germans educated in the classical gymnasia, was one way to escape the problem. The multiple and undeniable Roman influences were commented upon with numerous reservations and a distinct tone of melancholy, as it was evident that the Germanic people's original purity did not remain intact when confronted with the corruptive charm of Roman civilization. Kurt Breysig's work manifests the most desperation about this process, as he argues that the entire process of the Germanic people's assimilation into Roman law, culture, customs, and language, which actually denationalized a number of Germanic tribes (the Francs being the saddest example), can only be described as the posthumous revenge of the Roman Empire against the healthy peoples who had destroyed it. Only the northern Germanic tribes, like the Anglo-Saxons, who had limited contacts with the Romans, remained in his view uninfected by this poisonous impact.[24]

From Rome to Prussia

One of the key problems of nineteenth-century German historiography was the question of the birth of the German nation. Indeed, it seems that the nature of the problem was specifically German, and the answers these historians provided had a remarkable impact on future narratives about national history. To be sure, from today's point of view the question may seem inappropriately formulated and motivated by outdated—and politically compromised—nationalist ideology, which viewed nations as virtually unchangeable monoliths. In general, modern historians tend to view nations as essentially a modern phenomenon, and when they do not refuse outright to discuss national origins, they typically locate them in the Enlightenment and emphasize that it was only in the nineteenth century that modern nations became fully formed.

However, we do not need to be bothered with the question of whether these nineteenth-century authors, who assumed that the German nation had been formed in the early Middle Ages, got it entirely wrong, or why. In fact, I would argue that the problem they had in mind was different from the one today's historians discuss when examining the beginnings of national consciousness. Indeed, the issue of the beginnings of national identity nurtured the nineteenth-century authors as well, and we shall see that they interpreted that issue in a variety of ways. However, what they actually had in mind when debating the origins of the German nation was the beginning of German history. Thus, what they were really asking was where and when the continuity of German history began and when Germans became subjects of their own history.

The idealized Germanic tribes, who successfully opposed Roman domination and eventually contributed to the fall of the Roman Empire, satisfied the later German desire for a spectacular ancestry in the age of nationalism. Their glorious image was supplemented with a respectable ancestry of their own, allegedly reaching back to the Indian Aryans. However, as already mentioned, all Germanic virtues were anchored in their attachment to nature or, if you like, in the dark, impenetrable forests of northern Europe, sealed off from the poisonous Roman civilization. The forest was the nest of the people and shaped their glorious character, but it was not Germany yet. Once the Germanic people migrated to the territories controlled by Rome and formed the states that rose on its peripheries and its ruins, one could speak about "Germany." But which Germanic state, or state-like political organism, deserved to be considered Germany? A natural choice seemed to be those that were located on future German territory. But there were a number of groups that met that criterion, and picking one from that group seemed to be a process infused with local particularism, which the nineteenth-century German nationalists regarded as a destructive and backward concept. The powerful kingdom of the Franks, raised to imperial status by Charlemagne, was a tempting option. And yet it smelled of the French, the eternal rival and enemy of all things German. What was left was the Kingdom of the East Franks under Louis, created by the Treaty of Verdun in 843. But for some authors this country was still too cosmopolitan, as was the Salic dynasty, and therefore some historians considered Henry the Fowler to be the first truly German ruler—the one who was the first to understand what German national interests were and the first to pursue them.

In short, the origins of Germany were disputable. The patriotic historians were trapped by their own dogmas. They praised the Germanic people beyond reasonable limits and emphasized their kinship with the modern German nation, but they could not, however, deny their kinship with other European nations. Their problem was that they could not accept a shared national legacy, because they viewed German originality and uniqueness to be the fundamental aspect of their nationhood. They searched for a uniquely German element, and their goal was to find it in the epoch when the Germanic people had just left their isolated forest preserve and intermingled with strangers. So their question was this: What constituted a truly Germanic state?

A good example of this approach can be found in Oskar Jäger's narrative about the Italian Kingdom of the Goths under Theodoric the Great. The historian repeatedly emphasizes its perfectly Germanic character (even though it cannot yet be called German). His analysis first concentrates on the political order, which is based on the personal authority of the ruler and is supported, but not limited, by a council of representatives of the most powerful families. In the council, he observes, "the Roman element, with its culture and education, was extremely helpful." Still, he stresses that the Germanic Goths, a young and strong people, remained—despite their intense and invigorating contacts with the weakened Italians—a caste of their own: a community of warrior nobles and a pillar of the king's power. He crowns his argument with praise for Theodoric's personal policies. First, he claims, the king did not persecute anyone because of their religion (as was the notorious practice during the time of innumerable schisms competing for the title of Christian orthodoxy). Second, he limited the use of "tyrannical violence" to the political opposition, which, however, was also both very tolerant and very smart.[25]

My interpretation of this passage is that it was allegorical. A German reader at the turn of the twentieth century could not fail to notice an analogy to the Prussian monarchy of Frederick the Great or indeed the ideal promoted by Wilhelm II. This ideal was the German—that is, highly militarized—version of enlightened autocracy, in which a strong ruler, supported by the military and educated elite of the country, tolerantly respects his subjects' personal and religious liberties insofar as they refrained from any political activity that could undermine his power. The idea was to draw an idealized and timeless image of the German way of doing politics in general. In this context, Theodoric deserved to be called a perfect Germanic monarch: not because he ruled over Germans or in Germany but because of the way he ruled. One may ponder whether the analogies between the early Middle Ages and the Hohenzollern monarchy were subconscious or whether the author decided not to state them explicitly for rhetorical reasons, as he believed his readers would find them obvious.

German historians univocally emphasized the religious tolerance of the Germanic states established on the ruins of Rome during the epoch of intense and brutal competition between various Christian denominations (or schisms)—mostly

Catholic and Aryan. Needless to say, in the nineteenth century, when the last religious restrictions were disappearing from western Europe under pressure from progressive public opinion, this claim served as yet another compliment for the ancestors of Germans. It was for this reason, apparently, that historians avoided asking the question of whether the religious tolerance of the Goths did not in fact mark their indifference to the most hotly debated issues of their newly acquired Christian faith. Another typical claim, first introduced by Friedrich Kohlrausch in his 1816 German history text, was that the young and energetic Germanic race eventually saved Christianity from Roman decadence.[26] On one hand, his claim was a purely nationalistic idea, based on the assumption that all things Roman had been corrupted and were doomed, while on the other hand it was a Hegelian concept, according to which ideas are immortal and choose the fittest representatives, or bearers, in each epoch.

However, this idea was challenged by Heinrich von Sybel in his article "The Christian-Germanic State Idea," from 1851. In Sybel's view, the idea of a synthesis of Christianity and the Germanic political order was an ahistorical misconception, based on the study of feudal realities in the late Middle Ages, when royal authority was successfully checked by the Church and the estates. Quite paradoxically, and yet consistently, Sybel argues that the feudal order had been the culmination of despotism in German history, and he juxtaposes it against the idea of the *Rechtsstaat*: a state governed by a universal law for all its citizens. In his view, only a centralized and powerful monarchy was capable of building such a state and securing its proper functioning. He believes that feudalism, with its variety of laws embracing different estates and exercised by local lords or assemblies, limited individual liberties in a much more oppressive way than an absolutist monarchy. Moreover, the *Rechtsstaat* in his view is "a fulfillment of the Christian will, and an eternal goal of the Germanic spirit."[27] Sybel's criticism met with opposition from the Austro-German historian Julius Ficker. Ficker's argument is based on the standard German juxtaposition of the Romanic and Germanic political traditions. The former, he claims, prefers bureaucracy, hierarchy, and centralized government, whereas the Germanic people are individualists willing to give up their love for unlimited liberty only in extreme situations.[28] Again, Ficker's readers could certainly sense that his model of the Roman political order was related as much to the general image of the Roman Empire as it was to the French monarchy—the successor to Rome as the main enemy of all things German.

As noted, German historians avoided explicitly acknowledging that their image of the Germanic political order and society was full of inner contradictions. Nonetheless, they were aware that the legendary Germanic love for liberty was a problematic foundation upon which to build a stable political organization. One can easily see this in their debates concerning the emergence of royal power and the decline of the semimythical order based on assemblies of all free men. As far as this issue is concerned, serious differences could already be observed among the authors of the liberal generation of the first half of the century. The next generation of authors tried to resolve those issues by underemphasizing liberty and focusing on the problem of the (monarchical) state power.

Friedrich Christoph Dahlmann is perhaps the most radical in this respect, as he argues that among all the liberty-loving Germanic tribes the Saxons were the freest, for they did not elect any kings but only dukes of war (*Herzog*), and this was precisely why they respected the law more than did any other tribe.[29] According to Heinrich Leo, monarchy was formed as a consequence of constant war and conquests, which were also followed by significant changes in the social structure: the class of nobles (whom he compares to officers) appeared, as well as a class of partially free former captives, tasked to labor on newly acquired lands. As the institution of the monarchy evolved from that of a duke elected in wartime, it remained for the next thousand years a specifically German tradition to keep the throne formally elective.[30] Stacke, in promoting a paradox, is typical, or perhaps emblematic, of the entire interpretive tradition in this respect. On one hand, he claims that the Germanic people had adopted the institution of monarchy from the Romans and that it proved a necessity in times of constant war. On the other hand, he argues that it was the tradition of liberty and the communitarian constitution (*Gemeindeverfassung*) that gave the Germanic people the motivation and strength necessary to oppose the powerful Roman Empire. He also argues that the monarchy emerged in tandem with the "nature of the Germanic order" and soon became inherent in the national way of life (*Sein und Wesen*) without, however, damaging the "popular sense of liberty."[31]

Lamprecht analyzes in detail the Frankish monarchy's process of adapting Roman institutions and cultural patterns, even though he insists, in an overtly nationalist manner, that it preserved its national, "West-Germanic" character. Nevertheless, his conclusions are pessimistic: the Germanic people proved incapable of building a stable and durable state based on their natural virtues and inclinations, in particular the legendary Germanic liberty. Like Sybel and a number of others, he does not see any contradiction between a powerful and centralized monarchy and individual liberty, and he insists that it was feudalism—that is, the rising power of the estates and local landlords—that was its main enemy. The Frankish monarchy, despite being the most powerful and splendid of the Germanic states, disappointed him because it yielded to the pressure of feudal tendencies, which successfully limited the royal power and thus the storied Germanic liberty.[32] Dahn appears to be one of the few who recognized the inner tension between royal power and individual liberty. He solves the problem elegantly: in his view there was no difference between a monarchy and a republic in German history for a long time, as the power

of the assembly of all men preserved its prerogatives for a long period after the institution of monarchy had been introduced. Only the formation of nobility, along
with the subsequent exclusion of all landless men from the political community,
undermined the original political principles of the Germanic peoples.[33] Finally,
Johann Jastrow points out the fatal long-term consequences of adopting Roman
patterns in politics: the Germans remained mesmerized by the Roman idea of a
universal monarchy for centuries and thus neglected to establish a national one,
as other nations had.[34] As we shall see in chapter 2, this last point reappeared in
German historiography in many contexts.

Let us now reassess, in their contemporary political context, the German
historians' ideas about early national history so as to emphasize once again their
rhetorical-ideological positions. The so-called "liberal" authors, whose political
worldview was formed under the influence of the enlightened democratic ideas of
the pre-1848 (Vormärz) period, stressed the alleged Germanic attachment to liberty
and Christianity precisely because these were the values they desired for society.[35]
However, in the post-1848 context, liberty (in its Western sense) began to be sup-
planted as the German political ideal; its replacement was a centralized and powerful monarchy. Simultaneously, feudalism, with its dispersed power and strong local
particularism, remained demonized as Germany's most fatal disease. Thus, those
authors active after 1871, when Germany emerged united and imperialistic, kept
repeating that monarchy had been a product of constant war and conquests, but
they no longer seemed troubled by this fact. What they found regrettable was that
the early medieval monarchy had not preserved the original character it allegedly
possessed and instead yielded to the pressure of the centrifugal tendencies of feudal
elements. In their view, only a centralized power built up around a ruler surrounded
by a military elite guaranteed "German liberty" in the sense they ascribed to this
term. The legendary nature of the Germanic people—bellicosity, brutality, and vig-
or—was now being endlessly praised to establish a sort of ideal for the contemporary Germans. Militarism and autocracy were presented as timeless pillars of the
truly Germanic political order, as well as the guardians of German liberty.

Thus, in a number of texts discussed in this chapter, one can see an implicit desire to imagine that feudalism had never happened and that the Goths of Theodoric, the Prussians of Frederick, and the Germans of Bismarck and Wilhelm could
have marched together through centuries of national history. This is why the image
of the Germanic origins in Wilhelmine society is often called a myth in modern
scholarly literature.[36] This status arose not only because the image involved a number of fantastic elements that were products of early historians' and other authors'
imaginations; the image also evoked a circular concept of time, one in which the
Germanic society of the early medieval period was considered the ideal to be fulfilled in the future and the thousand-year-long period of feudalism judged a re-

grettable gap to be forgotten. As Mircea Eliade would have it, the main function of historical myths is to offer the chance for a national rebirth and a therapeutic new beginning by reverting to the original structure of the nation.

The Peaceful People

It may seem that Poles were no less fascinated with their early history (i.e., before the introduction of Christianity or rather, as we shall see, Catholicism) than were the Germans. This is particularly true with respect to Romanticism, which dominated Polish culture from the 1820s to 1860s, a period traditionally considered the era of the most spectacular achievements in Polish national literature, especially in poetry and drama. The most famous authors of the period—Adam Mickiewicz, Juliusz Słowacki, and Zygmunt Krasiński—chose the prehistoric realities and traditions—as they imagined them—to be the scenery and motifs of their dramas and poems, which remained highly popular among educated Poles until the second half of the twentieth century. Obviously, many of their less talented colleagues followed them in this respect, contributing to the establishment of the idealized and mysterious world of the pagan Slavs in the Polish national imagination.[37]

However, this trend had a different dynamic and scale than in Germany. In Poland and Germany alike, an uninterrupted tradition of cultivating and critically reassessing legends, chronicles, and other sources concerning early national history continued from the Renaissance to the Enlightenment.[38] It involved some of Poland's most talented wordsmiths: from Jan Kochanowski, the most famous poet of the Renaissance, who was also a pioneer in critical studies of the medieval chronicles, to Bishop Adam Naruszewicz, the country's first modern historian, who spent a number of years trying to figure out what should be accepted as true and what should be rejected as fantasy in these accounts and who, deeply frustrated in the end, gave up the idea of publishing the results of his research.[39] As far as foreign accounts about early medieval Slavs are concerned, all that Polish historians had at their disposal were short passages by a few Byzantine historians (Procopius of Caesarea, Theophylact Simocatta, and the author of *Strategicon*, attributed to Emperor Maurice) and some more detailed narratives in medieval German chronicles (e.g., those of Thietmar and Adam of Bremen).[40] Some of them were also familiar with more recent Western authors' comments concerning the Slavs, and they were probably allergic to their suggestions regarding the alleged Germanic impact on the institutions of the Polish-Lithuanian Commonwealth, such as its parliament—the Sejm (an impact recognized by, among others, Gibbon and Corning).[41] Finally, and most importantly, nineteenth-century Polish historians had to face the legacy of the Polish-Lithuanian nobility's specific obsession with its origins. Their origin story was based on sixteenth-century theories of the conquest of the

Slavic population of the future Polish-Lithuanian lands by the bellicose Sarmatians, who were supposed to have been the ancestors of the nobles. This theory (or theories) was enormously popular among the nobles of the Commonwealth between the sixteenth and eighteenth centuries, as it nicely supported their belief that they differed from the rest of the population not only by their social status and culture but also by blood.[42] Modern historians generally abandoned it as a fantasy based on the scarcest of evidence. They also dismissed it for ideological reasons: nineteenth-century historians did not intend to flatter the nobility anymore by emphasizing their alleged racial uniqueness and instead sought a narrative that would be acceptable for the entire nation and that would preferably contribute to its unity. Still, the idea that social divisions of the past had to have their origin in foreign conquest returned to Poland as a theory developed in the West, most notably by the French historian Augustin Thierry, who based his studies on the histories of England and France. Ironically, the theory was adopted by some Polish socialists (including Bronisław Limanowski), this time not to flatter the nobles but to stigmatize them.

However, one needs to bear in mind that the Romantic myth of the pre-Christian Slavic world was, in early nineteenth-century Polish society, revolutionarily democratic, as it undermined social divisions that many considered to be eternal. To be sure, much as it was in Germany, the myth was inspired by a general European trend to rediscover and reevaluate storied national origins, a trend initiated by the discoverers of early medieval Scotland: James Macpherson and Sir Walter Scott (the father of the modern historical novel). Among their enthusiasts were the first ethnographers and archaeologists of Poland, such as the aristocrats Alexander Sapieha and Jan Potocki (famous for his novel *The Saragossa Manuscript*) and, most importantly, Wawrzyniec Surowiecki. Surowiecki, in his pathbreaking book *On the Study of History and the Ancient Slavs* (1812), argued that "in order to study and describe the Slavs one needs to be a Slav himself."[43] He also suggested that studying the nation's prehistory was necessary because "the latest generations inherit the attributes of their ancestors. The customs, opinions, prejudices, enlightenment, vices, and virtues that govern our behavior today are regularly rooted in the most distant epochs of our forefathers. Since this is indisputable, one can easily conclude how important it is to learn about the origins."[44]

As is evident, his appeal repeats the thesis we have already encountered in discussing the German historians' narratives on their early history: that the national character is essentially unchangeable and that it is best to study it in its formative years, for it is then that it can be seen in its pure, natural form. The most famous apostle of the Slavic ancestors of the Poles, however, was Adam Czarnocki, the author of *On the Slavic World before Christianity*, published in 1818 under the pseudonym Zorian Dołęga Chodakowski. The book, which describes the "ancient" legends, customs, and beliefs of the Polish peasantry, coincided brilliantly with the eruption of Romantic sensitivity and Romantic interest in history. The credibility of the work was supposed to be taken for granted, as the author claimed to have based it on the stories he himself collected while roving from village to village, dressed humbly and talking to the oldest peasants he could find (as his pen name, which means "The Roamer," suggested).[45] His enthusiasm for the legendary world of the ancient Slavs influenced such historians as Wacław Maciejowski and Joachim Lelewel (whose writings we shall analyze in more detail), as well as poets, philosophers, and economists, who imagined that the rural idyll ought to be the pattern for future society, which would then be free from both feudalism and the miseries of nineteenth-century-style predatory industrialism.[46]

Nevertheless, with the decline and passing of Romanticism in the second half of the century, the enthusiasm for Slavic prehistory also declined in Polish culture and historiography, whereas in Germany early national history remained very popular and crucial for the nation-building project that ensued following the unification of 1871. Innumerable monuments, paintings, novels, operas, and finally movies imprinted the idealized image of the ancient Germanic warriors in the German national imagination, making them one of the pillars of modern German nationalism. The final phase of their "career" in this role was under the Nazis, when all Germans were officially supposed to be as heroic, brutal, and healthy as their alleged forefathers had been, if not in the present, then at least in the future, due to careful racial and eugenic engineering.

Despite some efforts by Polish fascists in the interwar period to reinvigorate the Slavic myth (a move certainly inspired by the Nazis), in the popular imagination of the Poles it remained related to Romanticism. There were apparently a number of reasons for this failure of the ancient Slavs to occupy such a remarkable position in the Polish national pantheon. One reason, paradoxically, was perhaps the actual popularity and esteem for the Romantic poets among educated Poles, which lasted until the second half of the twentieth century: the ancient Slavs never emancipated themselves from their monumental shadows in the national imagination. Second, the fascination with the ancient Slavs was related to the anti-Western and antimodernizing ideology of native exceptionalism, which eroded in the second half of the nineteenth century in Poland under the pressure of technical and scientific progress, which made the idea of copying from the West accepted and unquestioned, at least in some aspects, among the Polish elites. Third, pan-Slavism had become the official ideology of tsarist Russia in the Romantic era, under Nicholas I, and it was exploited to deny the Poles any rights of independence or autonomy from or within the Russian Empire, which successfully alienated many Polish patriots. Finally, the essence of the image of the ancient Slavs, as we shall see below, was politically ambiguous and controversial for a number of Polish historians.

Moreover, in sharp contrast to their German colleagues, many Polish historians openly admitted how little they knew about their nation's early history. Some of these declarations are clearly accompanied by regret, and we can only wonder if their reasons were purely professional—as professional historians are supposed to feel frustrated if they are short of evidence and to rejoice when confronted with a huge mountain of manuscripts that no one has yet read—or whether they were also ideological. In any case, no source as respectable as Tacitus, Caesar, or Procopius was available, nor was there a story as inspiring and thrilling as the Nibelung saga. In contrast to the German case, the few interesting puzzles that were available for the historians of Poland's prehistory had to wait for modern archaeology to rediscover them. As Józef Ignacy Kraszewski, an amateur historian, journalist, political activist, and Poland's most productive novelist (his oeuvre comprises almost 600 titles, including 232 novels!), melancholically observed, "Until Poland emerges in its alliance and its wars against Germany, we have scarcely any information concerning her history but some dime novels. And even these stories are not available for us in their original form as folk tales, for the people have already forgotten them, so we can only approach them through the chronicles written in subsequent epochs, for the purposes of their own time."[47]

We begin our overview with Joachim Lelewel, the most famous Polish Romantic historian. Due to the broad impact of his writings on professional and amateur historians alike, as well as his political involvement and international reputation, Lelewel remains the single most studied Polish historian and the only one whose legacy has also been extensively analyzed by authors writing in English.[48] There is no need, therefore, to reconstruct the evolution of his ideas concerning Poland's prehistory. It suffices to say that in his later years Lelewel, apparently under the influence of the historian of law Wacław Maciejowski, developed a fantastic theory on the racial genealogy of the Slavs, which, to be sure, he used to elucidate their character and virtues. For the purposes of this book, however, it should be enough to focus on the ideas he discussed in his *Considerations on Polish History*, finally published in 1855 as an adaptation of the earlier French edition.

In *Considerations*, Lelewel's democratic and communitarian ideals, to which he owed much of his reputation, are already clearly apparent but remain within the limits of reason that the contemporarily accessible evidence allowed. Thus, it might seem as if the book lacked a first chapter—its readers are confronted with the image of a fully formed society that awaits the fundamental change that would introduce it into history proper. The narrative begins at an undefined moment that seems to immediately precede the reign of Poland's first historical ruler, Prince

Mieszko (Mesco), who converted to Christianity in 966. Eventually, the rhetorical effect of such a narrative construction is that of a primordial harmony, of a "natural" order that had supposedly existed since time immemorial until the moment when the country was confronted with the challenge of Western civilization and history itself, a confrontation that would question the values, structure, and indeed the existence of the original Slavic community. Like his German colleagues, Lelewel believed these values were timeless, and he wished them to be reintroduced into the social life of his own time.

What he values the most about prehistoric Poland, as he views it, is its alleged egalitarianism, epitomized in the communitarian political order, one that is based on the will of the assembly of all free men. As he stresses, "according to Slavic law and custom the captives were also included in the citizenry after a time," and land belonged only to those who actually cultivated it.[49] In the scholarly literature, Lelewel is typically considered a "republican," someone who highly valued the democratic institutions of the Commonwealth, in contrast to the "monarchists," who wanted Poland to resemble the absolutist monarchies that surrounded it and finally partitioned it. To be sure, Lelewel was also a republican in the literal sense of the word, as he wished the Poland of his own day to become a republic. However, his republicanism should also be viewed in a broader sense: as a belief that a perfect society is a community of free people who express their will through free voting, be it in an assembly of all or in a parliamentary institution. As such, he was a perfect product of the Enlightenment and shared the ideals one can also find in the writings of Jean-Jacques Rousseau, Immanuel Kant, or in Johann Gottlieb Fichte's *Addresses to the German Nation*.[50]

As mentioned above, Lelewel's history of Poland starts when the original idyll is endangered. The process of destruction begins with the introduction of class differentiation: the "noble class" appears and begins to exert pressure on the "free peasantry." However, Lelewel does not provide a full explanation of the origins of this process. On one hand, he suggests it was a result of the cultural transfer of "Western ideas," which included the authority of the monarch and the general idea of feudal social differentiation into legally separated social groups. On the other hand, he vehemently opposes all contemporary theories according to which the rise of the nobility was the result of a foreign invasion—by the Sarmatians or other Scythians (as Mickiewicz had it), the Goths (according to Naruszewicz and Jerzy S. Bandtke), or the Varangians (according to Karol Szajnocha).[51] This question is further complicated for linguistic reasons: Lelewel tends to believe that the Polish word *szlachta* (nobility) is related to the term Lach, which is associated with a tribe bordering Rus and used as a synonym for a Pole, especially in the East, up until his own lifetime (it is also the name of a legendary early Polish ruler). This might suggest that the social divisions among Poles had their origin in a sort of conquest by indigenes. However, Lelewel does not elaborate on this, and he insists that the nobility and the peasants had originally been one people and that the former's aspiration to attain a special status within society had been a usurpation in light of native traditions and law.[52] His analysis of the process whereby social differences arise is eventually based on his readings of later codes and legal arrangements. Noting the subsequent legal changes that strengthened the position of great landowners and the monarch vis-à-vis the ever less free peasants, he concluded that this process had its origins in prehistoric times and thus that there was once a time when all men had been free and equal.

Lelewel is not fully coherent in his analysis of the rise of the monarchical power either. On one hand, he claims that the despotism of the rulers of the first Polish dynasty (the Piasts), who considered the entire country to be their property, went "against the Slavic spirit, against the principles that had been observed for centuries." On the other hand, he also disapproves of the decline of monarchical prerogatives from the twelfth century on, as well as the simultaneous rise in the position and influence of the great landowners and holders of local offices. In this context, and in sharp contrast to what he would write on the partitions of Poland, Lelewel argues that "they say the despotism of one is better than the despotism of the plenty, who oppress the people eagerly and carefully. This is what developed in Poland."[53]

Lelewel consistently presents these two issues—the monarchical despotism and the oppression of the poor by the rich—as Poland's main civic ills throughout the centuries, up to the partitions of the Commonwealth. He also emphasizes that the source of the problem was in imitating the West or simply yielding to the pressure of Western patterns and, consequently, neglecting native traditions: "I have said many a time, as others have argued, that since Christianity was introduced in Poland due to the progress of Western civilization, the people have been losing their original freedom, and their rights have been regularly violated and discredited."[54]

The "others" he had in mind were most likely Chodakowski and Maciejewski. In order to support their claim, they developed an original theory explaining the nature of the popular turmoil in the first half of the eleventh century, when a number of churches had been destroyed, allegedly by pagans who had refused to accept the new religion of the country. According to their theory, which was also based on some archaeological findings (and therefore has remained a matter of discussion until today), before Poland officially accepted Christianity in its Latin rite in 966, it had already been present in the country in the Byzantine-Slavic rite. This earlier rite was supposed to have better fit the customs of the country and to have been more popular among the simple folk, and thus many of the internal conflicts of the time, known from the later chronicles as the dynastic struggle for power, were supposed to have actually mirrored the rivalry between the "elitist" Latin form of worship and the "popular" Slavic rite.[55]

It seems remarkable that in his *Considerations* Lelewel draws his most elaborate image of primordial Polish society in a passage concerning the end of the sixteenth century—the epoch when, in his view, the original Polish institutions and social order finally degenerated. In order to explain what had been lost, he tries to return to the beginning. His analysis is both strikingly naïve and insightful at the same time. On one hand, he constructs a poetic image of a primordial idyll: he emphasizes his beloved people's love for liberty and nationality, their hospitality and generosity, their limited inventiveness, and their talent for imitation. Finally, he argues that "because of their peaceful and honeyed disposition, it happened a few times they were forced to kneel down and yield to foreign pressure; one cannot say, however, it happened owing to their ineptitude." One the other hand, Lelewel remarks that he is himself incapable of grasping the greatness of their virtues, for they represent a world that has been lost due to the progress of civilization and its detestable concepts. To be sure, he does not employ this meta-argument to question his own claims but to defend his paradise lost against any possible accusations. "The mediocrity of their talents is illusive, for their customs and ideas do not match what the foreign civilization promotes," he writes, whereas "what are considered to be their flaws, are actually a result of their qualities and their virtue."[56] This two-faced strategy may seem symptomatic of the historical epistemology of the age: in one moment Lelewel, like Ranke, argues that all epochs should be evaluated according to their own standards, while in another he pursues his own standards as universal.

For Polish historians of subsequent generations, the issue of the originality and exceptionality of the native culture of the pre-Christian population of Poland was of relatively minor importance. Nevertheless, they unanimously repeated the main points of the characteristics of the Slavs as formulated by Herder, in exactly the same manner that their German colleagues reproduced the characteristics of proto-Germans as constructed by Tacitus. Needless to say, they also reinterpreted them according to their own political and ideological values.

Let us begin with the aspects they generally agree upon. According to Henryk Schmitt, "What distinguished [the prehistoric Poles], next to their peaceful nature, was their great love for personal freedom, which they preferred over the security of the community."[57] In summarizing Polish history up to the twelfth century, Schmitt argues that the original Slavic egalitarianism was in continuous decline but that the situation of the lower classes was still better than in the West. This is supported by rather incoherent reasoning, according to which the Poles did not know the institution of slavery, while the Jewish migration to Poland was to be lamented because the Jews traded slaves.[58]

Michał Bobrzyński is the only one to argue that the Slavs had lived a nomadic life before they settled down and proved their talents for agriculture and apiculture. He then continues with the standard claim that "the Slavs knew no respect for despotic authority and law, nor the strength that results from unity and organization." Reasoning like the ancient authors, he explains this by their relative wealth and prosperity and the fact that they were not confronted with enough dangerous challenges. As a result, he concludes critically, their "peaceful, noble, and hospitable nature" degenerated because of their comfortable existence, which made them "careless, joyful, sluggish, and inclined toward constant dancing and singing." Like others, Bobrzyński emphasizes the paternalistic structure of Slavic society and the Slavs' extraordinary respect for the elderly and for women (whose position in society, he stresses, was much higher than it was among Germanic peoples).[59] Analogically, Władysław Smoleński uses colorful terms to describe the bucolic qualities of the ancient Slavs' rural way of life, concluding, however, that they had no inclination for war and proved incapable of building a stable political organization, because of their "carelessness, sluggishness, and disorderly nature."[60]

In short, the ancient Slavs resembled Rousseau's noble savage, whereas the ancient Germans lived in Hobbes's natural conditions, which made them brutal and aggressive. In both images, nature is the major interpretive key, and its uses are openly tautological, combining ethical and epistemological as well as explanatory and apologetic functions, and, most importantly, masking the inner incoherencies in the argumentation.

The most troubling aspect of the Herderian image of Slavic society was its alleged anarchism and its inability to resist the foreign aggressions that resulted from it. As we shall see shortly, Polish historians invariably saw this problem in the context of German-Polish military conflicts in the eleventh and twelfth centuries. They accepted the basic points of racial stereotyping—according to which Germans were aggressive and Slavs peaceful by nature—and thus further complicated the problem for those authors trying to instill national pride or even simply to explain the intensity of the conflict. Another fundamental issue that caused interpretive difficulties with respect to the Slavs' alleged anarchism and peacefulness was the question of how they managed to build any sort of durable political organization. There was, after all, a striking discrepancy in the sources that determined their reasoning: according to the ancient authors, the Slavic people had been individualists inclined toward anarchy, hardly capable of tolerating any centralized authority; according to medieval chronicles, however, the Poland of the tenth through twelfth centuries was a despotic monarchy ruled by a Piast dynasty that considered the entire country to be its property and did not tolerate any political opposition. How Poland became such a monarchy was a problem for which the evidence provided no answer.

Polish historians answer this question in a manner parallel to what we have become familiar with in analyzing German historiography. First, they unanimously agree that the idea of monarchical rule was imported from the West. Second, it was adopted by the Slavs as a sheer necessity, in response to foreign military pressure. The parallel seems remarkable since, as noted, the Polish historians had virtually no evidence to support their reasoning in this respect, and their entire interpretive effort was eventually to make the two incoherent images consistent. A few comments are noteworthy. Bobrzyński, the most devoted advocate of Westernization among our historians, argues with clearly expressed regret that the entire process of building monarchical structures of power among the Slavs "was of course very slow"—too slow to save the West Slavs from German military pressure. Józef Szujski, in contrast, claims that the process was quick, owing to the "natural" conservatism of the Slavs (as if monarchy were a conservative institution by definition). He also adds, evidently having future developments in mind, that things did not go as they should have: the building of a healthy paternalistic monarchy was incomplete, and it soon degenerated toward "feverish anarchy" in Poland and "slavish passivity" in Russia.[61]

Clearly, the latter argument constitutes a parallel with the German historians' attempts to distinguish, as early as possible, the Germanic people who were to become Germans in the future from the future aliens, particularly the French. In contrast to the German historians, who desperately tried to assess the level of the demonized Roman impact on various Germanic tribes in order to explain the future antagonism between them, the Polish historians had a more precise argument at their disposal: the difference between the Latin and the Greek forms of worship. However, their views on the question of the internal divisions in the Slavic world were in fact highly ambivalent. This ambivalence deserves a closer look, for it perfectly mirrors various historians' ideological involvements.

Lelewel, as an enthusiast of Slavic nativism and a democrat, is highly critical of the developments in Rus. The original Slavic idyll, in his view, was first undermined by the Varangian conquest, which introduced the element of brutality and violence into the hitherto peaceful country. Subsequently, Rus fell under the influence of Byzantium, from which a cult of despotic power was imported. Interestingly, despite his strongly anti-Western stance, when discussing the Byzantine impact Lelewel employs the Latin stereotypes regarding Greek decadence, perfidy, and despotism, which he despised the most, especially where the subjugation of religion to political power is concerned. In this context, he even appreciates the role of the Catholic clergy, which, despite being a Westernizing factor, opposed the Polish monarchs' appetite for unlimited power.[62] In his later years as an émigré in Brussels after fleeing the oppression of the Russian tsar, Lelewel developed a theory that allowed him to escape the contradiction inherent in his sentiment for the Slavs and his animosity toward contemporary Russia. According to his theory, Muscovy essentially lost its Slavic character in consequence of the Mongolian conquest and thus was not really a successor of the lost civilization of Kievan Rus in the cultural or political sense.

Karol Boromeusz Hoffman and Józef Szujski emphasize the religious division among the Slavs more overtly, highlighting Catholicism as a factor that contributed to the Westernization of Poland. Hoffman is perhaps the only one to openly and approvingly claim that by adopting Christianity in the Latin rite, all pagans "rejected their native customs and laws and accepted the principles of the Church."[63] Szujski, the most devout among the Polish historians examined here, is even more effusive and explicit about the advantages of adopting Catholicism. He argues straightforwardly in the name of both history and the true religion: "Joining the Catholic Roman Church decided the question of participation in the cause of the Roman Catholic civilization and historical progress, whereas rejecting it would have constituted an enemy of progress, and a negative historical factor. This was the most important issue of the time, which clearly surpassed all others."[64]

Finally, the most anticlerical of the Polish historians under analysis, Władysław Smoleński, is the one who expresses the most regret about the division of the Slavs into two religious camps and, more scandalously, also raises some doubts as to whether Poland's choice was the right one. First, he reminds his readers that at the time when Poland adopted Christianity, the Western Latin world represented a lower level of civilization as compared to the more sophisticated Byzantium, which was also friendlier and more flexible toward the Slavs, as demonstrated by the use of separate alphabets and rituals, whereas Rome preferred converting its subjects by pure force. It was much later, he claims, when the East and South Slavs, surrounded by "barbarians," degenerated into backwardness and ignorance. Thus, he concludes, it was tragic that the struggle against fellow Slavs in the name of Western civilization filled up so many chapters of Polish history.[65]

Furor Teutonicus

Finally, let us take a closer look at one more problem that, according to Polish historians, was to determine Polish history from its beginning: the German-Polish antagonism. As a military aggressor and the main provider of cultural and technological innovations, Germany played a parallel role in Polish historiography to that of Rome in the German one. Consequently, one of the main interpretive challenges Polish historians faced in constructing their narratives was how to interpret the preponderant German influence on Polish culture and politics in the early stages of its national history. This is not to say all of our historians were enemies of all things German. However, they had to acknowledge that in the first stages of its existence Poland was constantly in danger of being dominated by its powerful neighbor, from whom it imported cultural patterns, technology, and, finally, numerous settlers as well. Thus, anti-German sentiment was above all viewed as a question of preserving the national identity and its most fragile element: national pride.

Finally, anti-German sentiment was also strongly present in the evidence the Polish historians had at their disposal, as part of the legacy of the century-and-a-half-long conflict between the Polish kingdom and the Teutonic Order over Pomerania (1308–1466). Apart from numerous military campaigns, the conflict was also manifested in a series of trials in the papal tribunal and councils (particularly in Constance, 1414–18) and was accompanied by an almost incessant flow of diplomatic memoranda and propagandistic pamphlets. The task of discrediting the Teutonic knights' pretensions and demonizing their methods was one that attracted many of Poland's most talented wordsmiths during the late medieval and early modern period, including, for example, Jan Długosz, author of the monumental *Chronicles of the Famous Kingdom of Poland*—a must-read for all Polish historians. Since the Teutonic knights were popularly viewed (in both Germany and Poland) as essentially German (or, more precisely, as predecessors of Hohenzollern Prussia), the anti-German sentiment became a pillar of one of the most respected and ancient Polish intellectual traditions, which the nineteenth-century historians could hardly ignore.

Joachim Lelewel followed it the most faithfully, or perhaps most obsessively, among the historians analyzed. His passionate prejudice against all things German may seem paradoxical, as he did not live to the age of aggressive nationalism, and he was not chauvinistic as far as other nationalities were concerned, despite his love for his native Polish culture. It was the Germans, in his view, who were primarily responsible for undermining and polluting the original purity of Polish customs and laws. The list of sins he ascribes to them is long and colorful and includes, *inter alia*, promoting the feudal concepts of social differentiation and the ambitions of the rich and powerful, as expressed in the importation of their habits and practices, such as dueling. Lelewel neither hides nor denies that, as a result of the massive influx of German settlers into Poland in the thirteenth and fourteenth centuries, German culture and law became predominant features in the majority of Polish cities. He simply finds this fact lamentable, an example of how ethnic "otherness" undermined national unity, complementing the growing class divisions. His final and most serious accusation against the German burghers of medieval Poland is that they "kept various contacts" with their fatherland (for example, they appealed to Magdeburg, Halle, and Lubeck when legal controversies arose), which eventually "posed a danger to the country"—in other words, smelled of high treason. Notably, despite his love for the purity of original Polish culture, he seems sympathetic, if not enthusiastic, about other immigrants to Poland; Jews, Roma, Armenians, Czechs, Italians, and Spaniards are all viewed as welcomed guests, and the historian recalls their settlement in Poland proudly, as evidence of the country's good reputation and wealth. In contrast, he claims, "the alarming influx of German foes deserves caution."[66] And indeed, it seems that throughout his entire oeuvre Germans are never mentioned without some alarming or disapproving comment attached.

Henryk Schmitt generalizes Lelewel's approach: in his narrative the former's anti-German obsession involves other nationalities, too, particularly Jews. Obviously, Schmitt also regrets that so many representatives of these "alien" races settled in Poland in the medieval period, which he views as the result of the coherent yet horrendous policy of the Piast rulers, who offered the newcomers numerous privileges and legal autonomy. Eventually his assessment of Polish monarchs is correlated with their military successes in conflicts against neighbors, especially against Germans. One can clearly see how much attention he attaches to this fundamental issue of national pride by reading his emotional comment concerning a singular opinion, which he found in a contemporary German chronicle, that the Polish Prince Boleslaus IV was supposed to have begged Emperor Friedrick Barbarossa to forgive his disloyalty with "great humility" during their meeting in 1157. Schmitt angrily dismisses this information as "pure fantasy."[67]

No other Polish historian created a more apocalyptic image of the German menace than did Karol Szajnocha in his very popular (perhaps the most popular historical book of the century) *Jadwiga and Jagiełło*. The book, apart from being an extended biography of Queen Jadwiga and her Lithuanian husband Jogaila, who was crowned King Jagiełło of Poland in 1386, focuses on the conflict between Poland, Lithuania, and the Teutonic Order, which is presented as a mortal threat to both countries. However, in the historian's view, the Teutonic Order is but an element of persistent German expansionism dating back to the dawn of Polish history. Arguing in accordance with the stereotypical image of the Slavs, Szajnocha informs his readers that the Germans had been lured by promises of "open frontiers, the benign nature of the people, fertility of the land, and lack of competition." He accuses the Germans of cruelty, perfidy, greed, pride, filth, and an unceasing and unlimited appetite for Slavic lands. Thus, he considers the "rapturous military invasions" and the "pressure of urban colonization and trade" to be elements of one process, animated by a pan-German dream to conquer or subordinate the entire Slavic realm.[68]

Szujski shows much more respect for the blessings of Western civilization than his colleagues and is therefore a better example of the spirit of animosity against Germany permeating the writings of Polish historians. Although, as mentioned, he considers the adoption of Christianity to be the central turning point in Polish history, he refused to relate it to the German influence on Poland. In contrast, he emphasizes that it was Germany that was responsible for introducing feudalism—an idea despised almost as much by Polish historians as by German ones. However, what Szujski means by feudalism in the context of German influence seems highly incoherent. Apparently he confuses it with yet another unpopular idea: that of despotism. In his view, the Slavs had been more democratic than the Germans; their rulers had simply been representatives of the people and "administrators of the national property," whereas the Germanic ones had been "owners of the entire country and the source of all dignity." Clearly his analysis aims at an explanation of the political order of the early Polish Piast monarchy, which, as mentioned, is quite inexplicable in the context of the Slavs' alleged democratic individualism. Interestingly, it also appears in parallel to the German image of Rome and its poisonous influence on Germanic institutions. Consequently, Szujski's ambiguous phobia against Germans may be observed in his comments about German medieval colonization in Poland: he does not complain about the germanization of Polish cities but rejoices over the successes of the "Polish spirit," like the emancipation of the Polish Catholic clergy from German influence.[69] In short, in his view cultural importation from the West was a blessing for Poland, particularly insofar as Catholicism is concerned, provided it had nothing to do with Germany. The polonization of imported institutions, and especially the Church, was also emphasized by Stanisław Kaczkowski, author of the first Polish monograph on the history of the Teutonic Order. However, Kaczkowski claims that the Teutonic knights were a just punishment the Poles deserved for having helped the Germans fight the West Slavs and Prussians—whom he considers "brothers," that is, Slavs.[70]

Finally, Bobrzyński's and Smoleński's attitudes toward the Germans differed from those of their fellow historians in that they were coherent and transparent. Like his colleagues, Bobrzyński values all Polish military triumphs in the conflicts against the powerful neighbor and regrets that the Poles assisted the Germans in their conquests of the Slavs living between the Oder and Elbe and passively watched the annihilation of their independence. However, he overtly argues that at that time Germans represented a higher civilization and a better political organization, and he despairs that the Poles did not learn their lesson from them because of their "hatred of the Germans."[71] He takes a parallel approach, perhaps shocking to his contemporary readers, with regard to German colonization. On one hand, he emphasizes the "most fortunate" impact of the colonization on agriculture and technological innovations, on the organization of labor, and even on the political administration (including that of the Czechs!). On the other hand, like a modern nationalist who witnessed and reconsidered the progress of Bismarck's realpolitik, he describes the process of cultural germanization of the western borderlands and the cities, stressing that Germans were actually enemies of Poland—enemies who should not be demonized but imitated.[72] Apparently, he would also have glorified Theodoric—who learned from his Roman advisors how to govern Italy—had Theodoric been a Slavic ruler.

Smoleński takes a similar approach to colonization, stressing its benefits for the Polish economy and Polish agriculture, on one hand, and on the other the menace it posed to Polish national identity, which, however, except for Pomerania and Silesia, was neutralized due to the cautious policies of the Polish monarchs. Importantly, he is the only historian under discussion here who openly distances himself from the idea of a natural antagonism between Germans and Poles. He is also the only one to observe calmly that German chronicles constituted a major part of the evidence on early Polish history available to historians of his time and to suggest that the idea of a bitter antagonism between the two peoples owes much to their authors' prejudices, motivated by their "patriotic anger" against Polish rulers who opposed the emperor militarily and politically. In other words, he implicitly suggests that some of the anti-German sentiment of his colleagues may be a result of their frustration with the anti-Polish propaganda they encountered in their sources.[73]

CHAPTER TWO

The Zenith

Semimythical origins and the early history of Germany and Poland constituted a challenge for historians who had intended to draw a glorious and invigorating image of the national past. The idea that the two primal groups enjoyed harmony and unity, and that those inherent virtues were pure and unpolluted by foreign elements, posed a question regarding the future development of these two peoples: Having achieved such ideal social conditions in their infancy as national peoples, would both Germans and Poles struggle to preserve such an idyll? Of course, our historians did not follow this dogma consistently. The idea of the original perfection of sociopolitical conditions remained in the background of numerous interpretations concerning future developments, although it did not overshadow the sense of drama and importance the historians featured in their work. After all, both the German and the Polish national histories still offered many exciting and indeed decisive moments and shifts to be narrated.

In this chapter, I focus on narratives concerning the late medieval and early modern periods. My analysis emphasizes two sets of problems. First I address territorial expansion, specifically, the efforts of medieval emperors to maintain control over Burgundy and Italy (in relation to their rivalry with the popes for formal supremacy in the Western Christian world) and the union of Poland with Lithuania under the Jagiellon dynasty. The majority of our historians obviously considered and presented annexations and conquests as episodes of national pride and might. Like it or not, territorial expansion brought forth much enthusiasm among the patriotic public (and sometimes still does), regardless of its costs and the reactions of inhabitants of the annexed territories. The idea that conquests testify to a country's glory and strength apparently dates back to the origins of history itself. Dionysius of Halicarnassus put it most straightforwardly in the preface to his *Roman Antiquities*: he had chosen Roman history as his subject, he explained, because he considered it the noblest one, given the unparalleled Roman conquests: "the most shining achievements that can possibly be treated of." His assumption was based on "an universal and unalterable law of history" by which "it is ordained that superiors shall govern the inferiors."[1] However, as we shall see, the overall assessment of these processes by our historians was not particularly timid: they claimed that the expansion of the Holy Roman Empire and the Kingdom of Poland (which became a part of the Polish-Lithuanian Commonwealth as a result of this process) was a conquest unlike any other—it was supposed to be the fulfillment of the national mission, beneficial for both the conquerors and the conquered and for Western civilization as well. Moreover, it was supposed to have had a profound impact on both societies and their political cultures—an idea apparently introduced into modern historiography by Augustin Thierry in his *History of the Conquest of England by the Normans* (1825). Finally, what makes these two discourses fascinating is that the idea that Germany and Poland benefited from their territorial expansion—and that nationally minded readers should be proud of it—was fiercely criticized in both countries. This idea was fiercely criticized in both countries. In Germany this criticism was first formulated by Heinrich von Sybel in the late 1850s and, in Poland, by Józef Szujski in the early 1860s.[2]

Second, I focus on what several historians considered to be Germany's and Poland's most spectacular contributions to universal history. In the German case, it was the Reformation, the significance of which Protestant authors believed to have been as universal as it was supposed to have been crucial for the formation of the German national consciousness and the German national mission. In the Polish case, it was the so-called noble democracy, along with the religious tolerance of the Commonwealth that was naturally viewed as its by-product. Finally, I discuss our historians' image of the social structure of early modern Germany and Poland, as it would prove crucial for their understanding of future sociopolitical and constitutional developments in the Empire and the Commonwealth, as well as for their analyses of the causes of the decline and fall of the two states.

The Marriage of Love and Might

Throughout Europe, authors in the Romantic mold idealized the medieval age as a time of legendary heroes *sans reproche*, of truly Christian morality, and of a mythical unity of the people and their rulers. In Germany and Poland, as in Scotland, where this sentiment was born, it had an important contemporary political context: it was a reminder of the epoch when both nations were supposed to have been united and powerful. What follows will address the ways this sentiment was represented in the narratives of our historians.

Before the 1860s, the vast majority of German authors, regardless of their ideological affiliations, located the golden age of their nation's past in the epoch of the Holy Empire's expansion, which they labeled the Kaiserzeit, lasting from the *translatio imperii ad Germanos* in 962, when Otto I was crowned Roman emperor as the first German ruler, to the fall of the Staufen dynasty. The concept of the Kaiserzeit had significant, if subtle, implications: it suggested the emperors' personal might and authority, as well as their diminished position during centuries that followed. Under the Ottonian, Salic, and Staufen dynasties, it implied, the Empire was still what it ought to have been: a united, hierarchical state.

The most famous practitioner of this approach was Wilhelm Giesebrecht, a Protestant professor from Königsberg and the author of the most impressive study of the medieval Empire, *History of the Imperial Age* (1855–80). The Germans, argued Giesebrecht in his preface, were looking back at their history with increasing sentimentality, with nostalgia for the times when their country had been united. The epoch of the Holy Empire's domination in Europe, and the peak of German influence, when Germany was "powerful, united, and great," naturally attracted their attention. Giesebrecht acknowledged the more recent critical voices among German historians but nevertheless insisted that the Empire formed an impressive pattern for all German patriots, for in that time "the German and his name mattered the most in Europe."[3] Indeed, his patriotism, combined with the scholarly qualities of his multivolume study, earned him great popularity among his compatriots, regardless of their religious and political affiliations. Wolfgang Menzel's popular *Germany from the Earliest Period* (originally published in 1824–25) may be another instructive example, for this Protestant author was extremely critical of the Catholic Habsburg emperors after the Reformation and sympathetic toward the Protestant princes. Obviously, he was also an ardent enemy of the Roman Church. And yet, Menzel was enthusiastic about the medieval Empire, its conquests, and its military glory. In his view, they represented the brightest moments in German history, which he expressed in the most oratorical manner: "The royal race of the Hohenstaufen, in which the highest earthly dignity and power, the most brilliant achievements in arms, extraordinary personal beauty, and rich poetical genius, were combined, and beneath whose rule, the middle age and its creations, the church, the Empire, the states, religion, and art, attained a height, whence they necessarily sank as the Hohenstaufen fell, like flowers that fade at parting day."[4]

To be sure, the union of Germany and Italy under the German emperors seemed more questionable for the Catholic writers who felt uneasy about the famous (or notorious, as they saw it) conflict with the papacy that resulted from it. Such historians as August Friedrich Gfrörer, author of the multivolume *Church History*, or Constantin Höfler, author of a biography of Frederick II, did not hesitate to condemn the Salic and Staufen emperors for their desire to control the popes.[5] However, they were still pleased to see Germany ruling over Italy and Burgundy, shining as Europe's unquestioned leader and greatest political and military power. Despite reservations, Johann Friedrich Böhmer, a Catholic historian, claimed in 1846, "And yet, German relations with Italy were rich and fruitful. What a splendor and glory is associated with the imperial idea in our history!"[6]

Analogically, many nineteenth-century Polish historians viewed the union of the medieval Kingdom of Poland and the Grand Duchy of Lithuania under the Jagiellon dynasty as the brightest episode in their national history. Evidently, the union aggrandized the forces of the two nations, creating the largest European state-organism of its time and allowing them to successfully oppose their mortal enemies: the Teutonic Order and Muscovite Rus. One of the immediate results of the union was the Polish-Lithuanian-Ruthenian victory at Grunwald (Tannenberg) in 1410—probably the most celebrated "decisive battle" in Polish history. Poland was transformed into the Polish-Lithuanian Commonwealth as a result of the final union of 1569 and was for some three hundred years a European power treated with respect by its neighbors.

However, spectacular territorial growth and military might were not the only reasons for our Polish historians to praise the union and indeed were not the principal ones. What was most vigorously emphasized was the uniqueness of the union, one of the fundamental indicators for the exceptionality of Polish history in general. In their view, the union did not in the least resemble the modes by which other countries expanded their territory. What the Polish historians had in mind was that the union with Lithuania had been a peaceful, benevolent, and mutually beneficial process, not a military conquest or an annexation. The idea that the union with Lithuania determined all future developments in Polish history, and colored it with a specific ideological and moral component, became known as the "Jagiellonian idea," for it was the Lithuanian dynasty that symbolized the ties between the two nations.

The most dedicated advocate of this approach was Karol Szajnocha, author of perhaps the most popular Polish historical work of the century, *Jadwiga and Jagiełło*. Characteristically, Szajnocha choose the marriage of the Polish queen and the Lithuanian duke, which eventually produced the binational union according to the standards of the time, as the metaphor for the historical process, emphasizing its benevolence and peaceful nature. In his interpretation, it was more than a skillful diplomatic maneuver: it was a revolutionary mode of doing politics of universal significance. "Jadwiga and Jagiello: the two nations marry each other in their names, history witnesses one of the most beautiful attempts at reconciliation and the free communion of unrelated peoples. What can be a higher task in history than the blessing of such a fraternization of the entire human family one day? What story could be more delightful than that of these two names?"[7]

The unique character of the union was stressed by the title of the French translation of the book: *Une annexion d'autrefois*. In the preface to a late nineteenth-century edition, Stanisław Tarnowski, rector of Cracow University (significantly, it is now known as Jagiellonian University), emphasized that medieval Poland was a country that expanded "without treason and lies, without violating the rights and liberties of others."[8] Romantic and post-Romantic Polish historians praised the peaceful, and therefore unique, nature of the union and the Polish expansion to the east that followed. Henryk Schmitt claimed, "This expansion was not accompanied by the rupture of military conquest, and this constitutes the most magnificent page in our history."[9] Lelewel argued the same: "the magnitude of the Commonwealth" was based on the fact it was not created by force, and he emphasized that the length of the unification, which lasted two centuries, or six generations, from the moment Jagiello declared that Lithuania and Ruthenia would be incorporated into Poland, till its final accomplishment, testifies that it was not a result of pressure or compulsion but of a free transformation in all classes of the population.[10]

The mutually beneficial character of the union, as our Polish historians saw it, was based on the following exchange: the Grand Duchy offered vast, sparsely populated lands for Polish colonization, whereas Poland offered its political liberties, attractive for the Lithuanian-Ruthenian nobility, hitherto living under the yoke of monarchical despotism (or, as Lelewel had it, feudalism). Thus, Antoni Chołoniewski could argue that the union represented the triumph of love, expressed not only by the marriage of Queen Jadwiga and Grand Duke Jagiełło but also, and more importantly, by the subsequent intermarriage of numerous Polish and Lithuanian noble families.[11]

Of course the emphasis our Polish historians put on the peaceful character of medieval and early modern Polish expansion had its own contemporary political context. First, stressing the exceptionalism of Polish history and the erstwhile national grandeur and might must have been particularly invigorating for a nation living under foreign rule. Second, defining this historical exceptionalism as the ability to expand without conquest was yet another way to delegitimize the partitions of the Commonwealth, as well as the Russian, Prussian, and Austrian claims to Polish lands. The partitioning powers declared that they represented order and civilization, which they contrasted with the anarchy of the last decades of the Commonwealth; the history of the Polish-Lithuanian union was supposed to remind the contemporary public that such claims should not be affirmed by force. And yet, Polish arguments for the uniqueness of the Polish-Lithuanian union were not that unique: according to our German historians, the medieval expansion of the Holy Empire was no less exceptional and had little to do with military conquest of foreign lands.

One of the German historians who argued that the Germans were actually destined to rule over the Italians was Julius Ficker, a Catholic historian from Innsbruck. The Italians, he reasoned, were a highly civilized and creative people, but they were also notorious individualists, incapable of making sacrifices for the community and lacking the "state instinct." Indeed, their principal political tradition was that of the Empire, and the concept of imperial dignity still aroused their sentiments. Thus, Ficker suggested just before the actual unification of Italy in 1860 that German domination suited the Italians in a way, because they liked to have "two kings" and to play them off against each other. Therefore, German expansion in Italy and Burgundy was not a conquest but a "specific solution to the problems of the West," and "the difficult task of reconciling the nation state and the universal state idea was solved by the Holy Empire in the most remarkable way in history."[12]

Eventually, the majority of our German historians who did not belong to the so-called Borussian school believed that the expansion of the Empire had less to do with German national interests and more to do with the idea of Christian unity; the expansion was therefore not a conquest but a natural political process, which occasionally had to be supported by imperial military forces. After all, Ludwig Karl Aegidi reasoned, the Empire was not a state like any other but "a postulate in the law of nations based on religious assumptions."[13] Oskar von Wydenbrugk developed this reasoning, pointing out that the expansion of the Empire was possible only because of the unity of the Roman Church, which superseded national and local particularisms.[14] Hans Prutz emphasized that the Holy Empire and the Roman Church, despite their occasional clashes, were two pillars and symbols of Christian unity, and Ferdinand Gregorovius argued likewise in his famous *History of the City of Rome in the Medieval Ages*.[15] Naturally, the same idea was stressed by Catholic historians, including Constantin Höfler, who wrote about the "spiritual marriage of the Empire and the Church."[16] In short, even if German historians could not argue that the expansion of the Empire had been peaceful, as military conflicts constituted an important element of the process, in their view these conflicts resembled civil wars within the Western European Christian family rather than foreign conquests: the Empire's goal was to maintain Christian unity, not to annex Lombardy to Germany.

The idea of Christian unity, however, was but one reason for Germany to strive for control over Italy and Burgundy. Another one was the Roman imperial legacy epitomized in the imperial title and the aspirations it symbolized. Combined, they constituted the idea of a unity of the West that needed to be protected against Byzantium and Islam. According to our German authors, Germany was predestined for this mission because of its status as Europe's mightiest and most centrally located nation—*das Herzvolk Europas*. It was thus Germany's destiny to dominate Europe for the latter's benefit. Aware, perhaps, of the questionable nature of this argument, some of our historians supplemented it with additional apologias describing the Empire as representing truly German virtues. In this case, however, those virtues had little to do with the bellicosity, spontaneity, and predatory vigor that were supposed to characterize the primordial Germanic tribes.

The reasoning took the form of an ahistorical syllogism. Had Germany failed in its attempts for supremacy in Europe, Ficker argued, this role would have been taken up by the next most powerful European nation—France. And the French are well known for their "enormous desire for conquests, which were never limited to their linguistic territory," he informed his readers.[17] The same argument was employed by Wydenbrugk, who contrasted French "mechanical unification from above," as well as "centralism," with "organic" German federalism.[18] Their reasoning referred to an opinion that was certainly well known to their nineteenth-century readers but was hardly relevant as far as early medieval realities are concerned. It reminded German readers about the demonized Louis XIV, the French Revolution, and Napoleon. What it implied was the abhorrent idea that if France had adopted the universalist ideology of the Empire, it would still have remained essentially French—absolutist and expansionist—whereas Germany guaranteed a more tolerant and federalist model of integration. The German medieval ambitions for supremacy in Europe actually had nothing to do with expansionism: as Aegidi or Prutz argued, they instead represented essentially German idealism and the German tendency for sacrifice.[19]

Polish ambitions were humbler but eventually similar. The country's eastward expansion was also supposed to represent a mission in the service of Western Christianity and civilization. In Polish popular mythology, centuries of wars against Muscovy, the Tatars, and the Turks—initiated by the great Mongol invasion of the thirteenth century and capped with the 1683–99 war of the Holy League against the Ottoman Empire—fused into an image of the nation as a bulwark of the West and a bastion of Christianity. This idea was combined with a sense of Western civilization's superiority over both Islam and Greek Orthodoxy, and the superiority of Polish political liberty over Eastern despotism. However, our historians' approach to this idea was nuanced and clearly evolved over time.

Apparently one can already sense the idea of Polish cultural superiority over Orthodox Ruthenia in the writings of Polish Romantic historians. Lelewel, who had no love for the Catholic clergy, despised the Orthodox clergy even more for its submission to political power and for its alleged decadence, which it was supposed to have inherited from Byzantium—the place that epitomized the idea of political and cultural decadence in Western literature for ages. However, Lelewel, Szajnocha, and other Romantic historians focused on more practical matters: in their opinion, the main factor that invited Polish colonization of the East was that the lands that had belonged to Kievan Rus before the Mongol invasion remained sparsely populated, underdeveloped, and little urbanized. In their view, Lithuania-Ruthenia consisted mainly of virgin forests and steppes that simply awaited carpenters and plowmen: it represented nature rather than any inferior civilization.[20]

However, Romantic historians did not actually present the Polish colonization of Lithuania-Ruthenia as a *mission civilisatrice* because they had serious reservations about the idea of Western civilization. In their view, it was a foreign and indeed oppressive force that considered non-Western people as inferior and demanded that they abandon their own native culture. As Lelewel argued, what Poland offered, instead, was its own language, customs, and, most importantly, its political liberty. Szajnocha expressed the same idea by comparing the Polish nobles' approach to the Lithuanians with that of the English to the Irish. Having conquered Ireland, the English created some new heraldic arms for the Irish "barbarians," who were unfamiliar with this aspect of aristocratic culture. The Poles, in contrast, shared their own armorials with the Lithuanians, recognizing them as equals or perhaps even family members (for according to medieval theory, bearers of the same coat of arms were relatives).[21] It was only in the second half of the century, when the Romantic paradigm was replaced with enthusiasm for the West as the source of all progress, that Polish historians openly claimed, as Władysław Smoleński formulated it, that "the union was inspired by the idea of elevating the Lithuanian-Ruthenian peoples to the level of Western civilization." Of course, this claim still upheld the idea that union with Poland liberated the subjects of the grand dukes from Eastern despotism and brought the flame of liberty to the dark Lithuanian forests for the first time.[22] However, as we shall see in the next chapter, Polish historians' enthusiasm for the political order of the Commonwealth was no longer unreserved. Thus, serving the universal cause of liberty was now but one of the admirable consequences of the union; the other one was defending the West against some barbarians and civilizing the others.

The idea that the Polish historical mission was to bring Western civilization to the East was perhaps best expressed by the Cracovian historian Józef Szujski. For Szujski this was a particularly dramatic conclusion, because, as we shall see, in his opinion the union was a costly enterprise that had had fatal consequences for Poland. One might argue that his praise for the benefits the union brought to Western civilization was an attempt at consolation. "We have perished and yet achieved a moral success that manifests itself till our day with our accomplishments: our cities and villages, our civilization, customs, faith, and morality. We broadened Europe two hundred miles eastward, from the Vistula to the Dnieper and Dvina. This success of our civilization and this struggle against space explain many failures in our political history."[23]

The parallel between Szujski's approach and that of our German historians was profound. Eventually, his reasoning was Hegelian: the task of defending and promoting Western Christianity and civilization (of course, he did not view the two issues separately: they were actually one) was simply there, awaiting its executor; Germany and Poland competed for this position. The laws of history were flexible and cruel: the nation that performed better automatically became the bearer of the historical mission, until some other power dethroned it. And so, in his view, it was no coincidence that Poland began its spectacular eastward expansion at a time when the spirit of the crusades was fading and the splendor of the Staufen dynasty was gone. "When the German Empire curtailed its mission and failed morally, Poland rose as the future *antemurale Christianitatis*," he noted.[24] The reason for the German failure, he believed, was moral: having given up its role as Christianity's protector against external enemies, the Empire concentrated its efforts on suppressing other Christian powers, departing from its historical mission and choosing instead to create an illusion of might—an abuse that must have been punished by Providence. Of course, in his view, the Polish case was different. "According to all laws, divine and human," he argued, "Germany had no right to denationalize the Slavs, whereas Poland, as a missionary of European civilization in the East, may lay claims for moral primacy among the Slavic nations."[25]

This reasoning was further developed by a younger colleague of Szujski, Stanisław Smolka. Smolka wholeheartedly shared the opinion that the union with Lithuania and the "Polish mission in the East" constituted the most magnificent chapter in Polish history precisely because of its moral and religious aspects. Still, employing Szujski's logic, he used it more consistently. After centuries of prosperity and glory, the Polish-Lithuanian Commonwealth ultimately fell, and there must have been an explanation for this decree of Providence. Smolka's answer was as natural as it must have been shocking for his contemporaries: the Poles enjoyed divine sanction and support as long as they acted morally and fulfilled their mission, so their final disaster must have been a consequence of a moral failure. The success, he argued, which was a result of "efforts and sacrifices," was followed by a decadent desire for pleasures, by greed, and by the exploitation of annexed territories, and then "the merciless logic of history struck us with disasters and failures, devastating the most splendid results of the union." Interestingly, and in a truly historicist manner, Smolka took the metaphor of marriage that symbolized the union quite literally. In his view, Polish history mirrored that of Queen Jadwiga, who personalized the Polish historical mission: the first four hundred years corresponded to her maidenhood, that is, a period of "concentrating forces for a great effort," which was to Christianize Lithuania and Ruthenia or, in other words, to give birth to the Polish-Lithuanian Commonwealth.[26] Moreover, Smolka crowned his reasoning with an interesting counterfactual scenario that was supposed to remove any doubts regarding the purposefulness of the union. Had Poland not brought Catholicism to Lithuania, he argued quite reasonably, Russia would have certainly brought Orthodoxy to Lithuania. Should this have happened, the Poles would have faced a dangerous enemy—"the tsar of Lithuania"—as early as the fifteenth century, and this enemy "most likely would have played the role of Peter the Great, but would have been more spectacular, and more devastating for the entire West."[27]

Finally, Smolka also directly compared the history of Polish expansion to that of the Holy Empire, although he did so in a way that was strikingly inconsistent with his highly moralistic interpretation of the process. Namely, Smolka observed that Polish expansion in the East had actually begun before the union, with the annexation of the so-called Red Ruthenia (Ruthenia Rubra in present-day western Ukraine) by the last of the Piast kings, Casimir (1340–49). He took advantage of the issueless death of the local prince who had recognized Casimir as his inheritor in exchange for political support. According to Smolka, this was not a local game of power but a fundamental change in Polish politics: after centuries of conflict with Germany, Poland looked toward the East and the Oriental trade routes from the Black Sea. In his interpretation, the origins of this change were directly attributable to the medieval Empire's most ambitious and indeed most controversial ruler: Frederick II of the Staufen dynasty, for Casimir's actions were eventually negotiated with his brother-in-law, the Hungarian king Charles Robert of Anjou, son of Charles Martel, prince of Salerno. Smolka emphasized that Frederick's Sicilian monarchy was widely considered to be the most centralized and, in a way, the most modern state of its time; moreover, Frederick's decision to abandon Germany for Sicily was clearly inspired by his fascination with Mediterranean culture and the Orient. Unfortunately, Smolka had no evidence to support his claim that Casimir's close ties to the Hungarian Anjou dynasty involved a fascination with Frederick's mode of governing or that the annexation of Red Ruthenia changed anything in the way his Polish kingdom was administered.[28] Still, this grandiose scheme, colored with an image of oriental adventures and richness, was an interesting departure from the highly idealized image of Poland as a martyr, or indeed as a pilgrim for Christianity, animated solely by the sense of its religious mission.

The Shirt of Nessus

In 961, Pope John XII requested military assistance from Emperor Otto the Great. This was the moment, Oskar Jäger argues, when the unfortunate relations between Germany and Italy began. Praised by many as a period of the greatest glory and splendor, it was instead Germany's shirt of Nessus: an unintended disaster. However, as the historian explains, the disaster was also unavoidable. The anarchy in Rome, the capital of Western Christianity, was a deplorable insult for all Christians, and it was natural that the task of restoring order and decency was undertaken by "the first monarch of the world" instead of "a prince of Benevento or Spoleto."[29] The same telling metaphor of the shirt of Nessus was employed by Józef Szujski to interpret the consequences for Poland of its union with Lithuania. Moreover, fierce debate about whether the period of territorial expansion, widely regarded as the brightest chapter in the histories of both nations, should instead be properly considered one of the darkest chapters, began to rage almost simultaneously in both Germany and Poland around 1860.

The question of the price Germany had to pay for its medieval imperial ambitions is indeed to be found among the writings of historians of all political and ideological affiliations. It was widely believed that Germany could not afford an Empire that had to control so many foreign territories, be ready to confront any European monarchy that wished to challenge its policies, and protect the Holy Land against the infidels. It was a beautiful dream that simply cost too much. As Gustav Freytag, one of the most popular historical authors of the century, observed rhetorically but soberly, "While the Staufen were successfully fighting the Lombardians, Normans, and Arabs, when they were raising their banners and flags over the Gulf of Naples and the walls of Jerusalem, the whole of Germany was full of unrest, crime, and robbery, and the Asiatic Mongols were breaching the defenseless borders of the Empire."[30]

Despite its bitter sarcasm, this was a mild interpretation; in the worst case, as we shall see, the imperial ambitions of the Empire were viewed as the nonsensical fantasy of religious fanatics. In Polish discourse, a critical attitude toward the union with Lithuania and its legacy was mainly advocated by historians of the so-called Cracovian school. Such a criticism was still considered an insult for the majority of the patriotic audience and was therefore pursued with sorrow rather than sarcasm. Nevertheless, it was still too drastic for some of our historians to consider. Oskar Halecki, who entered the historical profession in the first decade of the twentieth century, argued that such a criticism must have been a logical mistake: historians who supported it did so because they believed that such an unparalleled catastrophe like the partitions of the Polish-Lithuanian Commonwealth could have been explained only with an equally grandiose historical process—in this case, the uniquely successful and peaceful expansion of Poland. However, he claimed this criticism should not be accepted or even considered, simply because "it appears the most painful and detestable of all interpretations of the causes of our downfall."[31]

To be sure, there is no Polish analogue to the German assessments of the imperial expansionist policies' direct consequences. The union with Lithuania did not coincide with internal disorder, nor were other borders in danger of sudden attack from a foreign power. Quite to the contrary, Polish historians univocally agreed that the immediate consequence of the union, or perhaps its crucial strategic purpose, was to secure both countries against the deadly menace of the Teutonic Order (and, of course, occasional border conflicts between Poland and Lithuania ceased). Remarkably, no Polish historian argued that, in order to oppose the common enemy, Poland and Lithuania did not actually need to unite and might have simply formed a temporary military alliance. It was popularly assumed that neither Poland nor Lithuania could reasonably hope to oppose the Teutonic Order alone, and thus, as Bobrzyński put it, "our nation opted for the Lithuanian-Ruthenian union as its only chance for survival."[32] This was so, perhaps, because of the highly demonized image of the Teutonic Order in Polish historical tradition reaching back to the fifteenth century, as well as a popular belief that the order was Poland's most dangerous enemy in its entire history until the eighteenth century. To sum up: in the short run Poland and Lithuania needed each other for defense against the Teutonic Order—a peculiar German state of the northern crusaders— whereas Germany and Italy needed each other to support the proper crusaders, the ones fighting for the Holy Land.

As far as long-term consequences are concerned, German criticism of imperial expansionism was most radically formulated by Heinrich von Sybel in his 1859 essay on contemporary assessments of the Kaiserzeit, which provoked a fierce debate among German historians. Sybel sarcastically observed that the Kaiserzeit, which was so dear to the German patriotic public, constituted but a short period in the history of the Empire. In its final phase, however, which lasted much longer, the Empire was a source of German embarrassment rather than pride. However, his devastating opinion about the Kaiserzeit had little to do with such sentiments, and he declined to follow the historicist principles of approaching each epoch according to its own standards. He argued that while assessing the policies of past actors, historians need not bother themselves with reconstructing their objectives and mentality: what matters is the timeless logic of national interests. Consequently, he claimed that the medieval emperors might have been great men, but they had not respected this logic in their attempts to control Italy and Burgundy, not to mention the crusades (which he had previously studied). The medieval emperors were motivated by their irrational religious ideals, and they considered themselves leaders of the European Christian community rather than advocates of German national interests. Their policies, and their conflicts with the papacy, were disastrous for Germany, for they resulted in the growth of the power of the princes and regional particularism, which later became the nation's curse and the main cause of its incurable weakness. Moreover, in his view, the idea of integrating Germany, Italy, and Burgundy into one political organism was "unnatural" because of the fundamental linguistic and cultural differences between these countries. The result was, he believed, pushing Burgundy toward the "linguistically nearer" France. In short, in his opinion, the entire expansion southward was a costly waste of German energy, which should have been invested in what was Germany's destiny: the colonization of the Slavic East.[33]

Some of Sybel's arguments had been present in the writings of the previous generation of German historians, who liked to define their position as Ghibelline, stressing their emotional attachment to the Empire. Eventually, the observation that the medieval emperors' engagement in Italy made it possible for the princes to emancipate and build up powers of their own was ubiquitous in German historiography of the nineteenth century; only its assessment varied dramatically. Menzel, for example, considered the princely opposition to the Staufen emperors, which occasionally disturbed their expansionist policies, to be high treason. "The princes, who remained obsessed by mediocre authority," he claimed, "merely sought the advancement of their petty interests," and their actions "were warmly supported by the pope, whom they assisted in exterminating the imperial house."[34] Like other conservative-patriotic historians, he did not view the growth of particularism as an obvious consequence of imperial policies but simply as their unfortunate by-product. His followers, including the foremost radically nationalist-Protestant Heinrich von Treitschke, lamented the lack of unity and, like Oskar Jäger, emphasized the popes' devilish tendency to conspire against any centralized power in Germany.[35]

To be sure, the problem was viewed differently by Catholic historians. Gfrörer was highly critical of the emperors who, like Otto I or some of the Staufen rulers, had attempted a full subordination of the popes: he defined their policies as attempts to reshape the Roman Catholic Church according to the Constantinopolitan model. He admitted that the "political development of Germany and Italy" suffered from chronic conflicts between the emperors and the popes, but he stressed that this conflict had a positive effect on the rise of political liberties in Europe, as it prevented the continent from having been dominated by one centralized power and indeed questioned the validity of all such attempts.[36] Heinrich Leo, a conservative who occasionally sympathized with Catholicism, instructed his patriotic readers to be proud of Emperor Henry IV, who did penance in Canossa in 1077, recognizing the superiority of papal authority. This was a highly unusual interpretation of this most controversial episode in the history of the imperial-papal conflict, typically viewed either as the Empire's most spectacular humiliation or as a canny maneuver by Henry, who sacrificed his pride to keep his power intact. Leo rejected as unchristian the idea that the proverbial walk to Canossa might have been a political "comedy." What terrified him was the election of Henry's successor to the throne even though his son was still alive; this move introduced the idea of imperial election to the Holy Empire, and Leo viewed it as the true source of Germany's problems. In Leo's opinion, the elective throne "goes against natural and divine order, and thus causes destruction of the kingdom," because candidates to the throne are ready to trade their prerogatives for support during the election. A custom that is so destructive and perverse cannot be an element of God's plan for humanity, he argued.[37]

In the final analysis, the German historians' discussion about the consequences of medieval imperial expansionism was marked with a certain fatalism. In the long run, it was commonly believed that the emperors' engagements outside Germany, and their conflicts with the popes, were ruinous both for their position within Germany and for the unity of the Empire. The only ones who emerged triumphant from these conflicts were German territorial princes, whose aspirations grew with the declining powers of the emperors. However, Sybel's argument that the emperors should have simply given up their ambitions as leaders of Western Christianity was not welcomed. The opinion prevailed that imperial dignity was the German Nemesis: no emperor could ignore the challenge, and no one could satisfactorily and permanently respond to it.[38] It was perhaps best summarized by the authors of an entry in the 1914 edition of the *Encyclopædia Britannica*: "Instead of strengthening the allegiance of the Germans towards their sovereign, the imperial title was a means of steadily undermining it. To the connection of their Kingdom with the Empire they owe the fatal fact that for centuries they were the most divided of European nations, and that they have only recently begun to create a genuinely united state."[39]

One of Sybel's arguments that gained popular acceptance among our German historians was that the Empire, focusing its ambitions on Italy, fatally neglected its prospects for expansion eastward. This idea was based on reasoning parallel to a view advocated by Szujski, who claimed, as noted, that Germans had no right to denationalize the Slavs, whereas the Poles were morally entitled to rule over Lithuanians and Ruthenians because the Poles had their liberty and their superior civilization, which they were ready to share with these underdeveloped peoples. Analogical reasoning made German historians believe that their ancestors were actually predestined to rule over the Slavs—the principal difference being that German historians regarded violent conquest as an obvious prerequisite for the assimilation of the Slavic barbarians, as was actually the case with West Slavic peoples between the Elbe and the Oder.[40] Ludwig Stacke was the most radical of our authors in this respect, as he openly lamented the fact that the Empire's insufficiently aggressive approach to the East made possible the formation of the Bohemian, Polish, and Hungarian kingdoms, which would later block further German expansion.[41]

And yet, German historians' sentiment for the Kaiserzeit was not eradicated, and moments of glory were still appreciated and defended. Oskar Wydenbrugk brought forward the argument we have already come across: that the Empire's conflict with the papacy was unavoidable simply because the Empire was the greatest power of its time, and any other kingdom, had it enjoyed such a status, would have acted similarly.[42] Accordingly, Ludwig Karl Aegidi supported the overambitious policies of the emperors as "a historical necessity."[43] Hans Prutz claimed that the failure to establish permanent control over Italy was a consequence of the immense effort invested in the crusades, as well as the papal policies of building up a "universal church."[44] Johann Jastrow appealed to national pride by reminding his readers that, in spite of the apparent decline of imperial power, "when the French crown became a plaything of its vassals, our emperors were capable of leading the nation across the Alps."[45] Moreover, Protestant historians emphasized with bitter satisfaction that the conflict between the Empire and the papacy turned equally ruinous for both sides.

Furthermore, several historians, including Ranke himself, argued that the unity of Germany, allegedly destroyed by imperial expansion, was in fact illusory: the Germany of the Carolingians and of the Staufen was still a conglomerate of peoples and provinces, and the actual power of the emperors was limited to their dynastic domains. Imperial conquests—undertaken with the forces of the entire country and resulting in confrontations with foreign cultures—were in fact a crucial factor contributing to the birth of the common German identity.[46] Stacke interpreted this problem dialectically. In his view, German history between the ninth and the thirteenth centuries was determined by four factors: church, Empire, kingdom, and local peculiarities that dated back to tribal traditions. It was in the time of the Staufen dynasty when the provinces evolved into feudal principalities, which, within the structure of the Empire, were the actual subjects of the king-emperor. Thus, again, the period of expansion and alleged fragmentation coincides with the birth of German unity.[47]

Finally, let us consider Lamprecht's interpretation of the problem. Lamprecht rejected the supposition that imperial expansion caused a decline in the emperors' powers and therefore contributed to the fragmentation of Germany into semi-independent principalities. In his view, this was an independent and unavoidable process, typical for the feudal phase of development. He liked Germany's conquests and imperial ambitions and saw advantages in its expansionist policies. Due to the emperors' control over prosperous Italy, he claimed, they almost managed to solve their main problem: a constant lack of money. What he did not like were the moments when imperial policies became religiously colored, as in, for example, the attempts to establish a "universal monarchy," or the crusades. In his opinion, such policies were "Romantic"—in contrast to realpolitik. The imperial dream of building up a new, pan-European center of power in Rome, he believed, was fatal for the German kingdom, which, neglected by its own monarchs, remained "an abstract construction." He compared this to "contemporary constitutional monarchies in the Balkans or in Japan"—countries importing foreign political patterns that did not match their own traditions. Medieval Germany, he believed, was petrified of being halfway between a conglomerate of tribal states and the universal Empire. However, he did not blame conflicts with the papacy for this. In contrast, he claimed that "the emancipation of the state and the people from religious concepts" was a prerequisite for building up a national monarchy, and the conflict in question prepared the ground for "a revolutionary departure from Christian piety toward civic ideas."[48] In the final analysis, although he despised the idealistic aspects of imperial expansionism, he still viewed it positively as testifying to the Empire's strength and vitality.

The debate also involved a fundamental methodological discussion. The issue was whether past realities should be assessed according to modern principles: in this case, it was the idea of national interest defined by nineteenth-century standards. In an essay on the German nation and the Empire, Sybel rejected all reservations in this respect and mocked his colleagues for their tendency to side with emperors or popes as if that conflict had continued up to the nineteenth century. He emphasized that the Empire had fallen because of its own weakness and that the historian's duty is to evaluate past developments according to timeless moral principles and to pass painful but illuminating judgments rather than to provide fuel for patriotic pride.[49]

Sybel's denial of past agents' right to act according to the standards of their time was met with serious resistance from his colleagues. This was perhaps best expressed by Ranke, who noted, "Some claimed that it would have been better for the Germans if they had not engaged in the affairs of the Empire at all, at least until they accomplished their internal political development, so they could have entered into universal relationships united and strong. However, the developments of this world do not evolve so methodically."[50]

Ranke, who thought persistently about the problem of the European game of power, was indeed one who appreciated the idea of universal monarchy as a solution that would have satisfied Germany's aspirations and demonstrated its strength, if only Germany could have maintained its position as "leader of the Christian world in the fullness of its youthful energy." What worried him was that the Germans apparently had not understood their historical mission the way he did and that the obstacles were too many for this mission to have succeeded. Independent monarchies were rising up all around the Empire, unwilling to respect German claims for primacy, and aristocratic tendencies prevailed throughout Europe, including in the Empire. The spirit of the time was against imperial ambitions, Ranke concluded, providing Henry IV as his example: after his reconciliation with the pope in Canossa, it seemed for a moment that fortune embraced the emperor again. However, Henry's sons rebelled against him, demonstrating how tragically lonely the ambitious monarch was.[51]

Our last German historian, Johannes Haller, disagreed with assumptions such as those of Lamprecht, but he shared Ranke's conclusions. If we agree with Sybel that imperial policies toward Italy were a "theocratic dream," he claimed, then we should consider eight generations of Germans to have been irrational dreamers, for these policies were steadily pursued for 250 years. As a matter of fact, this was medieval realpolitik inspired by a healthy imperialist spirit, as well as the legacy of Charlemagne, which Germany naturally continued in its role as Europe's greatest power. The idea of universal monarchy was a propagandist umbrella for German expansion, which was focused on Italy as the richest and most civilized country of that time. It was only owing to the financial resources of Italy that the emperors could think of breaking the opposition of their feudal lords, he claimed, further developing Lamprecht's argumentation. Finally, in his view, one should not wonder why the emperors neglected to expand eastward: in that time, in sharp contrast to Italy, there was nothing of great value to gain there, except for land, and there were not enough colonists to put the land to good use.[52]

The German controversy concerning the prize, and indeed the purposefulness, of the Empire's territorial expansion has a clear-cut parallel in the Polish discussion about the costs and long-term consequences of the union with Lithuania. In short, Polish critics of the union—of whom the most notable were the Cracovian historians Szujski and Bobrzyński—claimed that colonization of the vast Lithuanian-Ruthenian territories absorbed and eventually exhausted all of Poland's energy, contributing to the formation of a dysfunctional political and social order dominated by a small group of magnates who exercised disproportional influence due to their huge estates in the East.

The troubles began, our historians believed, with the invitation extended to the foreign Jagiellon dynasty, whose members were ready to remodel the Polish political system by giving up certain traditional prerogatives of the crown in exchange for the political support of local elites. The problem was first noted by Julian Ursyn Niemcewicz, who still did not regard it as related to the union; he simply observed the policies of the first Jagiellon on the Polish throne with disgust. The king, in his view, was a weak man, notoriously paying his advisors and sycophants too generously, thus carelessly depleting his treasury, and he all too easily yielded to the nobles' requests to take part in governing.[53] Other historians, as we shall see, saw this process, which would result in the formation of the so-called noble democracy, originating further in the past, during the reign of the first foreigner: Louis the Great (of Anjou), a Hungarian who was the first ruler to seek an official approval of the aristocracy for the succession of his daughter in 1374. After the invitation for Jagiełło to marry Louis's daughter, the process of bargaining over constitutional matters and royal prerogatives only accelerated.

Józef Szujski was the one who formulated the most devastating critique of the consequences of the union. First, he emphasized that the trend of seeking political support in exchange for privileges, initiated by Louis, became commonplace under the Jagiellon rulers, whose position in Poland was long considered suspect. On one hand, they ruled as absolute and hereditary monarchs in Lithuania and, on the other hand, as elected ones in Poland, where they had to bargain over each election with the nobles, working to improve the position of the dynasty. Thus,

Szujski argued, the nation "lost the sense of unity of the monarch and the state, for the monarch pursued his own policies in Lithuania. What resulted were notorious deals privileging [the kings' favorite] individuals and antagonism between royal and national policies."[54] Such was the beginning of the Polish departure from the standard European way of development. In sharp contrast to the Romantic historians, Szujski, as well as other representatives of the Cracovian school, did not value historical exceptionalism too highly; indeed, in their view it was the cause of Poland's misfortunes. "By surrendering to the will of an individual," he argued, "the West arrived at liberty. We were to build up the state with the acclamations of the masses. It happened in the way we have described, the way of antagonizing the nation and its king and all things royal."[55] As long as the country was ruled by the native Piast dynasty, who ruled absolutely, they believed, and as long as it remained within the boundaries of the ethnic Polish territory, Poland developed "normally," that is, according to the European standard. Once it navigated toward the vast forests and steppes of the East, its problems began. The union promised the Poles more than they could afford; as Lamprecht would have said, it promoted Romantic policies instead of rational ones.

However, the Cracovian historians' criticism was not limited to political and constitutional matters. Eventually, it also involved elements of classical decadence theory. The Poles, Szujski argued, became spoiled by their easy and spectacular success, as well as mesmerized by the "enormous Lithuanian and Ruthenian territories." The result was disastrous for their political and individual mentality. "A nobleman in his migration eastward deteriorated, he became plump, contemplative, slow and fond of ease, and inclined to combine despotism and indolence," Szujski claimed.[56] This diagnosis was poetically reproduced by Władysław Konopczyński shortly after World War I: "The idle lifestyle of the gentry in the vast lands of the East, the extensive economy of the spacious meadows, fields, gardens, and lakes, gave rise to the uniquely Polish, cheerful indifference toward all things that do not constitute a threat to the peace of an individual's home. Life went on smoothly without passion, conflicts, sacrifices, and struggle against fate. The dispersed population lived in a sort of dispersed culture."[57]

Bobrzyński developed Szujski's reasoning in a fantastic way. He did it by proposing to his readers a counterfactual scenario of what would have happened had there been no union and no easy colonization of the East: "A denser population, having difficulty in winning their bread from agriculture, would have turned toward trade and industry, moved to the towns, and balanced the influence of the gentry. A harder existence would have sharpened our national character, inspired emotions, deepened thoughts, and encouraged action. The following civil wars would have resulted in formation of a strong government.[58]

The Cracovian historians' interpretations were certainly related to Polybius's theory of decadence. However, their main concern was in explaining the malfunctioning of the political order of the Commonwealth. As we shall see, they believed that its democratic character demanded particularly sterling qualities from its citizens. The vast territories of what is today Ukraine, Belarus, Latvia, and Lithuania provided an opportunity for the corruption of the Polish-Lithuanian citizenry; as we shall see, according to our historians the lives of the gentry were both too comfortable and too harsh for the nobles to practice their civic values.

As mentioned earlier, in the second half of the nineteenth century, with the passing of the Romantic generation, the positive reputation of Western civilization as the source of all progress prevailed in Poland. Simultaneously, fascination with Oriental cultures and interest in nature and nativism declined, and so did religious piety, which was replaced with the cult of rationalism and efficacy. As a result, the idea of the Polish mission to the East lost its exceptional lure. It was believed that Poles could certainly have promoted Latin Christianity and Western civilization in the wild East, but doing so would no longer offered any reward. Historians entering the profession at the turn of the twentieth century, such as Konopczyński and Eugène Starczewski, argued that constant wars against Muscovy, Cossacks, Tatars, and Turks had also had a debilitating impact on Polish society: first, because wars, by definition, make people harsher and more brutal, and second, because "one could hardly learn anything from such enemies."[59] In other words, this generation of historians did not see Greek Orthodox and Muslims as infidels anymore but as barbarians—and fighting barbarians is not a highly moral obligation that guarantees one's salvation but a sad necessity that brought down a number of Empires mightier than the Commonwealth.

Konopczyński also lamented that the energy wasted on colonization of the East was not invested in attempts to reconquer Pomerania and Silesia—territories lost to Germany in the late medieval period. His lamentation mirrored the German historians' regret that medieval emperors had not conquered more Polish land instead of struggling for control of Italy. Paradoxically, this problem had already been addressed by Lelewel, who, as noted, was an enthusiast of the union with Lithuania and an apologist for the notion of the virgin lands of the East awaiting the Polish plow. Still, he also stressed that the nobility, busy with their acquisitions in the East, refused to act when the Polish monarchs (Jagiełło and Sigismund the Old) were invited to annex Silesia (because of the Hussite revolution) and Ducal Prussia (because of the Reformation). Contrary to his usual way of arguing, Lelewel did not blame the monarchs—or the aristocrats—for having wasted the opportunity but instead placed the fault on the nobles, whose passivity he declared "unforgivable."[60]

Employing similar cultural standards, our German historians arrived at different conclusions: despite the numerous drawbacks of the union with Italy, it was a cultural blessing for Germany. Indisputably, Italy represented a superior civilization in the medieval period, as well as an opportunity for Germans to learn and copy from it. Stacke, for example, emphasized the influence of Italian city life, particularly the example of municipal self-government, on Germany, and the subsequent rise of German urban communities in the medieval period.[61] Needless to say, the same opinion prevailed on the subject of art and architecture, despite some authors' efforts to stress the originality of German artists and artisans, especially in Gothic architecture.[62] Although Ranke repeated a number of times that the popes' usurpation of the right to approve the election of the German kings was "humiliating" for the great nation, he nevertheless stressed the affinities between German and Italian political culture, originating from Roman imperial traditions. The Germans, he suggested, were simply impressed with the imperial legacy and flattered that they could maintain it. He ironically noted that some emperors did not use their title as the German king at all, and some princes presented their prerogative to elect the monarch as a consequence of being the successors of Roman senators.[63]

However, in the opinion of some of our German authors, the acclaimed Italian civilization had been corrupted. Apart from suffering the effects of the unhealthful Italian climate, they believed, the morally pure and fresh German warriors in Italy were also exposed to mental challenges and temptations. According to Johann Gustav Droysen, the moral degeneration of Italians was best seen in the cruel customs of aristocratic families, in which treason and poison often paved the way for the younger generations to displace the elders. "Had it lasted longer," he concluded, "the Christian world would have fallen lower than pagans once had."[64] Fortunately, according to Menzel, "the rough honesty of the German character" emerged intact from its confrontation with Mediterranean perfidy.[65] Still, Johann von Döllinger argued that two and a half centuries of attempts to control Rome, continuous contact with its morally corrupted inhabitants, and the regrettable efforts to fraternize with them had had a devastating impact on Germans, their culture, and customs. Thus, he considered the Kaiserzeit as the darkest hour in German history. It would have been better, he concluded, if Germany had adopted Christianity in the Byzantine rite, for then German national customs, language, and morality would not have suffered the deplorable Italian influences.[66]

The Fall of the Middle Ages, or the First Frost

Nineteenth-century historians took a clearly different approach to the concepts of nation and state than did their post–World War II successors, who often trace the nation-building process to a time when the Empire and the Commonwealth had already disappeared. Nineteenth-century authors embraced concepts of both nation and state with no ideological or methodological predispositions and viewed them as fundamental categories organizing their analyses; the two were interconnected and considered to be principal objects of historical inquiry.

Moreover, nation and state, like liberty and virtue, were regarded as historically changeable but essentially eternal phenomena. National character determined the national destiny and vice versa. However, subsequent generations chose various paths, and some of them, our historians felt compelled to observe, did not seem promising as far as the national ideal was concerned. In this context, the late medieval period appears remarkable: both the German and Polish nations reached maturity, and the directions of their developments were being determined for the next several centuries. Neither Germany nor Poland was to become an absolute monarchy nor would their dynasties, or their rulers, become truly national. Their interests would not be identical to those of the nation, as had still been considered true in the cases of Barbarossa and Casimir the Great. German particularism was already firmly grounded and would remain a decisive factor in German history for centuries, as would Polish involvement in Lithuania and Ruthenia. The cards were already on the table, and it was evident which trees in the garden of national history would blossom and grow and which would humbly vegetate in their shadow.

This situation arose mostly due to the formation of the estates. Because the monarchs' position would remain relatively weak and their policies would never achieve the consistency established by the western European national dynasties, the estates would play principal roles in both German and Polish national history. Obviously some important factors, such as religious relations and the international position of the two countries, would undergo dramatic changes in the early modern period. Still, their political structure and internal power relations would be based on the position of the estates and on the series of arrangements regulating them. Constitutionally, these positions were shaped by the Golden Bull of 1356 in the Holy Empire, as well as the so-called Kosice agreement of 1374 in Poland, and by the series of parallel reforms in both countries at the turn of the sixteenth century, in consequence of which the main institutions of the Holy Empire and the Kingdom of Poland were formed (most importantly, their respective parliaments). These arrangements regulated relations between the estates during the three centuries that followed; the only major innovations, which actually confirmed the tendencies articulated in the reforms of the late fifteenth and early sixteenth centuries, were the so-called Henrician Articles (concerning the status of the monarch), the formation of the central tribunals in the Commonwealth in the 1570s, and the principle of the sovereignty of the estates of the Empire in their external relations, introduced formally in consequence of the 1648 Peace of Westphalia within the Empire.

In this epoch both the Empire and Poland-Lithuania were still great powers;

their enemies were still relatively weak and their citizens lived a peaceful existence, enjoying relative wealth and prosperity. In short, it was the zenith of the two national histories. And it was in analyses of this period where the principal sympathies and antipathies of our historians were revealed. The first symptoms of the future decline were diagnosed, and those who were to blame for it were exposed and stigmatized. Positions were taken in the debate concerning the downfall of both countries, and ideological assumptions shone in the last hours of the epoch of national glory and greatness, indicating its rotten foundations.

Polish historians were unanimous in their opinion that the so-called noble democracy, as formed between the 1374 Kosice agreement and the 1573 Henrician Articles, constituted a unique and exceptional political order. The enthusiasts of the Commonwealth claimed that no other country of the early modern era granted its citizens so many political privileges, and no other country was as democratic as Poland-Lithuania. Antoni Chołoniewski, the most apologetic of our authors, argued that Poland-Lithuania was a world pioneer of democracy. He also stressed that in other European countries the percentage of the population enjoying political rights—especially the right to vote—only reached the sixteenth-century Polish level late in the nineteenth century.[67] Stanisław Kutrzeba, a legal historian, gallantly compared Poland to England. In his view, these two countries "saved the medieval principle of liberty" and guaranteed "the participation of the population in the government, parliament, and administration."[68]

The idea that Poland was a world champion of democracy, establishing a link between the ancient times and the ideals of the nineteenth century, certainly flattered the patriotic Polish opinion of the age, and thus neo-Romantic Polish historians of the early twentieth century emphasized this notion for political reasons. More than a century after the partitions of the Commonwealth and after numerous failed attempts to regain independence, Poland had essentially become an abstract idea and difficult for Westerners to locate on the map of Europe, exemplified in the French symbolist playwright Alfred Jarry wittingly locating his odious character Ubu in Poland (i.e., in a nonentity of no importance). Polish patriotism, these historians believed, needed pride more than any other therapy history could offer. Moreover, the unscrupulously apologist image of the past integrated the Christian idea of a paradise lost (but recoverable in the future) into the secular imagination of the epoch that saw democratization as imminent. In short, it was not only national independence—the particular dream of the Poles—but also liberty as a more general, international ideal of the age that was to be regained with the reestablishment of Poland-Lithuania. However, the view that the so-called Polish-

Lithuanian noble democracy was an exceptional achievement, unparalleled in any other early modern European country, also had had advocates in the first half of the nineteenth century, when democracy had been a far less popular political slogan. As we shall see, Polish historians were nevertheless capable of marrying this idealized image of the nation with ideologies of their own.

Let us begin with Lelewel. He was aware that the noble democracy was viewed with much suspicion by his colleagues precisely because it had been a unique political order in the Europe of its time. On one hand, it was supposed to have excessively limited the powers of the central government, which would become a source of the anarchy that would trouble the Commonwealth in the seventeenth and eighteenth centuries. On the other hand, it was believed that the nobility had misused its liberties, not only against the monarchical, or indeed any central power, but also against the weaker social groups—the burghers and the peasants—gradually building a system that was seen as unjust and oppressive. Thus, Lelewel's reasoning was about divorcing the two lines of argumentation and emphasizing that the democratic principles of the nobility had nothing to do with the Commonwealth's political troubles. Despite the obvious shortcomings of the Commonwealth's political system, which required scholarly investigation, Lelewel argues that "we should nevertheless insist that Poland represents a glorious view among all other republics that shone forth in various epochs of world history."[69] However, Lelewel's eulogy for noble democracy still contained a number of Enlightenment or indeed pre-Enlightenment concepts. For example, he spoke of "republics" instead of democracies, that is, "republics" in their early modern sense as countries whose citizens participated in government and legislation and which could formally be monarchies, like the Commonwealth itself. Moreover, he stressed that Poland-Lithuania was a uniquely "spacious" republic, in contrast to the opinion advocated by a number of early modern theorists (and shared by Montesquieu) that republicanism only works in small states, such as city-states, whose citizens can actually meet each other, whereas large territories need a centralized and preferably monarchical power.

Perhaps astonishingly, Szujski's opinion on noble democracy was also an apologia, despite serious reservations. Szujski, who was also the most religious among our Polish historians, drew a picture of the national past that was marked by dramatic contrasts. In his opinion there was a painful price to pay for greatness, and following moral ideals did not guarantee prosperity. As noted, in his view Poland's civilizing-religious mission in the East made the country "a martyr of Christianity" and resulted in serious internal troubles. Analogically, he believed that the evolution of the Polish constitution after the end of the Piast dynasty had fatal consequences for the efficiency of the government and that the quick development of parliamentary life was premature in a monarchy that had been freshly united and had not managed to fully form its central institutions. Still, he insisted that this development "elevated the Polish nation above its neighbors . . . , constituted an example of institutions unknown to its time, and splendidly resulted in realms of liberalism and civilization."[70] In this way he tried to integrate the constitutional developments of the fifteenth and sixteenth centuries into the framework of values of his own time. And yet, his overall assessment of the apparently golden epoch that gave rise to liberty, parliamentary rule, and spectacular territorial expansion was contradictory. In his view, the decisive period in the formation of the political order of the Commonwealth was the long reign of Casimir, Jagiełło's son (who reigned from 1447 to 1492), known for being anxious to preserve the prerogatives of the crown against the nobility's rising demands for power. Szujski argues that "Casimir did not manage to resist the surge in liberties and representative institutions, for this surge was a consequence of individual power and the reason for the nation's greatness, and the fatal destiny of the nation was to abuse them and destroy the organism of the state."[71]

Szujski was not the only one of our historians who emphasized the price Poland-Lithuania was to pay for its greatness, which they found so praiseworthy. Anticipating future developments, when, as Niemcewicz put it, the nobility would "transform its holy liberty into lamentable anarchy," they frequently expressed their regret that the Jagiellonian monarchs had been too liberal, compliant, and conciliatory, often yielding to pressure from their subjects.[72] Niemcewicz pointed at Jagiełło, the founder of the dynasty, Szujski at his son Casimir, and Bobrzyński at Sigismund the Old (r. 1506–48)—all of them long-lived monarchs who watched the prerogatives of the crown gradually be limited in exchange for taxes, support for particular political maneuvers, wars, and personal popularity. Szujski was the only one who crowned this reasoning with a logical conclusion, expressing his regret that no Jagiellon "was capable of a decisive, radical action that would reverse the current"—that is to say, restore his monarchical power by suppressing the nobles' aspirations by force.[73] Finally, this line of reasoning was serenely perverted by Adam Szelągowski, a neo-Romantic historian from Lviv who argued that one of the main reasons for the prosperity of the Jagiellonian epoch was the dynasty's legendary tractability and its indulgence of the dynastic subjects. These traits, in his opinion, made the Jagiellons the most popular dynasty in Europe besides the English Tudors (although their royal composure was in sharp contrast to the Tudors' cruelty, which he did not bother to explain).[74]

Bobrzyński and Smoleński were certainly more critical toward the Commonwealth and its legacy than Szujski; however, neither of them equaled his dramatic fatalism in their analyses. Eventually, Bobrzyński's strategy was the opposite. He was the only one of our Polish historians who rejected the idea of Poland's exceptionalism on principle and might thus be considered a representative of a "Whiggish" approach to history à rebours: he believed that history was about a western European–style progress of efficient, civilizing, and centralized forms of accountable and responsible government that emanated from the country's political elite. In his view, no deviations from this scenario could have guaranteed greatness, and thus none of them deserve our sympathy. Quite surprisingly, however, his evaluation of the crucial political reforms of the years 1504–6, which finally instituted the Sejm as the country's central parliament and determined its prerogatives and its mode of functioning, was enthusiastic: in his opinion they made Poland the most progressive nation in the Europe of that time. He argues that the medieval political order, based on an estate structure, was broken and replaced with the idea of citizenship: "Since that time . . . all inhabitants of the Kingdom were to be aware that they were citizens, and that it was the state law that they were to obey and that was to protect them, not their particular estates. The Polish sejm, unlike other parliaments of its time, was not a representative of a number of estates, but of the entire country and nation." Thus, he concludes, all prior privileges and agreements expired in their capacity as sources of public law and were replaced with the "unlimited idea of love for the motherland, embodied in legal obligations," of which the fundamental one was the duty to respond to a call to defend the country.[75] This was confused reasoning because, as Bobrzyński himself stressed, there was in fact no room for non-nobles in the Polish political system, except for the symbolic representation of a few cities (with no right to vote) in the parliament, which, in his view, however, was all that the cities actually wanted, given that they were alienated from the rest of the country by their German elites and much more interested in commercial rivalry against each other than in national politics, which they avoided also out of a fear of new taxation.[76]

What is perhaps most remarkable about Bobrzyński's enthusiastic account is his emphasis on the idea of the passing of feudalism and the emergence of a new, modern state based on universal law and citizenship—an idea he stressed more than any other Polish historian and that was more typical of the Protestant German historians' analyses of the early modern period.

Droysen's *Geschichte der preussischen Politik* may serve as the best example of this approach. Naturally, the great apologist for Prussia had an attitude toward the early modern Empire that was extremely critical, for it was only on the ruins of the Empire that Prussia could become the first truly German power. Thus, the image he drew was one of an apocalyptic downfall. The late medieval or early modern Empire of the age preceding the Reformation was, he claimed, a negation of the divine order. The moral depravation of the elites was accompanied by the complete vitiation of the ideas of German liberty and German law, which became synonyms for anarchy and perversions of the *raison d'état*: "the irresponsibility of all, and the impotence of the whole." Like the majority of his Protestant colleagues, Droysen diagnosed the tragedy of Germany as its inability to abandon the "old order" of medieval ideas: feudalism, dependence on Rome, and the fragmentation of power, which still rested with "the prelates and the barons." The key to the transformation that Germany did *not* experience was centralization and the emergence of a strong monarchy, such as occurred in France, England, and Spain. This was impossible, however, because the emperors of the cosmopolitan Habsburg dynasty lacked true German patriotism and, instead of working for the consolidation of Germany, cared only about spreading their power over foreign territories.[77]

This was a standard accusation German Protestant historians leveled against the Habsburgs insofar as the times after the Reformation were concerned, when Charles V would choose the wrong side in the religious conflict. Droysen's radicalism was about projecting this highly negative image centuries back: in his view, the Habsburgs had ceased to be true Germans long before they became the archenemies of Protestantism. Eventually it was the Habsburgs' position as the new Roman emperors that destined them to remain anti-national rulers and colored their dynastic ambitions with supranational aspirations. Their imperial dignity also made them spiritual allies of the papacy, despite numerous actual conflicts of the Empire and the Church. Since it was the Empire that symbolized national unity, all that Germans could cultivate under the circumstances was the "spiritual unity of the nation." This, according to Droysen, was achievable only in nation-like states within Germany, that is, the principalities building up modern state apparatuses and political consciousness "in constant conflict with the Empire and the Papacy," which was to spare Germany the fatal destiny of Italy or Poland.[78]

The decentralization of Germany was nevertheless a highly controversial issue. In Eduard Heyck's view, the political constitution of the Empire became, after the extinguishing of the Staufen dynasty, a vicious circle: as the throne became electable within the circle of German princes, their main concern was not to let any of them, particularly the emperor, rise above the others, and therefore they always preferred the weakest candidate. Although the Habsburgs managed to make succession to the Holy Roman crown hereditary in practice once again, their constant involvement in foreign affairs never let them become a truly national dynasty, and after the Reformation their Catholicism made them open enemies of the German nation.[79] Oskar Jäger also found decentralization, particularly as institutionalized by Charles IV's Golden Bull of 1356, alarming, even though in his view the so-called Great Interregnum was at least advantageous for Germany because the "irresponsible dreams" of the Staufen dynasty were replaced by "purely national policies."[80]

Jäger emphasized that the fatal election of the emperors was a result not of any political tendency or theory but of unfortunate coincidence: four German dynasties died out, leaving the throne vacant. Still, he saw contemporary political concepts as erroneous. First, he stressed the ideological and legal fiction of the imagined continuity between the ancient and the medieval Roman Empire, a fiction that inspired medieval Germans' false pride and discouraged them from reasonable reforms. Second, exactly like Droysen, he bitterly suggested that the idea of German liberty was fundamentally responsible for the rising fragmentation of political power and legal prerogatives, causing both anarchy and stagnation, as no consensus on any serious political initiative was achievable. What distinguished him from his Protestant colleagues was an element of perverse optimism: in his view the dysfunctionality of the Empire turned out to be advantageous for Germany in the time of the Reformation, as it prevented the Habsburgs from extinguishing the new movement.[81] Moral and ideological reproaches prevailed, however. The most radical and simple of them was, of course, that of corruption: as Hans Prutz formulated it, the moral downfall of the German princes in the epoch of the Great Interregnum might be comparable only with that of the time of Louis XIV, who harnessed them to his chariot with the aid of gold.[82]

The anti-Habsburg obsession of the Protestant German historians may perhaps be best observed in the passages of *Die Epochen der deutschen Geschichte*, by Johannes Haller. First, the historian mocks his colleagues' criticism of the dynastic policies of the time. The dynastic principle, he claims, was the only ideology that the monarchs striving for unification of Germany had at their disposal, as well as the only one that worked in practice; Albrecht I (1298–1308), for example, was, in his opinion, close to achieving this goal. However, thirty pages later Haller presents his readers with a ritually passionate critique of the Habsburgs, who had pursued the policy he praised, but their objectives were non-national and they never desired anything but building their dynastic *Hausmacht*. Still, his overall attitude toward the late medieval period is astonishingly positive. In his opinion this was the time of the birth of a local, provincial patriotism in the German territorial principalities that would later evolve into a national German consciousness.[83]

This idea had its predecessors among our German historians of the first half of the nineteenth century, when national unity was still considered just a beautiful dream. The dedicated conservative Heinrich Leo, for example, rejected all criticism of the feudal fragmentation of medieval Germany; in his view, this was the soil from which the "inner variety and depth of Germany" grew.[84] The liberal Friedrich von Raumer emphasized that the medieval constitution of Germany, based on the idea of German liberty, protected its contemporaries against "the two maladies of political life": the tyranny of an individual and general anarchy.[85]

Although starting from different premises, Karl Lamprecht also arrived at optimistic conclusions about the late medieval period. First, in his analysis, the decline of nobility that formed the basis for royal power went together with the rise of the cities, best expressed in their tendency to associate in various unions and leagues (such as that of Hansa or Rhine), which were fundamental for building up a supraregional sense of German unity. Second, he stressed that with the decline of royal power, along with its Rome-related imperial ideology, the influence of the papacy in Germany also deteriorated, and so the nation, "living in estates rather than in its kings," was discovering its true identity; he regarded anti-Romanism as an essential German feature. Finally, Lamprecht enthusiastically described and analyzed the expansion of German influence and power over the West Slavic territories east of the Elbe, which he compared to the American conquest of the West in his own lifetime. One of the most important facts of the social history of that time, he informed his readers with pride, was that in 1404 the last Slavic-speaking woman reportedly died in Jasmund (today a national park on the island of Rügen). He noted with satisfaction the first manifestations of an "instinctive antagonism" against the French in contemporary sources, identifying it as another essential component of the German national spirit.[86]

Anatomy of the Feudal Monarchy

As noted, the late medieval period is of fundamental importance in our historians' narratives, as it was the time when both the political structure that was to determine the functioning of political life in the Empire and the Commonwealth in the last centuries of their existence and the estate structure that formed its basis were established. This social structure attracted much attention from our historians; however, it was invariably discussed in the context of major political developments. The problems they always had in mind when regarding the estates were their relation to the political whole, their patriotic consciousness, and their role in strengthening or weakening the political system. Only the considerations concerning the peasantry were free from this ideological infusion, and thus they occupied a marginal position in the narratives of our historians. The life of the peasantry, which comprised some three-quarters of the population of both countries, was considered mainly from a material or legal point of view, based on the limited information concerning its condition that was available to our historians. One of the factors discussed, for example, was the rise of serfdom in the Commonwealth and eastern Germany.

German and Polish historians alike believed that the political and legal order formed in the late medieval period was the result of the aspirations and influence of particular estates, combined with the German and Polish national characters. Interestingly, the political deterioration that was on the horizon, which will be discussed in the next chapter, was regarded as a degeneration of the status quo caused by the ambitions and greed of the social elites. On the other hand, it was considered a consequence of the petrification of the existing system, and, taken together, these factors were presumed to have left both countries vulnerable to their increasingly aggressive, absolutist, and modernizing neighbors.

Modernity was barely visible behind the colorful hills of continuity. Bobrzyński, who, as noted, argued that after 1505 Poland was rapidly transformed from a patrimonial monarchy into a modern state of law (and then degenerated into a noble oligarchy), was a thorough-going outsider among Polish historians, and indeed he did not pursue this idea too consistently. Eventually, Protestant German historians desperately searched for a social transformation that would mark the end of the medieval order. To be sure, in their view the Reformation constituted the most spectacular turning point in German history before Bismarck's unification, as it made Germany the new "chosen people" and opened up completely new prospects for the blessed nation. In the realms of political, social, and economic developments, however, their hopes remained unsatisfied. Neither the Reformation nor the Peace of Augsburg (1555), nor that of Westphalia (1648), annihilated the old order, the ancient institutions, or Germany's traditional shortcomings. The Empire remained anchored in antiquated ideology, structures, and mentalities, earning an embarrassing reputation among the enlightened public, until Napoleon brutally dissolved it. The apologists of the Polish noble democracy, as noted, could not agree on whether it preceded modern Western democracies or if it was a remnant of feudal privileges that had been eliminated by Western monarchies.

The formation of the new political order was related to some reconfigurations of the social order. A crucial element in this process in Poland was the temporary victory of the middle and lower orders of the nobility over the aristocracy, whose representatives dominated the senate. However, as aristocrats did not enjoy a separate legal status and the 1569 union of Lublin officially forbade acquiring any new aristocratic titles (all in the name of equality among all noble citizens), the question of whether this stratum should be considered a separate political and social factor remained controversial among Polish historians. Niemcewicz, Szujski, and Smoleński barely referenced it as a social class in their narratives. The Romantic historians—Lelewel, Szajnocha, and Schmitt, as dedicated democrats—were highly critical of the aristocracy and the role it played in Polish history. Some differences in their approach were visible in their attitude toward the union with Lithuania: Szajnocha emphasized that the union constituted an ideal opportunity for the rich and powerful families to broaden the distance between them and the rest of the nobility, whereas Lelewel, as an enthusiast of the union, stressed the general striving for colonization of the East.

In the end, Lelewel was more egalitarian than democratic, and antipathy toward social elites constituted a distinctive hallmark of all his writings. As discussed in the previous chapter, his apologist's defense of Poland's early history was essentially based on his belief that primordial Slavic society had hardly any hierarchies, and the fact that social differences eventually appeared was, in his view, a bad omen for the future. Lelewel's approach was dogmatic enough for him to appreciate the despotism of the Piast monarchy, because he viewed it as a factor limiting "aristocratic pretensions" and "nasty abuses of the law" by representatives of the social elite. He would again employ this rhetoric of "unlimited greed" and "oppression of the people" when describing the policies and mentality of the nobility in the seventeenth and eighteenth centuries. Perhaps astonishingly, with respect to the fifteenth and sixteenth centuries, he sharply contrasted the demonized aristocracy and the nobility, which he frequently labeled "the noble populace" or "the noble community" (or *gmin*—a notion derived from the idea of a commune). Obviously, he enthusiastically praised the latter's aspirations for power and prosperity, which he considered to be marks of both democratization and egalitarianism.[87]

However, Lelewel had already prepared the groundwork for his bitter future criticism of the nobility in what seemed an idyllic apologia for the noble democracy of the sixteenth century. "One can hardly imagine a more favorable condition of the citizenry, whose soul enjoyed a state of bliss," he argues, adding a remarkable comment: "If only humankind was capable of doing so without abuse." His analysis is based on the ancient idea that prosperity ripens into decay and success fuels decadence. "Normally," he concludes pessimistically, "the one who enjoys prosperity is greedy to achieve more, and so he wrests from the other, causing his misery. This was the way of oppression of the peasantry and the burghers that the nobility entered into."[88]

As a matter of fact, Lelewel's criticism was closely related to that of Niemcewicz, a representative of the previous generation, whose views he opposed in many ways. Niemcewicz, himself a child of the epoch that first formulated open critiques of the nobility and its mentality, was quite radical in his attitude toward the magnates who, "because of the immense difference in wealth," as he claims, "governed all, notoriously made rivals of each other, envied the kings, and embraced the entire country with the folly of their passions, and so they sent it plunging from the utmost glory down into the eternal abyss." While appreciating the nobility's patriotism, courage, hospitality, and gratitude, Niemcewicz nevertheless bitterly criticized its "incredible antipathy against work, and indifference toward their own property and wealth," which he found as lamentable as it was bewildering.[89]

Schmitt, who is typically regarded as Lelewel's successor, represented essentially the opposite view. In summarizing the first century of the noble democracy, he emphasized its deficiencies, which would later lead to fatal outcomes. What he criticized the most was "the exclusion of the major part of the population from political rights" and the growing legal dependence of the peasants on the nobles, provoking "the excesses" of the latter. He also pointed out potential abuses in parliamentary procedure, in particular the right of an individual deputy to veto any decision. It was a regulation first put into practice in 1652, but it had formally been part of the Polish parliamentary tradition from its beginning—and was intended to promote the discussing of every matter until unanimity was achieved. And yet, Schmitt argues that in the sixteenth century all these shortcomings of the new political order were still neutralized by the moral qualities of the Commonwealth's citizens: "public virtue, patriotism, readiness for sacrifices, and noble brotherhood."[90] Such was also the opinion of Szujski, who argues that despite "the loss of the last jewels of the monarchical power," the sixteenth century is rightly regarded as the golden epoch in Polish history, for in that time the elites still represented the highest moral, intellectual, and cultural qualities. "In Polish history," he reasons, "in which all depended on the spirit rather than the forms, the people rather than the institutions, the golden epoch occurs when the best people, and a momentous harmony, are to be found."[91] Szujski further develops this idea that the elites' superior mentality and moral condition deteriorated and undergirded formal political structures and institutions only later, when he provides his explanation for the causes of the Commonwealth's decline.

Among our historians, the sole apologist for aristocracy in that epoch was Michał Bobrzyński. The Cracovian historian and politician shared neither his colleagues' democratic sentiments nor their antipathies toward the aristocracy. In sharp contrast to Joachim Lelewel, Bobrzyński emphasized the role not of the masses but of the individuals and groups who were their most outstanding or typical representatives. Therefore, his attention naturally fell upon eminent personalities and men of extraordinary qualities. Thus, despite his tendency to idealize the strong monarchy, he remained critical toward the monarchs as individuals and was still able to appreciate the achievements of the characters and groups who challenged them, as he believed it was for the benefit of the state. For example (and, again, in sharp contrast to Lelewel), although extremely critical of the medieval epoch and its political fragmentation, he was still able to appreciate the efforts of the elite, who saw the benefits of reunifying the country and strengthening its central institutions.[92] Their finest hour, in his opinion, arrived with the union with Lithuania, when a foreign dynasty was invited to rule, thus opening new prospects for the magnate families of southern Poland (Małopolska), both as colonizers of the newly acquired territories and as advisors and officials of the monarchs, who needed support from the locals to rule efficiently. Bobrzyński did not deny their greed for power and wealth, because in his view "wealth is only a means to political influence, which was the true goal of contemporary Polish aristocracy." It was due to their political agenda, and indeed their vision, that Poland abandoned the "narrow" policies of the Piast monarchy, acquired new territories peacefully (a fact he values not for moral reasons but for the low costs incurred), and became a great power to which "nothing seems unachievable." In short, by emphasizing the fundamental role of aristocracy as the true architect of the Jagiellonian policies and the authors of "the brightest pages of our national history," Bobrzyński takes a unique position among the Polish historians of his time.[93]

Polish historians univocally argued that the price Poland-Lithuania paid for the rise of the nobility and its political-legal position was the decline of the cities, which, as Fryderyk Papée claimed, still possessed "a vital force" in the first half of the fifteenth century, a force they subsequently lost as a result of growing pressure from the nobles.[94] The same applies to the peasants; their deteriorating legal and economic condition resulted in the introduction of serfdom. Schmitt, desperately trying to combine his patriotic and democratic sentiments, argues that the cities "scarcely participated" in the great political reforms of the age, which "badly marginalized" the position of the peasants in society and would cause "heavy oppression" in the epoch that followed.[95] Lelewel, as noted, related this oppression to the catastrophic impact of the progress of civilization, and he remained highly ambivalent about the dark side of the noble democracy. On one hand, he expressed his disgust and contempt for the class-based egoism of the nobles, which he observed in their constant focus on legal regulations concerning the condition of the peasants (an issue he researched carefully), while on the other hand he insisted that the peasants' situation remained relatively comfortable due to the general prosperity Poland-Lithuania enjoyed because of its booming exports of grain after the reincorporation of Pomerania (Royal Prussia).[96] As far as the deteriorating situation of the cities is concerned, Lelewel and Bobrzyński were in accord: the burghers had it coming, as they actually did not participate in the reform movement of the age and remained apolitical and disunited because all they cared about was their immediate profits and the competition of the cities against each other. The burghers therefore willingly offered political concessions to the nobles or the crown in exchange for economic privileges and protection against their commercial rivals. Last but not least, the most powerful cities were simply unable to engage in the political life of the country because of the German character of their elites at that time.[97]

Smoleński is the only one of our Polish historians who was free of the antibourgeois sentiments typical for Polish intellectuals at that time. In his view, the nobility was guilty of both excluding burghers from the political life of the nation and destroying national industry because they instituted numerous antiburgher commercial and legal regulations, monopolized landownership, and, last but not least, refused to pay taxes and customs. All this, he argues, was "economically as well as morally ruinous for the burghers."[98]

In German narratives, the positioning of particular groups in the structure of power seems even more important than in the Polish ones, particularly because after the death of Frederick II and the end of the Staufen dynasty, the power structure—regrettably, as the German historians believed—became opaque and complex. Therefore, our historians switch their attention from individual rulers and their policies to analysis of the system of influences, ambitions, and aspirations determined by five elements: the papacy and clergy, the Empire, the princes, the nobility, and the cities.

The first three elements have already been addressed. Generally, German historians vacillated between stressing that the papacy and the Empire were two interrelated pillars of the same medieval system and simply stigmatizing both the papacy and Catholicism as Germany's most dreadful and dangerous enemies. These two strategies were not necessarily coherent, however, and were often employed alternately. Fierce anti-Catholicism was a constant factor in Protestant historiography; it was a dogma constituting the background of numerous developments in German history at various times, occasionally coming to the fore as an explanation of a particular problem or simply as a memento for German readers. The fundamental alliance or kinship of the papacy and the Empire was the factor on which the historians focused when explaining why their struggle against each other was never resolved—a struggle that, given the demonized and anti-German nature of the Roman Church, might easily have been interpreted as a national struggle for independence. The ambivalence of the Protestant historians' attitude toward the Empire, as both the representative of German power and the essential partner of Rome in the medieval universe, is perhaps best seen in Ranke's writings. On one hand, as already discussed, Ranke rejected Sybel's accusations against the medieval emperors as non-national and treacherous; he found them simply ahistorical. In contrast, Ranke regarded the Empire's ambitions for leadership among Christian monarchies, which Sybel mocked, as admirable and flattering for the German national consciousness. On the other hand, however, he also noted all the symptoms of anticlericalism and resistance against Roman influence with great satisfaction and labeled them as the most remarkable achievements of this German consciousness, still in its infancy in the period in question. Moreover, he also commented briefly on the alternative that his professional credo would not let him elaborate on: that the ideal solution of the dilemma would have been a divorce from Rome centuries before the Reformation actually happened. This scenario did not encompass a theological revolution, as all Ranke cared about were the national-political aspects, and the alternative outcome he had in mind would have been, apparently, a German version of Anglicanism, or even national Catholicism.[99]

Wolfgang Menzel was the historian who was not afraid to let both his imagination and his national ambition flourish in this respect. Since it was the German race that had conquered Rome and saved Christianity, he argued, "why then should not Germany also be preponderant in the Church, and a pope be German by birth?" This scenario, in his view, was more than natural and a desirable solution to the papal-imperial dualism and rivalry that shattered the Christian world. Moreover, "the Germanization of the Church would have been effected by the emperors had they not been abandoned and betrayed by the princes of the Empire." Finally, he also felt compelled to comment on the long-term consequences of such a scenario: "It has been objected that the sovereignty and tyranny of the emperor would have been a worse evil, and that the Church of Rome would have been reduced to the state in which she is now in Russia: a consolatory reflection founded upon an utter misapprehension of the national feeling throughout Germany. Had the unity of the Empire and its external power been preserved under the emperor, civil and mental liberty would, in all possibility, have reached a much higher level than they possibly could have under a polygarchy influenced by an inimical and malicious foreigner."[100]

Analogous controversies concerned the German princes. On one hand, as noted, they were accused of high treason for undermining the national unity and conspiring with the Empire's enemies; on the other hand, it was the principalities that some historians viewed as seeds of the "spiritual unity of the nation," in other words, entities from which the future united Germany would evolve, as Hohenzollern Prussia was to demonstrate a few centuries later. Let us look at Ranke's and Droysen's writings for details on this ambiguity.

Ranke seems remarkable in this respect, at least for the fact that he considered the antagonism between the estates—the monarchs, the princes, and the cities—to be a natural consequence of each party's striving for power and influence, rather than a result of some diabolical conspiracy against Germany. On one hand, he appreciated the princely ambitions and pointed to the Hohenzollern, Wittelsbach, and Wettin families as the most successful administrators and dynastic planners, as they had managed to stabilize their power and expand their territories. He noted with satisfaction that the count of Oldenburg had achieved the dignified rank of king of Denmark in 1450, clearly signaling the growing international prestige of German aristocracy. On the other hand, however, he lamented their constant conflicts and brutal rivalry, which resulted in a state of civil war that devastated German provinces, one after another. Germany during that period, he claims, was not in the pitiful condition of Italy, but the internal anarchy was still "humiliating and unbearable for the great nation."[101]

Droysen's attitude was marked with relative ambivalence, but he stressed different aspects of the situation, mirroring his general obsession with national unity, as was typical of a number of German historians. As noted, he passionately condemned German aristocracy for its immorality and inclination to use violence as the basic method for resolving conflicts, both with other dynasties as well as within one's own family. He also lamented the lack of political unity at that time, yet this sentiment was hampered by his fundamental antipathy for the Habsburgs. Political unity in the Empire, although in theory the fulfillment of his most precious ideal, becomes a questionable objective in his narrative when the detested dynasty gains control over the crown, and so his attention turns to the princes as potential organizers of a modern, German monarchy within the Empire, a nucleus of the future united Germany. However, he concludes sadly that all efforts to build up such a promising state-organism in this epoch were of no avail. The German princes simply did not bother or lacked sufficient determination to undertake the task, and the few who did achieve some progress in consolidating their power and replacing the old feudal order with a centralized, modern state apparatus found no respectable successors. German liberty, which Droysen labeled as feudal anarchy, proved fatally resistant to all such initiatives. He concludes that individuals, no matter how extraordinary their skills and qualities, can do nothing against the spirit of the time.[102]

While the late medieval epoch was unanimously considered to be when Poland's nobility rose and its cities declined, it was, in complete contrast, viewed as the golden period in German urban history. As mentioned, however, in the nineteenth-century historical narratives, economic and cultural aspects were always seen through the lenses of great political ideas. Thus, the cities' strength and their ability to pursue policies independent of or even antagonistic to those of the Empire constituted a controversial issue. In general, the historians' approach in this respect varied because of two factors that we have already encountered relative to other issues. The first was their attitude toward national unity as Germany's timeless ideal, an attitude mitigated by their awareness of contemporary realities and mentalities. As discussed above, some, like Ranke, were more flexible or skeptical about judging the past according to the standards of their age; others, like Sybel, mercilessly railed against the past agents' ideological shortcomings. The second factor was their attitude toward particular social groups viewed as representatives of either the healthy or the deplorable tendencies in the "national spirit."

Menzel, invariably radical and grandiloquent, was enthusiastic about the rise of the cities, the flourishing of urban culture, and their struggle against feudal lords, who desperately tried to dominate them. The conflict, in his view, was partially economic, but in the final analysis it was part of the great struggle of the feudal princes and the Church to "annihilate the Empire," a struggle in which the cities lined up against the centrifugal aspirations of the princes and clergy.[103] Raumer and Stacke saw the rich, proud, and powerful cities as centers of culture and the "national spirit," which, according to Stacke, were accompanied by the "perversion" and moral downfall of the "bearers of medieval culture," that is, the clergy and the nobility.[104] Ranke and Droysen criticized both the cities' ambitions to emancipate themselves from any authority and their rising antagonism against the nobility and the aristocracy. Droysen, like Lelewel and Bobrzyński, claimed that the cities became so powerful that, had they united, they could have played a decisive role in the internal struggle for power within the Empire, but they were too preoccupied with their own rivalry for profit and thus remained tragically divided. As a result, they watched the political evolution of the Empire passively, occasionally supporting the weaker side simply out of fear that the victorious party would become too strong and limit their own influence.[105] Finally, Ludwig Häusser developed this idea by arguing that all the estates of the Empire of that time failed in terms of their political engagement. In his opinion, the late medieval period, being a time of stable economic growth, was also a time of political inertia, which the territorial princes skillfully used to acquire more power, gradually reducing the entity of the Empire to an illusion. It was a process that neither the cities nor the nobles actually opposed, busy as they were with consumption, trade, and leisure, and showing less and less interest in politics or their ancient liberties.[106]

This characteristic ambiguity in the German historians' approach can best be seen in Lamprecht, who overtly delineates the two perspectives: the then-contemporary one, stressing timely and social contexts, and the general one, emphasizing long-term tendencies and introducing concepts unknown during the epoch in question. In the former perspective, the economic and political rise of the cities resulted, most importantly, in the formation of an urban elite, a new nobility of wealth, marked by its strong, and occasionally aggressive, antagonism against the old, feudal elites as a fundamental element of its self-consciousness. One of the consequences of the new status quo, in which the cities, and particularly their leagues, such as the Hansa, achieved a position of equality with territorial lords, was the intensification of internal conflicts within the Empire. This was partly due to the cities' ambitions, which quickly surpassed their traditional legal and political positions, and partly due to the nature of their power, which was more fluid and fragile than that based on landownership. In this way German unity—the central idea of the meta-perspective—again suffered in this process. However, in the final analysis Lamprecht stressed that the rise of the monetary economy, trade, and commercial ties between cities located in remote corners of the country successfully counterbalanced these undesirable consequences and were in fact crucial in awakening the sense of German unity in larger sections of society.[107]

Toward God and Reason

The sixteenth century was a time when the German and Polish histories extended beyond their national frames, giving rise to pride and suspicion in equal measure on the part of our historians. In Poland this happened due to the establishment of the democratic order, which, as the majority of Polish historians viewed it, was a universal landmark in the history of liberty in all of Europe and indeed the world. In Germany the same process occurred because of the Reformation: a renewal of Christianity that was as much German as it was universal. What's more, in Poland-Lithuania the Reformation resulted in the rise of religious tolerance, which, as has been shown, Polish historians viewed as an indispensable element of democracy in the Commonwealth and a unique Polish-Lithuanian contribution to the progress of liberty. In short, this was a time of spectacular, unparalleled achievements in both countries, inspiring much satisfaction and pride in the patriotic readers of German and Polish histories, respectively. However, a number of our historians, having enthusiastically and indeed pompously announced the greatness and uniqueness of these developments, hurried to warn their readers about the complications that followed.

It should come as no surprise that the Reformation is a controversial moment in German history, when Protestant and Catholic interpretations of the national past openly collide. Yet the controversy was more complicated than the religious division suggests, and it should not be reduced to the two antagonistic religious approaches. Most importantly, the Protestant point of view prevailed and dominated the entire discussion, simply because of the undeniable importance of the Reformation's legacy for German national history. Regrettably or not, it was a turning point, and no Catholic historian could deny the Reformation's impact on German history. As Ranke argued, this history lacked a center: no institution, social group, personality, or province epitomizes it. In his view, each history needs a focal point, because through it we can grasp that history's most characteristic features, as well as its moral and ideological sense. He believed that the rule of Louis XIV played such a role in French history, as did the Glorious Revolution of 1688 in England's history. In the German case, it was the Reformation, precisely because the history of that process best demonstrated the essential divisions within Germany and the potential it had for the future.[108]

However, there were two more aspects of German historians' interpretations of the Reformation in which the Protestant point of view thoroughly prevailed. First, it symbolized and indeed epitomized the passing of the old, medieval order and the beginning of the modern age. This was the idea that dominated the image of the national past for a number of German historians, most notably Droysen, for whom the Empire, all its other shortcomings notwithstanding, remained implacably anchored in the antiquated medieval world. In short, a new era began with the Reformation, for better or worse, and no German historian could ignore it. Second, the Reformation was essentially and unquestionably a German product, and Protestantism was naturally believed to bear some distinctively German features.

Regardless of whether one viewed it as inspired by Providence or by the devil, the Reformation was the way Germany influenced the course of world history, and no Catholic historian could deny that either.

According to Oskar Jäger, it was Germany's central geographic location in Europe that made the Reformation the most important development in world history since the dawn of Christianity. Thus, even though the sixteenth century also brought about the birth of other (but still Germanic) great powers—England and Holland—Germany was the battleground for the modern age's decisive conflict, which was to determine whether humanity would turn "toward God and reason."[109] Accordingly, Wilhelm Wachsmuth emphasized that between 1525, when this battle began, and the Peace of Augsburg in 1555, Germany became the center and leader of Christian civilization, bringing light and inspiration to the disappearing medieval world. On the other hand, he also proudly stressed the national and folkish nature of Luther's teachings.[110] Heyck described the Reformation as the power "that unites and surpasses everything" and that would later be defined by Kant as the categorical imperative.[111]

Eventually, however, our German historians did their best to keep the history of the Reformation safely anchored within the paradigm of national history. One of the reasons that made it possible and indeed relatively easy for our historians to successfully marginalize the international aspects of the Reformation and focus on its German dimension was that its consequences eventually inspired developments that were ultimately interpreted as fundamental for the formation of modern nations. Obviously, the translation of the Bible into German and subsequently into other national languages and the introduction of national languages into Christian liturgies, along with the formation of national churches, played a crucial role in this respect. However, other sociopolitical questions were of no minor importance for our historians' narratives. Before the Reformation, Western Christianity had represented an undeniable cultural unity in many respects, and thus no matter how nationally inclined our historians were, they could not avoid discussing a number of developments regarding German and Polish histories in the broader, Western context. The evolution of feudalism and Latin culture, the crusades and Church reforms—they all clearly had their impact on Western countries. With the Reformation, the history of Europe becomes more national, because each country starts following its own individual path, determined by factors independent of foreign analogies (or, more precisely, the analogies could be ignored from the perspective of the nationally oriented historians). European nations began to develop their exceptional features in contradistinction to all others, rather than in accordance with any common pattern. As a consequence, England becomes Anglican, France becomes Gallican, and Spain fanatically Catholic, while the Italians remain as perfidious as they always were and gradually disappear from the framework of German history. Germany meanwhile becomes even more tragically divided than it ever was, and its fragmentation becomes a distinctive mark of its exceptionalism.

This is how we arrive at the basic dilemma of the Protestant historians. The Reformation might have been Germany's most precious gift to corrupted humanity, but it did little to contribute to the nation's recovery from its most lamentable malady—political disunity. Moreover, it either coincided with, or contributed to, the formation of the centralized, absolute, and powerful monarchies in France, England, and Spain, arousing even greater confusion among German historians when they confronted the chaos and anarchy reigning in their nation's post-Reformation history. Finally, it demanded a great deal of imagination and rhetorical skill to claim that it had created the modern German nation, or at least accelerated the process, since one of its most evident results was, after all, that Germans started hating each other more than they had at any moment before, and perhaps even more than they would at any moment to come. One might argue quite convincingly that the Reformation awoke the Christian identity and consciousness of the German people, which had been petrified by medieval formalism, indifference toward Latin rituals, and degeneration of the Roman Church. This, however, was clearly ruinous for their sense of national unity, which became overshadowed by religious identity for a minimum of two centuries. Thus, the Reformation constituted a conundrum for Protestant historians, who of course also wanted their interpretations of history to be more patriotic than those of Catholic historians. Let us now see how they dealt with it.

One way to solve the problem was to exclude the contumacious Catholics from German national history and thus get rid of the problem of disunity arising from religious divisions. More precisely, Catholics were not erased from German history, in which they were still expected to play their regrettable role, but they were redesignated as foreign agents. Remarkably, this was consistent with Protestant historians' more general claim that resistance to Rome had been a distinctively and profoundly German-national inclination since time immemorial. Such was the attitude of Droysen, who believed that the Reformation was essentially the most German phenomenon in all of German history. It was the Reformation that eventually united Germany: all provinces and all estates contributed to this unique achievement of the German people. It was also the moment, according to Droysen, when Germany almost succeeded in rejecting "foreign spiritual domination." However, this was only partially accomplished, owing to the political fragmentation of the country, which in turn was a result of the perverted concept of German liberty on one hand and the treasonous resistance of the cosmopolitan Habsburg dynasty and its supporters on the other. As a consequence, the Reformation remained an unfinished project, constituting only a foundation for what might and ought to have been: the unification of Germany in the spirit of the

national, Evangelical liberty. The Empire remained a vicious circle: its true unification was impossible because of the Catholic dynasty that occupied the throne,
which made the Protestants, that is, the bearers of the national spirit, a centrifugal
force. Remarkably, Droysen did not argue that the true unification of Germany
would necessarily involve the conversion of German Catholics; it would have been
enough if they had given up their aspirations for political domination. Evangelical
liberty, as he saw it, included religious tolerance, and so there would have been
some room for Catholics in the united Germany of his imagination. Nevertheless,
this scheme could not work the other way around, that is, with Catholics in the
position of power, because of the antinational nature of their confession and its
essentially intolerant character, which allowed only for tactical concessions.[112]

Häusser developed Droysen's argument in a less metaphysical manner. He admits that the Reformation is a controversial issue and that it both strengthened
and solidified Germany's fatal inner fragmentation. However, he claims that this
is a misapprehension that confuses causes and effects, for Germany was already
divided before the Reformation, so its impact in this respect is elusive. Had the
Empire been a real state, he argues, and had it had a truly German character and
monarch, it would have followed the will of the majority of the nation, which the
truly German ruler would not oppose, and the entire nation would have embraced
Protestantism. Finally, Häusser falls into a typical trap of counterfactual thinking,
questioning his own grandiose scheme with yet another alternative: in 1526, he
claims, Emperor Charles V could still have effectively changed the course of German history by backing Luther and his supporters. He comments bitterly, however,
that Charles had just won the Battle of Pavia and simply did not pay much attention
to the Luther controversy, which he considered resolved, and instead focused on
celebrating his victory and formulating his plans concerning Spain. The historian
concludes with a comparison that may seem astonishing coming from the pen of
a German nationalist: Charles was no Napoleon—by which he apparently meant
that the emperor was not a statesman capable of changing the course of history but
rather a product of the mentality of his age and his milieu.[113]

Wachsmuth also promotes the idea that the Reformation ought not to be regarded as a factor contributing to Germany's fragmentation, because Germany
had been fatally divided even before the Reformation. He claims that while these
divisions may have been sharpened by religious conflict, the Reformation was fundamental in building up German unity because of its deeply national and folkish
nature, which helped to smooth over social divisions within the country, bringing
various estates—and particularly the princes and their subjects—closer to each
other spiritually.[114]

Still, there were other painful accusations that the Protestant historians had to
repel. One such example was the idea that the Great Peasants' Revolt of 1524–25,

the most devastating popular insurrection in modern Europe before the French Revolution, was somehow related to the Reformation. Some German authors openly claimed that there was a causal relationship between the two revolutionary movements. Raumer, for instance, bitterly remarked that one should not wonder why the German peasants rebelled, since all worldly authority had been openly questioned by Luther and his followers.[115] Nevertheless, unlike Friedrich Engels, none of our historians had much sympathy for the rebels. While the majority expressed some criticism of the legal and economic condition of the peasantry, and particularly against the rising tendency to introduce serfdom in various regions of Germany, nonetheless in their unified opinion this was not a reason to justify the rebellion. First, the anarchic, revolutionary, and violent nature of the revolt insulted their liberal, and indeed univocally elitist, views. Second, it offended both their religious views and their sense of patriotism, which stressed duty, discipline, and hierarchy as pillars of a healthy society. The idea that a social revolution might have prevailed in Germany aroused detestable French connotations and ran directly against their most persistent beliefs regarding the German national character. Finally, it also ran against the fundamental conception of the Reformation as the great turn toward reason and progress. In short, it was as non-German as it was non-Protestant (the two being perfectly compatible).

It is therefore easy to see that the Great Revolt was interpreted as both an inexplicable folly and a foreign conspiracy. Heyck claimed that its causes were the folk superstitions and the poisonous impact of the Czech Hussite movement. His claim was an awkward attempt to retaliate against criticism of the Reformation by pointing a finger at its foreign predecessor. He also emphasized that the German Reformation had nothing to do with social revolution. Häusser ritually blamed the Habsburgs as guilty of bringing about all of Germany's miseries.[116] Jäger went further by discussing Luther's famous manifesto *Against the Murderous, Thieving Hordes of Peasants*, which encouraged the nobles to massacre the rebels like mad dogs. He felt compelled to affirm that, from the modern point of view, Luther's attitude may seem quite controversial. In the final analysis, however, he argued that Luther had been right: the rule of the mob (*Herr Omnes*, as Luther paraphrased it in a German-Latin idiom) would be the most ruinous and terrifying outcome of the Reformation—it would transform it into the German version of the French Revolution.[117]

All the contradictions in the Protestant interpretations of the Reformation may be seen in Haller's *Epochs of German History*, the latest of our narratives on German history. Haller did his best to combine all his predecessors' ideals: national unity, great power, religious tolerance, and, last but not least, the moral superiority of Protestantism. Naturally, it was his opinion that the Reformation should not be blamed for the Empire's disintegration: it was the independence of German territorial princes that made the Reformation possible, by protecting the movement against Habsburg oppression. Its only connection with German disunity was that in its wake, the illusory nature of the Empire's statehood became unquestionable. He claimed that, in theory, it would have been preferable if one of the parties involved in the subsequent conflict had prevailed and thus been able to restore the country's unity. However, with the Habsburgs on the throne and enjoying a militarily advantageous position, such a scenario could only have resulted in a terrible outcome, so one should actually appreciate that all sides involved—the Lutherans, the Evangelicals, and the Catholics—managed to firmly establish the German spiritual landscape. This situation produced a variety and depth of social, economic, intellectual, and moral patterns that no other European country experienced; they constituted the soil from which sprang German greatness. And yet, there was an obvious caveat to his praise for the variety of German experience: Catholicism unfortunately would persist and be tolerated, but fortunately it would not really be involved. Following the Reformation, Haller concluded, "The German spirit and German consciousness are essentially Protestant."[118]

Thus, in the final analysis we arrive at a paradox: the Protestant narrative on the Reformation manifestly dominated the German historical discourse, but it was still clearly defensive in nature. Its main theme was a counterattack against the Catholic faction's alleged accusations, as well as against the inconsistencies in its own arguments. Thus, the Catholic voice, though feeble, was effectively enhanced by the angry echo of the dominant side. As a matter of fact, the Catholic narrative, apart from the question of national unity addressed above, may be reduced to two issues. Its first argument, as political as it was theological in nature, emphasized that the Reformation "made religion a maid of the state."[119] It could do so, the argument went, because Protestant clergy submitted themselves to territorial rulers and because of the nationalization of the Protestant churches. The second argument, also as political as it was ethical, stressed the physical and spiritual price Germany had to pay for the religious conflict, as well as the fanaticism of the war waged by German Protestants against the "Roman beast" and the "international revolutionary party."[120] These arguments were echoed in the narratives by Protestant authors, who retaliated vigorously and, once again, incoherently.

Certainly both sides accused each other of fanaticism, cruelty, and superstition, and indeed some authors were ready to agree that all the involved parties were to blame for these inclinations and methods, with some authors arguing that the prime culprits were the Catholics and the Lutherans, with the Evangelicals typically falling victim to those two groups. However, the most painful accusation was that of inviting foreigners to intervene in German affairs. This charge included both asking for help from foreign armies and making secret treaties with Germany's enemies, particularly the French archenemy. In this respect, the Protestant position was hardly defensible, simply because promoting nationalist values was supposed to have been one of the main merits of the Reformation, whereas the Catholics never denied their cosmopolitanism. Moreover, although the Habsburgs indeed employed foreign military, particularly Spanish contingents, to battle German Protestants, nevertheless their international involvements, as the Protestant authors emphasized themselves, significantly hampered their efforts to crush the Reformation in Germany. The movement survived because the emperors focused on their conflicts with France, and indeed against the popes, as well as on their interests in Spain, Italy, Hungary, Bohemia, and the Netherlands. It was, as Oskar Jäger put it, "a wonderful spectacle: the emperor and the heretics fighting against the pope; the pope and the heretics against the emperor!"[121]

The most immediate impression one gets when comparing the German and Polish discourses on the Reformation is the lower temperature and less emotional tone of the discussion in Polish historiography. This is perhaps to be explained with one observation that German and Polish historians shared: that the Reformation was an essentially German phenomenon. And it was exactly its German character, Polish historians believed, that doomed it to failure in Poland-Lithuania. As Szujski argued, the Reformation "did not manage to become firmly rooted in the national soil."[122] Obviously, this kind of argument was itself deeply rooted in a more general image of the Polish national character—an image shared by both its apologists and its critics. Bobrzyński certainly belonged to the latter, yet he still emphasized that Polish society, or more precisely the landed gentry, was incapable of embracing the Reformation in its theological depth and actual zealousness. The gentry, as he ironically observed, "were not inclined to have passionate discussions of any religious or political matters, and thus they remained indifferent to the truly German dogmatic controversies. They were unwilling to insult Catholic dogmas, and they did not hate the clergy; indeed they wanted to preserve the Church hierarchy and, most importantly, Catholic rituals, appealing to their imagination so poetically and vividly."[123] In other words, Bobrzyński suggests that it was instead the intellectual and theological sluggishness of their patriotism that prevented the Polish-Lithuanian nobility from embracing the Reformation. Feliks Koneczny, the most zealous Catholic among our historians, argued similarly in order to ridicule the Polish Reformation or perhaps the rise of Protestantism in general. The way he argued, however, was to win the sympathy of the religious skeptics of his own time: he depicted the Reformation as pointless, irrational religious ferment causing social anarchy and confusion.[124]

Accordingly, a dominant tendency among Polish historians was to present the

Polish Reformation as a secular intellectual and political movement, rather than a monumental turn in the spiritual life of the nation. This claim was based on the observation that the Reformation managed to gain popular support among the elite of the gentry for only a few decades—from the mid-sixteenth century till the first decades of the next century, when the Counterreformation clearly prevailed, attracting numerous noble families back to Catholicism and making Protestantism a temporary, and allegedly superficial, adventure of the Polish-Lithuanian gentry, except for a tiny committed minority. At the same time, the more permanent success of the Reformation in the cities was interpreted as yet another proof of their German character, which, regrettably, contributed to their lasting alienation from the rest of the country.

Thus, one can see hardly any traces of German religious fever in the Polish narratives on the Reformation. Major political turning points, such as the union with Lithuania or the Constitution of May 1791, inspired much more passionate debates and controversies. Like their German colleagues, Polish historians of the time were typically inclined to view the religious zeal of the past centuries with great skepticism, and they had a contempt for fanaticism, which they unanimously regarded as obscurantist. Moreover, our devotedly Catholic Polish historians—Szujski, Koneczny, Halecki—were in a clearly more favorable position than their German colleagues: Catholicism had unquestionably won in Poland, and thus they could safely show some sympathy for the Protestant party, demonstrating their own unprejudiced attitude. The other historians, more critically inclined toward Polish Catholicism—such as Bobrzyński, Smoleński, or Szelągowski—could also discuss positive aspects of the Reformation without fear of insulting their readers' feelings.

While the tendency of Polish historians to present the Polish Reformation as more of an intellectual and political trend than a true menace to Catholicism may be seen as condescending and deprecating, it nevertheless testifies to their relative respect and sympathy for the movement. This was a way to put aside religious zeal and fanaticism and to focus on the secular aspects surrounding the religious controversies of the past, which a liberal nineteenth-century audience could find reasonable and insightful. Finally, another factor that shed a relatively positive light on the Reformation in the Polish narratives was their authors' awareness of what was to follow: the Counterreformation. The latter was regarded even more superciliously by Polish historians than by their German colleagues, precisely because it eventually prevailed. As we shall see in the next chapter, most of our Polish historians believed that the triumph of the Counterreformation was one of the most fatal afflictions of the Commonwealth and one of the causes of its final decline and fall.

Most importantly, however, international comparisons concerning religious conflicts of the sixteenth and seventeenth centuries filled Polish historians with great pride. In contrast to what occurred in other European countries, the Polish Reformation did not result, as Schmitt put it, "in a severe civil war" but in "innumerable paper conflicts and dissertations."[125] The majority of Polish historians appreciated that the Reformation caused much ferment among Polish nobles and made them read, discuss, and think about the most pressing issues in contemporary Europe. As Bobrzyński brutally formulated it (in contrast to his own opinion cited above), "An entire generation of gentry woke up from its provincial stupor and anarchy."[126] However, the most positive and promising thing to come out of the issue was religious tolerance, as codified in the so-called Warsaw Confederation of 1573, which guaranteed equal rights for citizens of all denominations, as well as "eternal peace" between them—in sharp contrast to the practices and regulations in then-contemporary western Europe. Obviously, what the Polish historians emphasized with patriotic pride and satisfaction was the uniqueness of Polish tolerance, which in their view testified to the exceptional nature of the Polish national character. As Lelewel argued, it was this "national spirit" that inclined the Poles "to guarantee freedom of all denominations and all opinions, without privileging any one of them." According to Chołoniewski, tolerance was the natural consequence of the Polish national character and noble democracy, while according to Halecki, Polish tolerance was, quite paradoxically, "truly Catholic in its nature."[127] Szelągowski, in contrast, drew a picture of the Reformation that could please a Protestant. In his view it was a development, or a continuation, of one of the fundamental aspects of Christianity: "the sense of individual freedom and dignity." And yet his idea was not to insult the Catholics, nor did he actually intend to take sides in the religious controversy. Typically for Polish historians, what he stressed in his analysis of the Polish Reformation were its secular and indeed modernizing aspects. In his view it equaled "an integration of the principle of religious freedom into the concept of political freedom of an individual" or "a social and political revolution, as was the case in Germany."[128] To sum up: the majority of Polish historians suggested that embracing the Reformation was a natural consequence of the principles of political liberty adopted by the nobility on its way to power in the Commonwealth, and religious tolerance in sixteenth-century Poland-Lithuania was so perfect and admirable because, as a matter of fact, it had little to do with religion: it was simply an extension of the rights of the individual that all citizens of the Commonwealth enjoyed.

Szujski was the only one of our Polish authors who attempted a serious consideration of the problem regarding its truly religious aspect. He did so in his usual manner: exposing his Catholic principles and his profound pessimism about the prospects of their implementation in practice in the midst of worldly realities. Inasmuch as the secular aspect of the Reformation was just another aspect of Polish liberty, Szujski stiffly remarked, "The Poles had had their liberty before the Reformation, and so when it came they easily obtained citizenship for it. Having been accepted, it failed because it inspired no more interest." However, Szujski's interest was not limited to the political context. In his view, the Reformation was a dual tragedy: first, it was a heresy that hardly deserved to be called Christian; second, it had a lamentable, and indeed debilitating, impact on Catholicism. It "abandoned Christ's path of love." Like all other Polish historians, Szujski had a highly negative opinion about the Counterreformation, which he regarded as a spiteful overreaction against the erroneous enemies of the Roman Church, which had become "a powerful and formidable fortress, armed with medieval pretensions and the idea of absolutism."[129]

Despite their pride in the exceptionalism of Polish tolerance and all their laudatory remarks about how the sixteenth-century religious controversies invigorated the national intellectual life, some of our nineteenth-century authors were still confused about the religious zeal of the conflict. Thus, they arrived at an idea that was clearly parallel to the one advocated by the German historians: that the conflict lacked a positive resolution. Of course, the actual course of developments was dramatically different in Germany versus Poland. The draw between the Catholics and Protestants in Germany turned out to be permanent and might have been viewed as either a relative victory of Protestantism or a painful wound in the body of the nation, which finally divided it into two (or three) parts. As discussed, the latter aspect caused some German authors to conclude that it would have been better if *any* of the parties involved had prevailed. The parallel draw in the Commonwealth was temporary and was soon overshadowed by the triumphs of the Counterreformation, which almost all Polish historians regarded with extreme regret. At the same time, however, that regret did not make them advocates of Protestantism—a solution to the dilemma that might seem logical theoretically but would still be mentally and culturally anathema to our Catholic authors and their predominantly Catholic audience. What remained in play was an idea that had indeed been considered by a number of important political figures of the 1550s and 1560s, including King Sigismund Augustus himself: a Polish version of Anglicanism, which would not depart too far from Catholic theology, liturgy, and rituals but would still be independent of Rome and, therefore, truly national. Of course, the majority of our historians, both German and Polish, realized that both imagined scenarios, which would have united the painfully divided nations, were scarcely imaginable in the sixteenth-century realities of the Empire and the Commonwealth: only a strong, centralized monarchy could afford such a revolutionary solution. Decentralized power, in contrast, favored subsequent splits among Protestant churches. Moreover, while nineteenth-century readers might have been liberally minded and viewed religious fanaticism with disgust, they did not wish to see their religious feelings openly insulted. Thus, the Polish historians' longing for a Polish national church was only signalized *avant la lettre* in their melancholic suggestions that it would have been better for the Commonwealth at the time of the religious controversies if, instead of the tolerant, honest, and intriguingly indecisive Polish Hamlet—Sigismund Augustus—the country had been ruled by a local incarnation of Elizabeth I, or at least a Polish Henry of Navarre. This, however, was but one more timid expression of criticism about the famous liberalism and peacefulness of the Jagiellonian rulers.

In fact, Lelewel was the only one to openly voice his regrets that no national church had ultimately been established. Ironically, he supported his opinion by reminding his readers that "the most orthodox Catholics" of the sixteenth century had advocated his favorite idea: subtly redefining the idea of the Catholic orthodoxy. Apparently, the orthodox figures he had in mind included not only the king but also Archbishop Jakub Uchański: the two figures who would indeed have immediately profited from the establishment of a national church and the removal of Roman influence.[130] Moreover, he did not hesitate to consider yet another alternative scenario. "Some speculate," he informs us, "that Sigismund Augustus could have saved Poland had he opted for Calvinism or Lutheranism, for they believe that Poland fell because it remained Catholic, whereas the Protestant countries prevailed." Still, this was an alternative that Lelewel—who manifested his antipathy toward Protestantism as overtly as his dislike of the Catholic clergy—rejected as illusory. Since the majority of the gentry remained faithful to Catholicism, he claimed, the king's turn toward Protestantism could only have resulted in a civil war, and so the Commonwealth would have disintegrated, like the Holy Empire did.[131] Feliks Koneczny employed the very same logic to reject the idea of a national church: it was a purely political project, he argued, one that would have to be imposed on the entire nation by force, in sharp contrast to the idea of tolerance.[132]

One more version of this scenario was considered by Bobrzyński, the most dedicated advocate of centralized power among our Polish historians. In his opinion, the centralization of royal power, and the rise of its prerogatives and authority, was the most notable result of the bloody religious conflicts in the West. He reasoned that "the religious zeal was so intense that each party offered their unlimited support for the ruler, providing he was willing to crush their opponents. . . . Thus, a modern and efficient administration rose on the ruins of religious wars and oppression, concentrating all authority and all resources of the nation for its future development. . . . Such was also the task of the Polish Reformation."

Obviously, this scenario never materialized. Poland-Lithuania witnessed no religious war that would transform it into a centralized, absolutist monarchy. Like Lelewel, Bobrzyński pointed to Sigismund Augustus and his tactics of constant compromises, turbid promises, and torpid authoritarianism as being responsible for keeping Poland-Lithuania regrettably peaceful. However, the bloodthirsty historian did not limit his criticism to the king, who, as he himself famously stated, did not want to rule over his subjects' conscience: it was the entire nation, sluggish and indolent, that was disinclined toward "passions" and "violent actions."[133] The triumphs of the Counterreformation, and the civil war that took place under Sigismund III of Vasa, did not satisfy his imagination, for their result was precisely the opposite of what Bobrzyński advocated: the limitation of royal prerogative and the rise of the notion of the golden Polish liberty. Apparently, Bobrzyński did not convince his colleagues, as he found no followers for his line of reasoning in this respect. The civil wars of the seventeenth century, and the rise of religious intolerance that accompanied them, invariably horrified Polish historians (as we shall see in the next chapter). Moreover, disrespecting the splendid uniqueness of Polish tolerance was an attack on one of the most precious elements of the national tradition. The most vehement defense of national pride was formulated by Chołoniewski, with a precision and consistency he rarely demonstrated: "Since imposing one's religion on others by force is rightly considered nowadays to be brutal, barbarian, and stupid, and our ancestors arrived at this opinion hundreds of years ago, it would be reasonable to conclude that their legal and ethical notions surpassed those of other contemporary nations, in spite of attempting dubious accusations against the Polish national character."[134]

CHAPTER THREE

The Decline and Fall

The year 1648, when the Thirty Years' War ends and the great Cossack uprising begins, is the moment when German and Polish histories get most visibly entangled. It is the turning point, or the point of no return, or what the Greeks called *trope*, after which the Holy Empire and the Polish-Lithuanian Commonwealth are doomed. The subsequent century and a half is a time of decline in all spheres; political and military impotence, territorial cessions, internal conflicts, religious fanaticism, and, perhaps most importantly, a weakening of the public spirit and of patriotism all shred the fabric of society. There will be, according to our historians, only a few bright moments in this period, for example, the common victory against the Ottomans at Vienna in 1683, and a few names (in the German case, mostly of artists and scholars) highlighted against the black firmament of ignorance and immorality.

In German history the Peace of Westphalia of 1648 signals the end of the period when the Empire could still have been saved, according to a number of alternative scenarios based on the assumption that the war did not end in a draw between the Catholic and the Protestant parties. However, even these scenarios are pessimistic and timid, for the idea that the opposing party could have won seems too depressing, and thus the majority of German historians accept the actual result of the war with ambivalence, a mixture of regret and relief. Consequently, in the major part of the narratives in question the history of the Empire after 1648 becomes marginalized and German history focuses on the rise of Prussia, its "German mission," and its antagonism toward Austria. All that remains to be said about the Empire is that it was so dysfunctional that it ceased to play any significant role in German history.

German historians are virtually unanimous in their opinion that the constitution of the Empire that emerged from the Peace of Westphalia and a series of subsequent treaties paralyzed its main political institutions, so much so that it effectively ceased to exist as a body political. Germany became fragmented into a mosaic of independent states and three main religious communities (which overlapped as long as the *cuius regio, eius religio* principle allowed the rulers to oppress and discriminate against all denominations but their own). Some authors, as we shall see in this chapter, emphasize that Germany nevertheless not only remained a spiritual community but that the misery of political fragmentation was a stimulus for the rise of modern national identity—a process often related to the rise of Prussia. The Empire was locked into a structure of the past, and German history as a process of change and conflict was now related to the developments within particular German states, most notably Prussia and Austria, whose rivalry no longer had much of anything to do with the Empire. This image was a prefiguration of the situation after the Congress of Vienna and before the Battle of Königgrätz. The historians claim either that the formal dissolution of the Empire in 1806 merely confirmed that it had been long dead or that the right of the sovereign German princes to conduct foreign policy independently, introduced in 1648, "included the seeds of the Empire's breakdown."[1] These were two ways of saying one thing: that after 1648 the Empire was a legal fiction.

In the history of the Commonwealth, 1648 marks its apogee, as well as the moment when the fragility of its political, military, and social construction suddenly becomes evident, Vladislaus IV's death being, as Józef Szujski has it, "the end of Poland's happiness."[2] The swiftness of the country's subsequent deterioration called for catastrophic metaphors. And so Ludwik Kubala introduced the period of painful turbulence to come by asking, "Who would expect the rapid appearance of clouds over sky that had been so blue, and that a foreign storm would soon devastate our land?"[3] Władysław Konopczyński chose another classical motif: "The year 1648 presented Europe with an unexpected spectacle of the vast, rich, and splendid Commonwealth crumbling down into ruins in the fires of the Cossack rebellion."[4] The civil war of 1648 opens a period of steady decline in all aspects of society and results in the physical destruction of the country. However, in contrast to the German case, some alternative scenarios are still discussed, and historians point to a number of "lost chances" for reforms that could have saved the Commonwealth. However, the later such chances are located, the less rosy the scenario. John Casimir Vasa's plans for a profound reconstruction of the political institutions of the Commonwealth in the 1660s are considered seriously, even if the king and his ambitious wife inspire little sympathy from Polish historians. John III Sobieski, Augustus II, and Stanislaus Leszczyński's analogous ambitions for reform—slanted toward monarchical absolutism, a national dynasty, or a strong parliamentary government—were being recorded by historians for the sake of accuracy, and with various signs of melancholy, regardless of whether the author favored such reforms or not. Obviously, our historians look back before 1648 to pinpoint the cause of the Commonwealth's malaise. However, between 1648 and the second decade of the next century the suspect cause takes the shape of a powerful and rapturous virus, devastating all fundaments of the country's political order: the monarchy, the parliament, the army, and, last but not least, the public spirit and the citizens' mentality. All attempts to stop the general deterioration seem more and more desperate and unrealistic. Finally, the last years of Augustus II and the reign of his son, Augustus III, are dominated by ahistorical stagnation: the Commonwealth, like the Empire, becomes a fallen state, and all a historian can do regarding this period is to express regret and condemnation. As Michał Bobrzyński observed, "We already know the results of all that, we have no more hope, nothing can astonish or scare us any more."[5] Characteristically, the analyses of political developments in this period, including the formation of the reformist movement, are often transferred to chapters concerning the reign of the last king, Poniatowski, when history regains its natural dynamic and predilection for change.

The most characteristic method of rendering this lamentable condition of both the state and the society was an organicist-medical metaphor of lethargy and torpor. Historians of the time frequently employed such metaphors to emphasize that stagnation was reciprocal: dysfunctional institutions and demoralization of society alike paralyzed any initiatives for change and contributed to the general stagnation in all fields of public life. According to Joachim Lelewel, in early eighteenth-century Poland "the rich and powerful, and the poor and weak, suffered from political torpor, an inertia of all emotions, a lethargic stillness."[6] Szujski argues similarly: "Next to the total passivity of the court, another characteristic feature of the time strikes us: that of a popular moral languor and weariness of the entire nation, a true lethargy."[7] Bobrzyński diagnoses "a complete apathy."[8] In Friedrich von Raumer's view, after the Thirty Years' War "the state, the Church, sciences, and arts vegetated, deprived of fresh air."[9] Ludwig Häusser adds that this "vegetal condition" was a result of foreign powers' purposeful policy of conducting intrigues against Germany.[10] Ludwig Stacke, like the Polish historians, claims that the post-1648 stagnation paralyzed "any new thought" within the Empire.[11]

The most evident aspect of the general decline of the Empire and the Commonwealth in the post-1648 era was the permanent crisis of their central political institutions. What the historians emphasize is the rising dysfunctionality, which effectively made the two political entities shadows of what they had been in the previous epochs. "We can observe," Henryk Schmitt notes, "the old forms deprived of their original sense, and replaced with vain illusions."[12] The parliaments constitute the best example of this regrettable process. Beginning in 1652, the Sejm became notoriously paralyzed by obstruction due to the *liberum veto* principle, which effectively introduced the requirement for unanimity in voting and so gave a single deputy the right to protest all decisions of the given session. In total, seventy-three sessions of the Sejm were nullified this way in the seventeenth and eighteenth centuries, radically limiting the parliament's capacity to introduce new taxation and legislation and reducing it to an arena resembling nothing but a political salon. Analogically, the Reichstag became paralyzed by its division into three religious *curiae* that also had the right to veto each other's initiatives and that, as

Häusser claimed, preferred the Empire to break down rather than to agree on any controversial issue.[13]

The decline of central power in both countries resulted in political anarchy but also strengthened local centers of power. Within the Empire, territorial states governed by local dynasties became de facto independent states, which was formally confirmed by their gaining the right to negotiate international treaties without the approval of the emperor or the Reichstag. As Johann Gustav Droysen ironically notes, the Empire survived the Thirty Years' War only to initiate its own dissolution by recognizing the sovereignty of its estates.[14] Raumer, who viewed this situation with much more regret, argues that it eventually perverted the meaning of "German liberty" by establishing "a mixture of anarchy and tyranny" under the princes.[15] In the Commonwealth, actual governing power was also captured by aristocracy, which did not have any formal prerogatives but exercised it through a system of clientelism and bribery, which made possible the nobles' control of the local dietines (*sejmiki*). This situation, Smoleński argues, "perpetuated a radical decentralization that deprived the Commonwealth of any government and invited infiltration by the aristocracy and foreign powers."[16]

As far as interpretation of the crisis is concerned, however, an important division among German and Polish historians needs to be mentioned. The German authors differed radically in their approaches to the Empire. Some favored the "Prussia's German mission" view and emphasized the Protestant character of Germany's destiny, thus paying no further heed to the Empire. Others, however, still mourned its downfall for a number of reasons, whether their political beliefs or just general patriotic sentiment. For authors of the "Prussian school" the Empire ceased to represent German national interests and, as Johann Jastrow put it, "was robbed of its Germandom" and increasingly yielded to foreign influences.[17] From the nationalist-Protestant point of view, the Empire, with its Catholic monarch and federal structure, was as non-national as it was anachronistic. Therefore, its decline was supposed to have been a natural and in fact a desirable process. Häusser, for example, argues that it represented the final phase of the passing of the feudal order, based on the alliance between the Empire and the papacy, an association to be replaced by a constellation of "nationally consolidated" states.[18] Eventually it was not the Empire's crisis they found problematic but its survival and the fact that it was hampering the formation of a national, Protestant Germany. Thus, the Empire needed to be either demonized or marginalized. As Kevin Cramer has insightfully demonstrated in his study of German narratives on the Thirty Years' War, this conflict served the former purpose quite well, being the core element of a "continuous and coherent history that identified the struggle with Rome and Catholicism as the defining conflict that shaped German identity."[19] And yet, the pro-Prussian historians were aware that the Empire constituted a powerful symbol of national unity, and it thus enjoyed some sympathy from their contemporary readers. Their main effort while discussing the post-1648 period was nevertheless to draw as negative and discouraging a picture of the Empire as possible and to thus prepare their readers for its triumphant replacement by Prussia, which was assuming the role of the true Germany. This was a subtle rhetorical operation, as the ideal of national unity was particularly dear to nineteenth-century Germans and could not be overtly disregarded. They needed to be persuaded that the Empire had become so awful, and the order it represented so intolerable, that the ideal of unity needed to be sacrificed and put aside to allow for the rise of the new, essentially modern German state of Prussia on the imperial ruins.

A parallel dividing line ran between the Polish "republicans" and the "monarchists." These labels derived from the historians' views on the causes of the Commonwealth's decline. Generally speaking, the former were favorably inclined toward noble democracy and highly critical of royal policies, particularly about a number of attempts to transform the Commonwealth into an absolutist state. In other words, in their opinion the causes of Poland-Lithuania's problems were incidental rather than structural. They simply believed that the country could have survived if only it had been governed more wisely: unnecessary wars and internal conflicts could have been avoided, irresponsible politicians could have been curbed, and so on. The tendency to seek the causes of the Commonwealth's ills in deficiencies of human nature naturally led to the blaming of a number of prominent figures, most notably the kings and their courtiers, as well as notorious magnates who dominated the political scene at the time. The monarchists, in contrast, were highly critical of noble democracy and believed that the only way to save the Commonwealth was to transform it into a state ruled according to the standards of the epoch, that is, a strong monarchy.

The post-1648 period of rapid deterioration experienced by all central institutions of the Commonwealth, particularly the monarchy and the central parliament, constituted an evident challenge for the historians in the republican category, of whom Lelewel was certainly the most radical. It was a difficult task to blame the monarchs and their policies for all the misfortunes of the Commonwealth at a time when royal power was in decline and its impact on political developments was undeniably limited. Lelewel solves this problem by creating an astonishing tautology: in his view the monarchs and the magnates, despite dozens of open conflicts between them, with some resulting in civil wars, were actually representatives of a particular aristocratic-cosmopolitan tendency. "The royal and the aristocratic egoisms," he argues, "had one goal: running against the national spirit," that is, against the spirit of noble democracy, religious tolerance, and the idea of a national church.[20] Schmitt adds that blaming noble democracy, and the anarchist implications of the idea of noble liberty, is a misunderstanding based on an overestimation of the prevailing political doctrines of the time. In his opinion the popular belief in the omnipotence of nobility in that period is illusive, for in fact the anarchical conditions privileged the few, who were "free to execute any injustice they wished."[21] Clearly, what both historians desired was to reverse the popular belief that the seventeenth and eighteenth centuries were triumphs of noble democracy, which would imply that democracy had something to do with the decay of the Commonwealth. Instead, they suggested that the magnate families did not represent the most successful and prominent members of the nobility but were in fact opponents of the nobility and its political ideals, acting independently or in a sort of "objective" or unintentional alliance with the monarchs, which proved ruinous for the country. Finally, Polish historians of both orientations were united in pointing to the public morality of the age as a complication that suited both the structural and the individualistic interpretation.

Before we turn to morality, however, let us first take a look at the physical devastation of both Germany and Poland resulting from the seventeenth-century wars, which our historians lamented. Apparently, they did so not only because of their sense of duty as historians, who could not ignore the most terrifying catastrophe in the modern history of both countries to that time. The horrendous images of devastation they found in the sources at their disposal were truly shocking, but they were also a useful point of departure for the story of moral ruination of the age. On one hand, images of popular misery caused by war served as an explanation for some aspects of the moral downfall, such as religious fanaticism; on the other hand, they were confronted with images of irresponsibility, egoism, and frivolity of the powerful and the rich, which made them appear even more scandalous than they would have seemed in a more peaceful and prosperous time.

What seems the most striking in German historians' narratives on the war in comparison with Polish ones, apart from the depressing brutality of the images they evoke, is the direct link between the physical and moral devastation they establish. Indeed, many of the historians found it difficult to express its scale. Stacke, for example, concludes his remarks on the war by writing that one could wonder that anyone remained alive in Germany in the aftermath of the war.[22] According to Raumer, "a single day of war brought destruction of what had been built for ages," so people became so desperate that they dreamed of any power capable of establishing an order, be it "Austrians or foreigners."[23] The list of atrocities, as enumerated or described in detail by various authors, included mass murder, rapes, robbery, purposeful famine, torture, kidnapping and trading infants, untreated epidemics, slaughter and arson of entire towns and villages, cannibalism, devastation of fields, and a dramatic decrease in the human population and the number of cattle, horses, and all other domesticated animals. Eduard Heyck emphasizes that, "as always happens during war," the peasants suffered the most, and as a result of this war, the "traditional folk cheerfulness," typical for the German culture, was extinguished.[24] According to Stacke, Germany needed two hundred years to make up for the material losses of the war, particularly the ruination of its agrarian culture, whereas Karl Grün estimates that as a result of the war the country regressed a hundred years, back to the time before the Reformation, and he sadly concludes that the resulting demoralization was probably greater than the material misery and depopulation of the country.[25]

Polish historians drew similarly depressing conclusions regarding the consequences of the mid-seventeenth-century wars against the Cossacks, Sweden (the so-called "Swedish deluge"), Muscovy, and Transylvania, as well as the Great Northern War against Sweden in the first decade of the next century. In order to emphasize the scale of destruction, Franciszek Bujak, a leading social and economic historian during the first decades of the twentieth century, employed the same shocking metaphor of reversed progress, his calculations being even more spectacular. In his view, Poland in the first half of the eighteenth century fell to a level of civilization typical for the early medieval period. Because of popular misery, nonmonetary forms of trade were reintroduced, and most peasant families turned to an autarchic economy (i.e., consuming only what they produced themselves), as had been customary before the fourteenth century.[26] Szujski concludes that "one cannot imagine a more horrendous condition" than that of Poland after the Great Northern War, adding that peasants abandoned their villages en masse and volunteered to enlist in any army that plundered the area, "preferring to rob others than be looted."[27] Schmitt notes that "the misery of the country was evident for anyone who had ever seen the prosperity of foreign lands."[28]

On one hand, the analyses of destruction brought upon both lands by the seventeenth and early eighteenth centuries, and particularly as a result of foreign invasions, are to be safely located within the enlightened paradigm of progress as the main principle organizing the course of history. From this point of view, the epoch in question is a shocking anomaly, as is emphasized by the historians' calculations of how far back in time each country regressed or how much time each needed to recover what had been lost in consequence of the conflicts. Importantly, however, the anomaly does not invalidate the principle: catastrophic breaks or reversals of the general trend do not stop the progress of civilization and culture, which restarts anew after atrocities have occurred. No catastrophe is tragic enough to annihilate the general principle of progress, and nothing can prevent a nation from following its destiny. However, this is not the only perspective, or tendency, the narratives on the war represent. Some of them evidently lean toward a more pessimistic view, one in which war resembles a natural catastrophe—as stressed in the popular Polish labeling of the Swedish invasion of 1655–60 as a deluge—and the destruction caused by it is in a way viewed as irreversible. Fires may have been extinguished, houses rebuilt, and the number of cattle may have started rising again, while some things, like traditional folk humor or, perhaps more importantly, both countries' prominent position on the world stage, were lost forever. What was reconstructed was not exactly what had been there before, and the time, money, and energy needed for the reconstruction exacted their own heavy toll. Kevin Cramer's conclusions regarding his analysis of the "atrocity narratives" may seem radical, but if they are right, they constitute a remarkable parallel with the Polish case. "Germany's experience in the Thirty Years' War," he claims, "was the reason that a pervasive fear of physical annihilation as a nation and the extinction of German culture became a distinctive characteristic of the German national consciousness."[29] Analogically, the period of the "deluge" was widely viewed in Poland as a prefiguration, or a prelude, to the partitions of the Commonwealth, which for many was a true *finis Poloniae*. One should not, however, become confused about the centuries-long distance between the processes constituting this parallel. National histories necessarily involve a great dose of mythical and symbolic thinking; thus, what happened once may happen one more time, either in the future or in an event yet to be discovered in the past. Eventually, analytical thinking about history that seeks signs of long-term processes, tendencies, and lines of development does not contradict this idea, as it also extends specific conditions of a given time to other periods. Indeed, what is merely possible in the former way of reasoning becomes probable in the latter.

Acedia or Nadir

Nineteenth-century historians, continuing a tradition going back to ancient times, paid a lot of attention to public virtue, which they regarded as an important factor in political behavior. A modern reader may find this practice anachronistic and perhaps naïve, for modern social sciences avoid such concepts, employing instead statistical data and a number of analytical constructs, such as mentality, behavioral patterns, social imagination, and values as related to the interests of particular social groups. Indeed, statistical data do enter syntheses of national history in Germany and Poland on a broader scale late in the nineteenth century, though they remained a marginal source of information for the majority of our historians. This marginality may be explained by slow progress in research methods and practices, particularly because individual scholars were able to access and review only a limited number of documents. In addition, their findings remained isolated for a time, until the results of their research formed a coherent map, allowing for a synthetic view. The absence of large-scale data may also be attributable to the historicist paradigm of history, one focusing on individual agents, their choices, and their impact on history. Thus, one may consider the tendency of our nineteenth-century authors to focus on what they called public morality (including various issues such as education, consumption patterns, corruption, or the presence of violence in public life) as an early, preliminary stage of what was to become social history in the twentieth century. One should, however, keep two things in mind. First, as we shall see, despite the fact that public morality as an analytical concept may seem awkward to us, the speculations and interpretations it inspired were often the most sophisticated the nineteenth-century authors produced, and they were certainly no less insightful than those provided by modern social history. Second, their work was evidently rooted in a more general approach to the past that organized their entire intellectual and narrative effort. Generally speaking, the authors of the age believed that virtue not only ought to be but actually is rewarded by Providence, and if history at some moments does not develop in accordance with this principle, it is to be regarded as a paradox demanding further study. In such cases, there were two frequently asked questions: What was the right thing to do? and, What would be the most virtuous attitude in a given situation? History is a science (*Wissenschaft*), Droysen argued, because we believe that God leads us, and history's purpose is to lead us to realize the direction and the paths indicated by Him.[30] Thus, history was not only about what actually happened but also about what ought to have happened—the past was to be a lesson for us. One illustrative example of this approach may be Józef Szujski's interpretation of the causes of the French Revolution. He describes the epoch preceding the revolution as follows: "Nowhere in history can we find such dishonesty, disrespect for the law of nations, distrust, insincerity, and open cynicism but in that time covering its moral poverty with the glitter of enlightenment. . . . Next to the depravation of the elites, the bestiality of customs, and the loosening of Christian morality, silently rose the revolutionary idea."[31]

Such assessment of the Enlightenment epoch was highly popular among both Polish and German historians. Moreover, emphasizing the immorality of the age played a specific role in Polish narratives. Certainly Polish readers saw more than the causes of the French Revolution in Szujski's lines: in their minds the moral poverty of the Enlightenment was also responsible for the partitions of the Commonwealth. This was a diagnosis that was supposed to make the bitter pill easier for the Polish public to swallow, which all Polish historians were ready to confirm. As Władysław Konopczyński argued half a century later, "Polish anarchy" paralleled "European anarchy."[32] Employing the same word, *anarchy*, was supposed to mask the fact that two different phenomena were in question. "Polish anarchy" was a common label for the decline of central government in the Commonwealth, whereas "European anarchy" was supposed to denote the lack of any moral principles in international relations in eighteenth-century Europe. Analogically, drawing a detestable image of *ancien régime* Europe was a necessary prerequisite for German historians, who claimed that the moral corruption that plagued their country during that time was ultimately a cultural import adopted predominantly by social elites, who were regrettably influenced by French cultural patterns. Such was also the opinion of some Polish historians, particularly Lelewel, who believed that civilization in general was an ambiguous and dangerously cosmopolitan idea, bringing "enslavement" to the people.[33]

Last but not least, stressing the immorality of the Enlightenment was a way to signal what was considered a paradox: that the progress of civilization was not necessarily paralleled by the progress of morals and that abandoning "prejudices" such as religious fanaticism did not make the enlightened ethically superior to their "backward" ancestors. One of the authors of the 1918 volume on the causes of the partitions of Poland-Lithuania felt compelled to inform his readers, "In that time education had little to do with honesty. The best educated steal and cheat." He would probably find it difficult to pinpoint the time when education and honesty were strongly interrelated, but he nevertheless assumed that such a relation was somehow obvious. And his conclusion must have seemed ambiguous indeed for his Polish readers, as in nineteenth-century Poland the term "enlightenment" was frequently used as a synonym for education.[34]

And yet, there was another aspect of the general progress of civilization that our historians regarded as obvious: the rise of modern patriotism. If societies were not necessarily getting better with time in terms of their members' relations to each other, they were nevertheless believed to be transforming into nations in the modern sense of the term. Individuals were now supposed to be aware of their nationality and to be ready to make sacrifices for their country, especially because the country badly needed them. "The moral condition of the nation in this dreadful epoch must be evaluated according to its ability to act patriotically," claimed a Polish historian.[35] Eventually these expectations were contradictory. On one hand it was believed that, in the immoral epoch, patriotism was the ultimate moral standard according to which individuals should be judged; on the other hand, it was also assumed that a fundamental reason for the moral crisis of the time was that national consciousness was still in its infancy and that patriotism in its modern sense was a rare phenomenon.

German and Polish historians were of one mind in their contempt for the general demoralization of society in the late seventeenth and early eighteenth centuries. They reserved their harshest criticism, however, for the elites of both countries. On one hand, as mentioned, the elites were blamed for the political deterioration of the Empire and the Commonwealth. On the other hand, because these critiques were formulated in the postrevolutionary age of intense class tensions, extreme contrasts in social behavior were also emphasized. This trend may be summarized by Wilhelm Wachsmuth's conclusion: "The people were supposed to work hard, with sweat and tears, whereas the society at court was having incessant fun."[36] Interestingly, the most sensitive of our authors in this respect were active in the pre-Marxist era and were unaware of the theory of class struggle. In their view, Lelewel argued, oppression of the people was simply a result of the unlimited greed of the lords.[37]

Let us begin, however, with the political aspect, as German and Polish historians approached this subject differently. Nevertheless, they identified and emphasized strikingly similar vices, which they saw in the context of both countries' ruination and political decline. However, since the political structures of the Empire and the Commonwealth were different, the diagnoses of their malfunctioning stressed different factors. These factors were determined by an unfulfilled ideal. In the German case it was national unity; in the Polish one it was political efficiency.

The Polish historians, except for a few monarchists among them, unanimously accepted that the Commonwealth was a body politic governed by the entirety of its citizens—that is, by the nobility. Thus, these historians also regard the nobility as a "collective monarch" responsible for the condition of the Commonwealth.[38] Obviously, our historians realized that the equality of all noble citizens was just a theory, or an ideal that had been dear to the masses of poor nobles, who had nevertheless been easily manipulated by the powerful and the rich. As Tadeusz Korzon puts it, "Poverty and ignorance made the lower strata of the nobility and the bourgeoisie politically passive elements."[39] Consequently, most Polish historians were as proud of the Commonwealth's democratic structure, particularly in comparison with contemporary absolutist monarchies, as they were confused that the nobility had made no good use of their privileges. They could not, after all, deny that noble democracy had deteriorated into a malfunctioning system that paralyzed the basic political institutions of the Commonwealth and made it powerless against its aggressive neighbors. Even the most enthusiastic apologist of the Commonwealth among our authors, Chołoniewski, admits that "for about a hundred years" the perfect mechanism of noble democracy, which was based on "high moral standards," ceased to work properly, and "the good intentions of the citizenry" were not enough to guarantee its smooth functioning.[40]

Polish historians univocally emphasized that in the democratic Commonwealth political virtues played a special role: the condition of the decentralized state, in which liberty was valued so highly that an individual member of parliament had the right to block the entire legislative process, was eventually supposed to be a function of "public morality." Schmitt, for example, explains that "virtue determined everything" in the Commonwealth and that its institutions were merely form, while the citizens' activities and attitudes were its true content.[41] Thus, Lelewel argues that there is no point in criticizing the political institutions of the Commonwealth: it was the "demoralization and decline of virtue that was responsible for the fall of the state."[42]

This type of reasoning is apparently to be located at the intersection of various political philosophies. One can see in it elements of a modern democratic approach emphasizing the role of participation and popular activism as fundamental for the functioning of political structures, as well as negotiating their practical dimension. However, one can also view it in the context of premodern political-philosophical treatises, stressing the practice of virtue as the true goal of any public activity. Furthermore, elements of religious thinking can also be traced in this approach, in which the state seems to be a structure parallel to the church. It has its hierarchy and its organization; however, in the final analysis, it is an ethical community to be valued according to its members' moral record. This last element is particularly present in the thinking of Józef Szujski, the most Catholic of our historians. In his opinion, the institutions and laws of the Commonwealth were "a constant temptation and the source of public demoralization." Liberty and the sense of personal dignity and common power, as obtained by the Polish nobility, were no less an ambiguous privilege than the freedom to choose between virtue and sin. Szujski had no doubt that the nobility had yielded to the temptation of evil, and the *liberum veto*, a privilege as dignifying as it was abusive, was his central example. Once this happened, he claims, "outrage followed indignation, and there was no way out" for the Commonwealth.[43] However, he was not fully coherent in his pessimism, as he believed that "the source of evil is not to be found in human nature, but in the laws," which made him arrive at conclusions that were the opposite of those proposed by Lelewel: "The vicious circle of Polish institutions was responsible for the increasing chaos in the country and confronted the citizens with numerous immoral temptations, undermining its pillars. . . . The spirit of liberty, immanent for these institutions, having conceived the great and the virtuous, started animating the dim and the scoundrel, so that in the second half of the seventeenth and in the eighteenth century baseness becomes notoriously popular, and public virtue is rare."[44]

Evidently, Polish historians' emphasis on public morality as a crucial political factor in the history of the Commonwealth's decline was based not only on their general belief that virtue matters in public life but also on their sentiment for the democratic form of government. In their view, democracies were much more morally sensitive than autocracies, which were immoral, or perhaps amoral, by definition. Democracies rested upon their citizens' qualities and were easily corruptible, whereas autocracies rested upon the corruption of men who gave up their liberty for other privileges. In this context, their unanimous antipathy against aristocracy—or magnates, as they were typically called in the Polish context, as the Commonwealth did not officially sanction but a few aristocratic titles, so as not to disturb the ideal of equality—seems highly consistent. Not only were the magnates immodestly sinful in comparison with those who could not afford spectacular errors and ostentatious consumption, they were also an indefinable element in the political system of the Commonwealth. The undeniable fact that political initiative shifted from the king and the noble masses to a few powerful families in the course of the seventeenth century did not fit any of the political ideals of our historians, neither the democratic-republican one nor the monarchical one. The clash of these two political theories left no room for a cool analysis of the actual developments in the political history of the Commonwealth in the seventeenth century, which included the formation of a de facto oligarchy. The republicans believed that the democratic institutions of the Commonwealth were essentially good, although their spirit was perverted by the excesses of noble liberty. The monarchists believed these institutions were irreparably dysfunctional and should have been replaced by a strong, centralized monarchy. Our historians were aware that what actually happened was the rise of the informal power of the few aristocratic clans on the ruins of formal political institutions, which actually coincided with the decline of the Commonwealth. They had no theory to explain this, however, except that of a moral degeneration of the entire structure. Luckily for them, the many magnates had indeed been frivolous, treacherous, and hideous, providing our historians with a basket of detestable facts to support their argumentation.

German nobles were not expected to meet such high moral standards. Their political position, it was silently assumed, was much humbler, and thus German historians did not expect them to play any significant role, until Prussia made its nobility one of the pillars of the much idealized "indigenous" monarchy in the early eighteenth century.[45] Moreover, German historians paid much more attention to the bourgeoisie, whom they regarded as the most promising candidates to be the bearers of German national consciousness. Following the same logic that governed the analyses of Polish historians, they focused on the Empire's estates, particularly the dynastic princes, as the group in whose hands rested the actual power. They were unanimous in viewing the rise of these princes to the status of de facto sovereign rulers as a gradual process, dating back to the time of the Staufen dynasty and crowned with official agreements following the Peace of Westphalia. As mentioned earlier, the Protestant historians viewed this process with much sympathy, as it was combined with the decline of the Catholic emperors' influence. What troubled them was the increasing fragmentation of Germany. As Jastrow observes, after 1648 German unity became a mere illusion, because any consensus of the estates was technically impossible, for there were now about two thousand of them: principalities, duchies, cities, bishoprics, and other territories, typically inhabited by a few hundred souls.[46] Wachsmuth ironically remarks that some of them were doing pretty well: Peter Holstein-Gottrop, for example, won the title of emperor of Russia, remaining an estate of the Empire in his capacity as a German prince. "Such a splendid illusion, and such an actual misery!" he comments.[47] Häusser observes that up to the end of the eighteenth century, five foreign monarchs became members of the Empire, and if the French or the Ottoman did not, he argues mockingly, it was simply because they did not want to; the Empire certainly couldn't have opposed it.[48] Even though political disunity was nothing new in German history, a new, alarming tone appears in the narratives concerning the post-1648 era. The increasing political fragmentation, foreign influence, and permanent internal conflicts, our historians believed, would in the long run be dangerous and even deadly for German national identity and the sense of German community. "The national character of the Empire," Häusser argues, "was replaced by the European one."[49] According to Otto Hintze, "Germans were gradually becoming a nation of poets and thinkers, their Empire a state of another world, and the people [*Volk*] a cultural, and not a political community."[50] Wachsmuth offers the diagnosis that Germany had less patriotism than any other European nation at that time, as demonstrated by the numerous alliances of German courts with foreign powers, particularly France—alliances that in his view should be labeled high treason against German national interests.[51]

Corruption is infectious, and it spreads most easily from the top down the social structure. The omnipotence of the aristocracy in the Empire and the Commonwealth was supposed to have been demoralizing for its members, as well as for the groups that remained under the direct influence of the powerful and the rich. Our historians were unanimously scandalized by the moral condition of the upper classes—servile, egoistic, and vain. Their analyses were monotonously dark and pessimistic, even though they employed a large number of epithets and metaphors available in the classical rhetorical repertoire. When they described the lower strata, they emphasized their poverty, misery, brutality, and ignorance. When they focused on the upper strata, they stressed their egoism, frivolity, and national indifference. Apparently, this depressing picture was frustrating enough for some of our historians to seek any brighter element. Was there any social group that remained irreproachable? Tadeusz Korzon claims that "the lower we get in the social hierarchy, the busier a given social group, the healthier it seems."[52] Obviously, he did not have the peasants, indeed the most hard-working and the largest social group, in mind, but instead some members of the lower nobility and bourgeoisie. German historians' intuition was similar in this respect: it was the lower middle class, which was neither debilitated by poverty nor demoralized by aristocratic influence, that was supposed to remain a healthy fundament of society. This image was especially dear to the Protestant historians, for whom humble piousness and private virtues went along with patriotism. It was among the provincial *petit bourgeoisie*, with their idyllic "silent life," Droysen argues, where German genius and the national awakening were born.[53]

Let us return for a moment, however, to the vices of the elites, as they were the ones who dominated the picture. The era that witnessed the rise of the aristocracy and nobility, Stacke informs us, was the worst in modern German history. Aristocratic titles, he adds, were regularly obtained for money by the ones who got rich during the war due to army contracts and bought land from those ruined by the same conflict. The freshly ennobled competed with the old aristocracy in ostentation and luxury, eagerly patterning their lifestyles after those of the deplorable French. The most precious goal of the poorer nobility and bourgeoisie was to get closer to the aristocrats, win their lordly attention, and ridiculously imitate their lifestyle in minor, affordable details. The only bright aspect of this situation Stacke notes is that "the people laughed at the carriages with brand new coats of arms on their shields."[54] Heyck observes with melancholy that the upper middle classes easily gave up any pretensions to political involvement and participating in public affairs. Their liberty was eventually the freedom not to be involved in public life but to live in a closed circle of family and associates, indulge in social games, music, and other private pleasures, such as a cup of recently popularized tea or coffee. When the authorities or some aristocrat openly mistreated them, they were rewarded with money, which generally did not insult their sense of justice.[55] Supposedly, Heyck was influenced by the nineteenth-century critiques of the Biedermeier mentality of the pre-1848 era in his analysis: the type of mentality he described was widely mocked by Romantic authors and German patriots of the early nineteenth century. Its most criticized aspects were political indifference, opportunism, and snobbishness.

In Polish historiography, the criticism of social and political elites was no less intense, colorful, and emotional. It was also perhaps more anxious, as it commonly stressed one of the classic ideas: that of gradual decadence, resulting in each generation being more degenerate than the previous one. This idea was fundamental for Lelewel's view of the general course of Polish history, in which moral decadence and political ideology were intermingled. In his opinion, in the seventeenth century the noble estate "abandons its mission," blindly imitating the aristocracy and allowing for "humiliation and numerous violations of the republican principle." As far as the elites are concerned, he draws a "hideous image of the entitled, decorated, powdered, cosmopolitan, effeminate, greedy, and treacherous figures."[56] Schmitt claims that the nobility lost its ancient pride in their relation to the magnates, who became "slavish," and that they spent all their money on luxurious consumption, such that scarcely anything was left to take care of public needs. "Those who spent everything they had," he adds, "frequently sold their votes to anyone who was ready to pay for them," including foreign agents. As a result, "the Commonwealth, which had shone so brightly before, sank into darkness, and widespread ignorance gave birth to prejudices, pietism, and fanaticism, which inspired filth, hypocrisy, snobbery, corruption, and many other vices."[57] According to Szujski, the traditional virtues of the nobility were replaced with "moral corpulence" and "comfortable patriotism." In his view, this was a consequence of imitating aristocracy, which "ignored any moral principles, both in private and in the public life," as well as of parroting the royal court, for example, that of Augustus II, who "inspired the joyful nation to sink into the abyss of careless idleness." He supports his claim with a passionate description of the nobility's style of life, with its incessant celebrations for all possible sorts of occasions—private, public, and religious—and their love for disputes, dueling, intrigue, and *vain parler* (i.e., lengthy speeches, shining with anecdotes and classical erudition rather than any practical objectives, obligatorily delivered at any public occasion), which they confused with engaging in politics.[58] Smoleński confirms this opinion more calmly, concluding that the "idle and ignorant" noble masses limited their public activity to the services they could render as clients of the powerful magnate families.[59]

According to Franciszek Bujak, an economic and social historian, the attitude of the magnates and the nobility toward their state resembled that of the "unenlightened peasants" toward communal meadows and pastures: their strategy was to gain as much profit from it as quickly as possible and not to cultivate it or invest in it in any way.[60] In Tadeusz Korzon's opinion, "the Polish magnates undeniably spent more of their income for luxurious consumption than any other European aristocracy." Despotic landlords and irresponsible citizens lived an idle, carefree life of profligacy. "Half a century of such a lifestyle," he concludes, with the first half of the eighteen century in mind, "ruined Poland's reputation and international position, so that a Pole was ashamed of his nationality abroad."[61]

Yet another aspect of the nobility's lifestyle was criticized by the cultural historian Władysław Łoziński, who, interestingly, reformulated that classic idea of decadence as a by-product of political and economic growth and a mark of the last phase in each culture's natural development. Łoziński assumed that Poland represented a youthful branch of Western civilization, and it therefore could not in principle produce the decadent culture that is naturally a product of any civilization's advanced age. Polish decadence was a paradox, and thus it lacked the subtle charm that decadence, despite all its shortcomings, presents, especially to the refined eye of a cultural historian. He argues, "Had their luxury, at times scandalous or lighthearted, blossomed from a fertile soil, . . . had their apparent elegance corresponded to the elegance of their minds, and finally, had it all been a product of an old culture and accumulated wealth—it would have some internal and social logic. However, in a young, fresh, and poor nation of limited enlightenment, this was but a perverse contrast, which was particularly painful as it coincided with the most tragic epoch in our history."[62]

Oppression Does Not Go Unpunished

Corruption, political apathy, lack of patriotism—these were significant vices of the social elites in the opinion of our historians, but there were many more. The elites' attitude toward lower social classes was no more sympathetic than their attitude toward their country. The wartime physical devastation of both countries had its counterpart in the oppression of the people. That oppression was universally described by our historians as lamentable injustice (caused by the class-driven egoism of the ruling classes), incompetence and corruption of the government, and lack of imagination among both the elites and the administrators in power. Images of misery and injustice in our historians' narratives are passionate enough to suggest that the entire social system of the time was rotten: it was a moral scandal, implicitly delegitimizing the political structures standing behind it. Again, our historians' analyses in this respect are to be located at the intersection of traditional Christian morality and classical rhetoric with modern social sensitivity. As we shall see, however, it is difficult to differentiate between those who referred to traditional moral notions when presenting their readers with shocking images of social contrasts and those who viewed such regrettable conditions as typical of past ages in general and who believed the progress of civilization to be the sole remedy for such conditions. In other words, dramatic images of the exploitation and oppression of the people make it difficult to draw a line of distinction between the historians who believed that the true cause of such suffering had been sinful human nature and those who attributed it to ignorance or backwardness, resulting from the deficiencies of the socio-economic system of the time. This difficulty also arises because all historians considered relations between the rich and powerful and the masses in that epoch to have been as deplorable as they were irrational: conditions were supposed to have been in too much turmoil to expect any stability in the sociopolitical order. In any case, the problem of social inequality enters our historians' narratives precisely in this period, preceding the breakdown of both the Empire and the Commonwealth, as well as the French Revolution, which certainly influenced the historians' approach to social issues, even if they were not particularly enthusiastic about it. Indeed, none of our authors represented a socialist-revolutionary point of view. Still, as we shall see, revolutionary perspective mattered no less for the liberal than for the conservative historians: it sharpened their social sensitivity precisely because revolution was what they feared.

Among German historians, the most passionate critic of social conditions in the post-1648 era was perhaps Wolfgang Menzel, a progressive liberal. German princes of that time, he argues, spent all their money for celebrations and frivolous nonsense, and when the treasury was empty, they refilled it by raising taxes, introducing new ones, and selling public offices. Naturally, those who paid for them did so because they were greedy for bribes and a share of their lords' revenues, and so they immediately abused their newly acquired positions. The rise of administrative apparatus naturally followed the rise of fiscal obligations, even if some older feudal fees were removed. "The most terrible abuses were committed in the minor states, where they attracted less notice," Menzel claims. "The follies perpetuated in almost all the petty courtships, several of which were gradually raised to principalities, are perfectly incredible," and, as Protestant readers would have assumed anyway, "the ecclesiastical courts had long fallen to the lowest depths of depravity." Most hideously, the rulers profited from selling recruits, or indeed anyone they could arrest or kidnap, and these unfortunates ended up in the Prussian army, known for its harsh discipline, or as soldiers for British or Dutch forces in the colonies.[63] This particularly loathsome practice was frequently addressed by German historians, who emphasized that it demonstrated that the princes regarded their subjects as slaves. Oskar Jäger comments bitterly that Germans sold for colonial service might easily find a better life overseas than in their native country.[64] Stacke emphasizes that aristocrats considered their subjects "second-class people" and that, as a consequence of increasing poverty, "the higher thoughts and deeper emotions" evaporated from the minds of German peasants, the vast majority of the "so-called German nation."[65]

There were more reasons for the rising misery of Germany's population, however. As Wachsmuth demonstrates, numerous new taxes, regularly introduced under "frivolous names," were needed to cover the costs of ostentatious consumption in the court of many a noble, but the new, professional armies demanded even more money. Therefore, he observes, although the kings of Prussia were certainly the most decent among German rulers, their subjects were heavily exploited, as they had to cover the costs of building Prussia's large military force.[66] Karl Grün labels the quickly expanding armies an epidemic of modern Europe, one that was emptying German rulers' treasuries even faster than the luxuries of court life.[67] Stacke indicates that ruthless fiscal policies were regularly accompanied by the issuing of new, deficient currencies, thus contributing to inflation and further ruination of the people, who were of course obliged to pay their taxes in hard currency.[68]

Our historians' collective list of accusations about and laments concerning the aristocracy in the post-1648 period is long and depressing. As demonstrated, the issues addressed by both German and Polish historians were essentially the same. However, their approach was asymmetrical. Polish historians stressed political indifference, ignorance, anarchism, and the lack of patriotism as the most scandalous vices of the social elite of the Commonwealth, equaling or perhaps surpassing class egoism. They leveled such charges because they believed that the elite were responsible for their own condition and for their continued decline, which the historians considered to be the most characteristic, and regrettable, large-scale process of the time. German historians focused on social inequalities and oppression of the masses because, in their opinion, traditional political activities within the framework of the Empire and its institutions at that time were pointless. There was no reason to despair that the Empire was doomed because, in the Protestant historians' view, the rickety feudal structure, serving cosmopolitan and Catholic influences, deserved its demise, and it was in the best interests of Germany to get rid of it as soon as possible to make room for the Hohenzollern monarchy. Finally, a number of German authors, including such prominent figures as Droysen and Heinrich von Treitschke, paid hardly any attention to social issues at all. What mattered for them were diplomacy, alliances, wars, successions, annexations, and the questions regarding the "national spirit" or the "spiritual life" of the nation, which, broadly speaking, corresponded to the problem of national consciousness. In this kind of historiography there was scarcely any room for mention of ordinary people—except as recruits for the Prussian army.

Analogically, although Polish historians univocally claimed that conditions among the peasantry were steadily worsening, they eventually paid little attention to the details of these developments, focusing instead on the nobility in their role as the political class. The conditions of peasants' life were presented as a function of the nobles' deteriorating morality. As Henryk Schmitt claims, "the oppression of the people, which had been limited by public opinion and personal virtue in the past, grew enormously because of the ignorance and greed of the landlords."[69] As far as details from the life of the peasantry are concerned, Polish historians focused primarily on the devastation caused by constant wars. They had a similar view with regard to the cities, even though historians broadly commented on the deteriorating legal status of the burgher estate in the sixteenth century, as well as on the prospects of reforming their status in the second half of the eighteenth century. Nevertheless, dramatic descriptions of the ruinous effects of wars on city life in the Commonwealth may be seen as microcosmic illustrations of the miserable conditions throughout the entire country. Let us consider, for example, Bujak's remarks regarding the first half of the eighteenth century: "A general picture of the cities is that of a total ruin. Empty squares and houses, typically wooden, crumbling down, dirty streets, and misery in the houses, accompanied by drinking and idleness. . . . The majority of older towns in the eighteenth century possesses no more than one-third or a quarter of the buildings they possessed in the second half of the six-teenth century."[70] Such images must have been appalling for nineteenth-century readers, who lived in the age of rapid urbanization, saw the city landscape changing radically in their lifetime, and believed those changes to be marks of progress. In their minds, urbanization equaled civilization, and they must have been shocked to learn that the process might have been stopped and society forced to regress.

Still, a number of Polish historians raised the question of whether the lamen-table condition of the peasantry did have an impact on the political deterioration of the Commonwealth. The sturdy social and economic barriers that divided the peasants, constituting some three-quarters of the population, from other estates eventually excluded them from the body politic of the nation, thus limiting its potential in any confrontation with the Commonwealth's powerful enemies. Hence, a number of our historians believed that the nobles' exclusivism, so char-acteristic for Poland-Lithuania, was not just immoral, since it justified econom-ic oppression of the peasantry, but also politically suicidal. "The noble nation," Smoleński argues, "prepared the tempest that devastated the country by its op-pression of the lower classes and religious minorities."[71] This was a tricky question, and various factors discouraged our historians from responding with a clear-cut answer.

The issue at stake was the actual meaning of the political legacy of the Com-monwealth, or, in other words, it was negotiating the actual image of historical realities as it emerged from the evidence with the political message that would define modern Polish patriotism. The majority of Polish historians were proud of the democratic legacy of the Commonwealth and patriotically juxtaposed their state's noble democracy against the absolutism of neighboring countries. Discuss-ing its deficiencies, such as the rising dysfunctionality in the Commonwealth's central institutions or the shocking contrasts between aristocratic luxury and peasant misery, was a matter of both professional accuracy and smart rhetoric. And yet, claiming that the fact that the Commonwealth *belonged* to its nobility made it dysfunctional and contributed to its collapse would imply delegitimizing the entire legacy of the Commonwealth. Moreover, it would reek of the arguments that nationalist German and Russian authors used to justify the partitions of the Commonwealth, which they typically presented as a sort of police action for the benefit of the many inhabitants oppressed by the greedy, egoistic, and anarchic Polish-Lithuanian nobles. On the other hand, however, Polish historians, except for a few radical traditionalists, saw the idea of the noble nation as anachronistic, and they praised the idea of modern patriotism embracing and indeed unifying all classes of society. Leftist sensitivity was helpful in this respect, particularly in condemning all kinds of social divisions of both the past and the present, but, in the age of modern nationalism, striving for national unity as a political idea for all times was simply ubiquitous and unquestionable. Thus, our historians hesitated between the two principles that were difficult to negotiate.

One can see this hesitation in, for example, Tadeusz Korzon's argument regarding this problem. Korzon was perhaps the best Polish economic historian of the late nineteenth century. He pored through an untold number of documents concerning material conditions in the eighteenth-century Commonwealth, and doing so allowed him to support his argument with an impressive array of statistical data. And yet, even though he claims that the Commonwealth's resources were sufficient "to conduct a Seven Years' War against the entire world" and that this remarkable potential was largely wasted because "more than 80 percent of society knew no civic duties and remained politically passive," his conclusions appear ambiguous and quite irrelevant to his economic analyses. Political activism may be helpful, he suggests, but if the authorities are energetic and determined enough, they can mobilize the masses for national purposes, regardless of the statistics. Implicitly, this was as if to say that if only Poland-Lithuania had had a more efficient central government, it would suffice, and no more social equality would be needed to save the country, even though more politically conscious citizens would have been of some help.[72] As a result, the question of whether the nobility as a class was responsible for the country's political weakness was dismissed.

Others, however, were less ambiguous in this respect. Class egoism of the nobility, they argued—although none of our authors employed this Marxist term—did harm the Commonwealth politically. Moreover, they viewed it as the direct cause of the catastrophic Cossack uprising of 1648, which devastated and depopulated half the country and undermined its military capability and its political system. They all agreed that the fundamental reason for the uprising was the unwillingness of the nobility, and particularly the magnates in possession of the large estates in Ukraine, to satisfy at least some of the Cossack demands, due to their false pride and petty egoism. Several scenarios were considered: from enlisting more Cossacks into the army of the Commonwealth, to ennobling their leaders, to the formation of the Duchy of Ruthenia from the Ukrainian lands of the Polish Crown and its elevation to the status of the third member of the Commonwealth (as was actually agreed to in the 1658 Treaty of Hadiach, which, however, was typically regarded as a belated attempt to meet the Cossack expectations). They all failed, though, and Polish historians univocally believed the nobility's blindness and stubbornness were to blame. Antoni Chołoniewski, whose *Spirit of the History of Poland* earned its fame as an uncritical apologia for the Commonwealth, nonetheless argues that its policies toward the Cossacks constituted an "abuse of the principles to which the Commonwealth owed its fortune and strength" and that the failure to implement the 1658 compromise, which was to transform Poland-Lithuania into the Polish-Lithuanian-Ruthenian Commonwealth, was "one of the gravest mistakes."[73] Another apologist of the Commonwealth, Oskar Halecki, repeated this assessment in 1917.[74]

More importantly, for a number of authors, "the Cossack question was related to the peasant question."[75] Thus, it was an opportunity to discuss a broader problem and was simply a convenient pretext to introduce the issue of social inequality for historians who were not Marxists, were mainly concerned with political history, and intended to construct a standard narrative organized around a series of events. The Cossack rebellion was a remarkable catastrophe for the Commonwealth, given the bloody battles and subsequent loss of eastern Ukraine to Russia. Therefore, it provided a more dramatic introduction to discussing the unfortunate consequences of the nobility's class egoism than would a lengthy structural analysis of social inequalities; the tragic consequences of those inequalities were painfully apparent.

This ambivalent approach to the peasantry and the Cossacks' role as a catalyst of the issue is best seen in Joachim Lelewel's narrative. During his lifetime, he was famous for his leftist political views and involvements. It is therefore no wonder that he fiercely scolds the nobles for their blindness, stupor, and greediness and for their strategy of compensating for the war losses by increasing the *corvée* obligations, so that "what had been done by twenty people before, must now be done by ten," which embittered the peasants. However, he emphasizes that the peasants "having their humble needs satisfied," they did not despair, and lived an apparently happy life. Moreover, he repeatedly insists that their condition was still "more comfortable than in other countries." The only example he provides is Russia, from which peasants continued to migrate to the Commonwealth, prompting Catherine the Great to complain about it several times. Finally, he crowns his argument by stating that peasants under the Russian partition felt nostalgic about the Commonwealth because "republican tyranny is less hideous, humiliating, and detestable than the despotism of an individual. The oppressed masses can sense this difference."[76] Ironically, as noted in chapter 1, while discussing the rise of feudalism in medieval Poland, Lelewel argued the opposite: that monarchical despotism is in principle tamer and more benign for the people than oligarchy. This is not to say that he was right or wrong in any case but to demonstrate that in traditional historiography it is ideology and emotions that precede factual observations rather than "principles," or "rules,"' which are typically introduced to support and elevate them to the more general status.

The ambiguity of Lelewel's conclusions seems based on clear ideological premises: he wanted to negotiate his leftist-republican sensitivity, his patriotism, and his enthusiasm for noble democracy as a uniquely Polish political order, rooted in the supposed Slavic inclination for democracy. In this context his attitude toward the Cossack uprising appears remarkable. He believes that the nobles' stubbornness was a fatal mistake and that a compromise based on concessions might have saved the Commonwealth from the misfortune that soon followed. Still, he is strikingly ambivalent in his analysis of the uprising: it was "splendid" as a popular rebellion against oppression, "which rarely happens in history," and it was "terrifying" when it deteriorated into a spectacle of mass violence, motivated by both class antagonism and religious hatred against Catholics, Uniates, and Jews. As far as the reaction of the Polish-Lithuanian nobility is concerned, his remarks are full of pessimism, which is quite remarkable in the writings of a truly idealistic author: "The noble estate fought a bloody battle to preserve its prerogatives and possessions intact. In no other conflict did they suffer so many failures, obstacles, and humiliations. Nor was there a conflict in which they demonstrated so much stubbornness, bravery, and sacrifice as in this fatal struggle. The youth were decimated, estates devastated, families slaughtered, the best warriors perished, the resources exhausted. And still they vote unanimously, and hurry from all corners of the country to continue the bitter struggle."[77]

Bobrzyński, considered to be Lelewel's main scholarly adversary, put it more straightforwardly: in his view the Cossack rebellion was a catalyst for the loss of fundamental deficiencies of the Commonwealth that suddenly became apparent: "the freedom of the people, the freedom of the Orthodox Church, and efficiency of the government"; thus, "the Cossack issue could not have been resolved but through an inner renaissance of Poland by reestablishment of the people's freedom, religious freedom, and the royal authority." Therefore, his evaluation of the actual developments—that is, the civil war of the nobility against the Cossacks— was no less pessimistic than that of Lelewel: "The most heroic efforts were inconsequential, as there was no persistence or order in them. Despite its fury against the Cossacks, the nobility did not abandon its anarchy."[78]

The Cossack uprising, as well as the failed attempts at a compromise that would have involved a reconstruction of the Commonwealth's political order, prompted debate over several issues: the efficiency of the government, the noble identity and its political responsibilities, the weakening potential of the Polish-Lithuanian union, and religious tolerance. The uprising's role in the Polish narratives may perhaps be compared to that played by the religious divisions resulting from the Reformation in German historiography. It was a fierce, bloody struggle that undermined national unity and strength and was fought in the name of principles that were no longer valued in the nineteenth century, which made its assessment highly problematic for our historians. To be sure, the religious division of Germany, even though by this time no one was willing to fight to the death over it, was still a controversial issue. Indeed, it concerned essential problems of German national identity, and answering the questions it inspired required some psychoanalytical sensitivity; it was like traveling inside the German soul to find out whether there was some room there for the other part of the divided nation and whether the old hatred had been mitigated. There was no comparably sharp and dramatic division in the Polish narratives on the history of the Commonwealth. The marginalization and oppression of the peasants did not exclude them from what the historians viewed as the Polish nation, nor did their treatment modify what was regarded as the Polish identity. They were supposed to integrate within the national community consciously and spontaneously a bit later. Their misery from the past was metonymically represented by the Cossacks, because they could not formulate any aspirations themselves. Politically, the failed attempts to include the Cossacks in the political structure of the Commonwealth might have been a fatal or indeed a mortal mistake; spiritually, however, they never belonged to the Polish or the Polish-Lithuanian nation, and the struggle against them took place outside the boundaries of the national community, in which some problems can never be resolved and need to be readdressed by subsequent generations. More precisely, this struggle marked the end of Polish-Lithuanian expansionism: the brilliant formula of marriage-like peaceful unions became exhausted and deteriorated into a bitter and bloody civil war, paving the way for the fragmentation of the Commonwealth.

Alamodezeit, or the French Folly

In contrast to the Polish narratives on the history of the Commonwealth, which stressed the problem of the political order, the principal idea organizing the German narratives was that of national unity. Therefore, German historians ferociously criticized all alleged crimes against this unity. Since, after 1648, political unity remained out of the question, what was left was the cultural and spiritual unity of the national community; however, that unity was in danger too, and the biggest threat it faced was intense foreign influence. Karl Grün argues that imitating foreign cultural patterns, but simplifying and misusing them in the process, became typical for Germans, who had been "a people so spontaneous, a country of the Reformation," in the previous epoch.[79] The principal source of the poisonous foreign infiltration was France. German historians unanimously presented it as reaching into all spheres of life for the social elite, and they viewed its scale as terrifying.

In that time, Wolfgang Menzel informs us, when a French governess caught her student speaking German, she would reproach her saying, "Fi, on vous prendroit pour une Allemande!" There were, to be sure, more French agents in the German upper class of the time, according to our historian: teachers, chefs, hairdressers, and spies.[80] The anti-French phobia was ubiquitous in nineteenth-century German historical narratives, and it culminated in the passages regarding the epoch of France's most spectacular international successes under Louis XIV, labeled mockingly by German historians as Alamodezeit (the à la mode time). Eventually they were highly irritated that France, its most famous king, and all things French had been held in such esteem by contemporary Germans and that some remnants of this admiration were still present in literature available for German readers. Louis XIV, Oskar Jäger informs us, was in fact no great monarch at all but a bigot whose reign prepared the way for France's downfall: he understood neither liberty nor art, and all he loved was glamour. In German memory he symbolizes greed and the brutality of the French conquests, and Germans should not forget that while pompous baroque and rococo palaces were being constructed in France, French troops were devastating some of Germany's most precious architectural monuments, such as the cathedral of Speyer and the castle of Heidelberg. French power, Jäger concludes, was dangerous for Germany not simply because of France's territorial expansionism but also because of the "secret alliance with Catholicism" within the Empire.[81] French policies, Raumer emphasizes, were always perfidious: in the time of the Reformation, King Henry II presented himself as a protector of religious tolerance, and a hundred years later Cardinal Mazarin pretended to be a protector of German liberty. What they both actually had in mind, however, were simply territorial conquests in Germany. This is what the famous *raison d'*état (*Staatskunst*) is eventually about, the irritated historian argues, and he comments bitterly that the people are valuing highly what should be deplored.[82]

German historians sadly agreed that after 1648 the Empire became a space of political and diplomatic infiltration and manipulation by foreign powers: England, France, Sweden, and, the Protestant historians stressed, Rome and its agents, most notably the Habsburgs. What truly annoyed and scandalized them, however, was the supremacy of French fashion and the high reputation of French culture among the German upper classes. The decline of the Empire, the humiliation of Germany, the moral degeneration of the elites, the deterioration of patriotism—all were viewed as the result of French influence. Indeed, it is hard to say whether the French impact was the source of all evil or was merely the most detestable symptom of the decline. Eventually, new rivals on the horizon were being observed: bellicose Sweden, powerful England, and the wealthy Netherlands. However, for the Protestant historians the loathsome Sun King overshadowed them all, including the ritual complaints against Rome and the Habsburgs and their Spanish etiquette.

In the Renaissance epoch, Wachsmuth argues, the German princes retained a national spirit even though they were conducting foreign policy independently, which involved forming alliances with the French kings of the Valois dynasty. The nobles and aristocrats cultivated "the German habits of hunting and drinking," and they refrained from "the French frivolity, the Spanish *grandezza*, and the English frigidness." The "conventional education," promoting a pan-German, or even an "unnatural" European identity, was still marginal at that time, although the custom of traveling abroad for educational purposes had already started to shape the nobles' manners, artificially polishing them, introducing them to the ideas of courtesy and elegance, and discouraging the traditional virtues of chivalry and roughness.[83] The historian might have found the phrase "Spanish *grandezza*" in his sources, whereas "English frigidness" seems to have been a concept typical of his own time. Raumer provides us with yet another exciting example of demoralization coming from abroad: in his opinion, Emperor Charles V deserved a better reputation than the typical complaints offered by the Protestant historians. He might have had his shortcomings, to be sure, but privately he was a decent man. In contrast to foreign monarchs such as Henry VIII of England or Francis I of France, or "any pope of his time," the historian informs us, Charles had only two children out of wedlock.[84] Interestingly, in these catalogs of moral corruption infiltrating from abroad, France is located on the top of the list but does not dominate the picture completely.

And yet this is exactly what happens when we turn to Eduard Heyck's analysis of Renaissance culture. As far as ethics is concerned, in his view France and Germany were never more antagonistic than during the Reformation. The country of physically and morally degenerated Valois rulers was dominated by an immodest and colorful court culture, following Rabelais's credo *fay ce que voudras*. The only principle the French of that time knew, Heyck claims, was honor, "of which they talked so much, including King Francis, when he became prisoner after the Battle of Pavia, and which they in fact hardly respected, but by discretion." In his view, the court of Louis XIV was not so immoral anymore: it was too obsessed with formalities, hierarchies, etiquette, and fashion—"a war declared by Louis against nature."[85]

Unfortunately, the German elites—aristocracy, nobility, and bourgeoisie— embraced this folly enthusiastically. An invasion of governesses and cooks, as well as wigs, corsets, and slippers, followed the French advisors and courtiers. "The French fashion," Stacke explains, "inspired vices, frivolity, and immodesty." The Prussian court of Frederick William was the only one that appeared immune to demoralization. Still, the high society of Berlin, including its women, especially in the time of Frederick the Great, yielded to it enthusiastically. One should not, Stacke informs us, be misguided by the severity of the Empress Maria Theresa's manners. She was an exception at the Viennese court, whereas her husband (Francis I), as well as Chancellor Kaunitz, "were prisoners to the French gallantry." "It was a miracle," he concludes, "that the bourgeoisie survived among this folly."[86]

The moralist historians eagerly provide us with horrendous details. Oskar Jäger departs from a general observation that "one wonders how the Germans tolerated what was intolerable," namely, the odious French impact on the lifestyle of their elites, and especially those at the various courts. A list of the "peculiar symptoms of degeneration" follows, including three main categories: alliances with Louis, following the French fashion, and various other symptoms of moral decadence.

Among his examples one can find a colorful description of Dresden court life under the Wettin dynasty, with activities such as comedy performances, masked balls, and fireworks. Jäger also describes the rule of a mistress and a Jewish banker named Oppenheimer in Württemberg under Eberhard Ludwig (1693–1733) and Charles Alexander (1733–37), crowned with their conversion to Catholicism (the Saxon rulers also converted when Frederick August was elected king [Augustus II] of Poland-Lithuania in 1697). The historian is eventually confused by Frederick the Great's apparent love for French culture and finds some difficulty in interpreting this embarrassing fact without insulting the memory of the great German hero. It was just a "trivial entertainment," he claims, and explains that although the king wrote in French, his texts were "thoroughly German spirited," and his correspondence, because of its clarity and humor, resembles that of Bismarck. He emphasizes with satisfaction that Frederick quickly became disillusioned with Voltaire, because of the latter's "inclination for suspicious financial speculations."[87]

Droysen sadly concludes that a new nation came into existence at the German courts: it was the *nation de qualité*, whose sole inspiration was France and whose morality was reduced to the sense of honor and the *bon ton*. The dominant aspect of its culture, he argues, was its unnatural character, expressed by its adherents' predilection for wigs and uncomfortable dresses, for French gardens, Japanese temples, and Chinese porcelain. It was a culture, he sums up, totally alien to the German bourgeoisie and peasantry, and so was the state, controlled by aristocracy and serving exclusively its interests. "The state," he argues, "moved out of the nation."[88] The state he meant, of course, was not the Empire but the territorial principalities, which were nonetheless still its legal components.

The writing about the French impact might have seemed obsessive, yet there was logic in it. The French intrigues played a crucial role in undermining German unity. Having achieved this, the French proceeded to alter what had been left to the Germans: their national culture. No conspiracy was needed in this case. Guardians of national purity always label the imitation of foreign patterns, or any cultural transfer from abroad, as unnatural, since in their view the national culture must remain indigenous and pure. Thus, the French impact was believed to have been destructive simply because both national cultures were supposed to be antithetic: any transfer between them would pollute the recipient's culture. Still, in the post-1648 period this process, regrettable as it was, intensified terrifyingly because of its scale and because of the character of French culture in that epoch. It was not simply unsuitable for the Germans; it was itself unnatural. Its adaptation by the Germans was therefore a double perversity. In a way, German historians suggested, this was possible only due to the diminished political condition of Germany in that epoch: the Empire, as Samuel von Pufendorf claimed in his famous 1667 treatise *De statu Imperii Germanici*, was a monstrosity, and it was its perverted political organization that inspired demoralization in all spheres of life. Cultural identity was all that remained after the loss of German unity, and the mighty French cultural impact was a powerful threat to this last vestige of Germandom.

The main factors that constituted and determined a national culture were, according to nineteenth-century standards, language and literature. Thus, German historians were devastated at the expansion of French linguistic influences at that time, as already noted in the discussion of correspondence by Frederick the Great. However, there were other moments when the poisonous impact of the French was observable. The treaty ending the Great Northern War, during which the Swedish armies subsidized by the French plundered northern Germany, was, Wachsmuth notes, the first in German history written in French. It happened so despite the fact that "the Empire's honor rested with Latin" and despite a protest attached to its final version, approved in Vienna.[89]

According to Heyck, contemporary resistance to the French influence ironically testified in a way to its perverse attractiveness. A number of societies and academies that attempted a codification and purification of the German language by replacing foreign terminology with indigenous vocabulary, he claims with an air of suspicion, in fact imitated the policies of Cardinal Richelieu (the "French Bismarck"), and his Académie Française.[90] Grün represents a more practical opinion: in his view these attempts were simply belated, and occasionally naïve, for new "Germanic" terms were unsuccessfully promoted to replace words of foreign origin that had already entered popular use—due to the regrettable French influence.[91] As Jäger adds, however, "German is predestined for the high calling of poetry and scholarship like no other language."[92] Still, Latin and French polluted German language, and a cosmopolitan spirit penetrated German literature in the "age of Louis XIV" and the Enlightenment. German historians' painful task of unmasking cosmopolitan trends goes so far as to attack a number of monumental figures typically considered emblematic of German national culture: Kant, Goethe, and Schiller. Even Frederick the Great, as already noted, was not spared such criticism.

One of the severest critics of the most respected German authors of that time was Ludwig Stacke. During the Franzosenzeit (which roughly corresponded to the time between the Peace of Westphalia and the French Revolution), German national literature did not exist, he claims, because there was no German nation as defined by national consciousness. Poets and writers popularly considered founding fathers of modern German national literature—such as Goethe, Schiller, Herder, and Klopstock—were in fact adherents of cosmopolitan idealism, praising abstract ideas that had nothing to do with the real life of the nation, "as if Weimar were located on the Moon." Moreover, the Enlightenment, "which the philosopher Kant liked so much," was essentially a foreign, Anglo-French idea that was unhealthy for Germans and anti-Christian as well. It might have contributed, he argues, to the intellectual development of the country but certainly not the moral progress of the people. One should not, he explains, blame Frederick the Great for his support of Enlightenment ideas, for his intentions were certainly decent; however, in promoting tolerance, he invited demoralization.[93] Wachsmuth bitterly explains what was worst about Frederick's policies: the monarch supported French education, literature, and translations from the French.[94] Jastrow also argues that the patriotism of eighteenth-century German authors was so highbrow, philosophic, and idealistic that one can hardly understand which country they had in mind when describing their *Heimat*. In his opinion, the young Goethe did not care for his country at all, and the only writings of Klopstock (famous for his patriotism) that he finds "authentic" are his odes to the German language. It is remarkable, he observes, that the abstract German literature of the time, despite all its social and political miseries, offered no Jeremiah (i.e., no prophet) who would warn his contemporaries against a catastrophe, nor did it produce an Aristophanes who would mock the snobbery, fashion, and injustice of the epoch.[95]

Obviously, however, historians were not unanimous in their views on this matter. A number of authors believed that, next to the kings of Prussia, the writers and poets of the period were the biggest contributors to the German national revival and thus deserved a special position in the national pantheon. Before I discuss this problem in the next chapter, let us have a look at the analogous pessimism and xenophobic trends in Polish historiography of the time.

Foreign Elements

Our nineteenth-century historians were too focused on their respective national histories to approach them systematically in relation to general European trends and developments. More precisely, the apparent lack of international contextualization was predetermined by the concept of national history as a unique and singular process that shaped unique national identities. To be sure, numerous foreign analogies were allowed within this paradigm, elucidating particular policies or attitudes that resulted and that the author wished to confront in the context of the realities of his own country. Historians were always eager to have a look at Spain to illustrate the consequences of religious fanaticism, or Italy for political fragmentation and intrigue, or Russia for despotism. However, even if they realized that some national developments, such as religious movements, were parts of broader, international processes, they typically avoided discussing this multinational factor at length, focusing on the national dimension instead. National histories were too individualized to be viewed as elements of any broader trends. One could observe this tendency in the previous chapter's section concerning the Reformation, which was viewed as an essentially German phenomenon. Apart from religious motivations, this national hyperfocus was the reason German historians refused to discuss its international consequences, and the Polish historians remained skeptical about it: the Reformation might have been a pan-European religious movement, but its national impact was what dominated the picture.

Therefore, German and Polish historians did not present, or even consider, the post-1648 troubles of the Empire and the Commonwealth as elements of what modern historians consider the general European crisis of the seventeenth century.[96] In their view, foreign influences were poisonous by nature, for they undermined the purity of their respective national cultures, as well as the coherence of national history that was supposed to develop according to unique indigenous patterns. Foreign powers were present in their narratives predominantly as rivals of their countries. Thus, the general tendencies they observed, such as centralization of power and the rise of absolutism, fiscalism, bureaucracy, and professional armies, as well as the economic potential of some countries, occasionally accelerated by a demonic genius such as Richelieu in France or Peter the Great in Russia—all this was being introduced in the narratives on national histories of Germany and Poland to make readers realize the alarming shift in the European balance of power, which made their own countries' position more and more unfavorable vis-à-vis their greedy neighbors.

═══════

As already noted, Polish historians were scandalized by their seventeenth- and eighteenth-century ancestors' eagerness to accept bribes from foreign diplomats and agents. They were also shocked by their forebears' naïveté and unwillingness to see that, from the second decade of the eighteenth century, various powers collaborated to promote the idea of "golden liberty" among Polish-Lithuanian nobles, as it guaranteed that the Commonwealth would remain anarchic and defenseless. Władysław Konopczyński, for example, argues that, next to Austria, Prussia, and the "Byzantine perfidy" of Russia, Turkey, because of its "stupidity," and France, because of its "lightheartedness and perfidy," supported this suicidal ideology through their agents.[97]

As far as foreign influences in general are concerned, however, the Polish historians were more ambivalent than their German colleagues. The reasons for this were twofold. First, one can argue that a number of them had a profound sense of Poland's peripheral condition as a recipient of ideas and trends emanating from the center of Western civilization, be it France or Britain for the progressivists, or Rome for the Catholics. Their nationalism, to be sure, made them believe that these ideas should be modified and adapted to local conditions and negotiated with the Polish national tradition. Still, their image of this tradition involved cultural transfer, and they indeed took some pride in copying from the West, if only the process was cautious and, needless to say, beneficial. Second, it was the specific developments of Polish-Lithuanian history in the epoch in question that mattered. Constitutionally, the Commonwealth was a European anomaly in the last two centuries of its existence. As long as western Europe was plagued by religious and civil wars and intolerance, Polish historians emphasized the uniqueness of the Commonwealth with pride and satisfaction. However, France, England, the Netherlands, and finally also Prussia, Austria, and Russia emerged more powerful, united, and richer from the crisis, whereas Poland-Lithuania was now being devastated by that same crisis. Naturally, this raised doubts about whether Polish-Lithuanian exceptionalism was indeed the best path to follow.

There were various answers to this dilemma. One of them safely protected the national pride by suggesting that the Commonwealth's exceptionalism provoked aggression of the absolutist monarchs, who feared the impact of Polish-Lithuanian liberties and therefore concocted the partitions and inspired (or, more precisely, paid) some talented authors to mock the Polish nobles. "There was nothing more antagonistic toward the spirit of contemporary Europe" than the Commonwealth, Szujski claims: adherents of both absolutism and liberalism hated it (for its liberties and its backwardness).[98] The most dedicated apologists of the Commonwealth, such as Lelewel and Chołoniewski, believed this hatred to have been the main cause of the partitions. There were, to be sure, good reasons to support this belief. A number of famous French philosophers (such as Voltaire and Diderot) and other Enlightenment authors who commented on the Commonwealth were indeed inspired, and financially supported, by Frederick and Catherine the Great (as they were driven by more general prejudices against the barbaric East).[99] Moreover, the Constitution of May 1791 and the subsequent uprising of 1794 did eventually cause some panic in St. Petersburg and Berlin, as they were viewed in the context of the French Revolution and therefore suppressed under the banners of restoring order and fighting "Jacobins."

And yet, many believed that even though some influential foreigners did not like the Commonwealth, that did not explain its internal problems, nor was Polish liberty the singular factor that differentiated the Commonwealth from its neighbors. Indeed, a number of Polish historians melancholically comment on the Polish-Lithuanian nobility's rising megalomania and their refusal to learn from the foreigners in the time of the country's most desperate decline. Franciszek Bujak, for example, sadly observes that while the Germans (he actually had Prussia in mind) invited "the hardworking and intelligent" French Huguenots, expatriated by Louis XIV, and purposefully copied a number of French fiscal and administrative policies, Poland-Lithuania under the Saxon kings, wallowing in its false sense of superiority and singularity, "conducted only unreasonable policies."[100] Michał Bobrzyński was the one who most steadily promoted the idea of imitating Western patterns. Thus, he emphasizes with sorrow and disgust that the nobles, who had been so open-minded and reform-oriented in the sixteenth century, by the end of the next century had abandoned any political ideas but the one of cultivating and stabilizing their perfect political order, while they ceased to regard any foreign country as a point of reference in their debates. The most regrettable symptom of this tendency, he notes, is the rapid decline in the number of nobles sending their sons to study abroad. Those who still did travel, he reasons, did so exclusively "for the foreign demoralization, language, and fashion."[101] Władysław Smoleński concludes his essay on the Polish religiosity of the baroque epoch with sadness: in his view, superstitions, religious fanaticism, and national megalomania debilitated the nobility of the time, diminished indigenous intellectual traditions, and successfully prevented the reception of the most progressive foreign ideas. We had no philosophers like Locke, Descartes, or Bacon, he laments, "and their voices could not reach our fathers' ears."[102]

Joachim Lelewel was the historian whose attitude toward foreign impact on Polish history was openly hostile. This was a logical consequence of his love for all things indigenously Polish and Slavic, rather than antipathy against any particular nation. In his view, as already discussed, the entire history of Poland was about preservation of the original Slavic ideals of communitarianism and equality, which he believed were embodied by various political institutions and social groups throughout the ages and were in constant conflict with aristocratic and royal aspirations for power, as well as oppression of the people. If there was a nation he disliked, it was the Germans, whom he also viewed as the primary promoters of Western cultural patterns in Poland. However, the era in which this antipathy was most often expressed was the Middle Ages: the period of military conflicts against the Empire and the Teutonic Order and of the German colonization of Polish cities and the western borderlands. The late seventeenth and eighteenth centuries provided little opportunity for blaming the Germans for any of Poland-Lithuania's miseries. The culturally dominant interlopers of that period were the French and the Oriental patterns that dominated the nobility's imagination; politically, Sweden and Russia were evidently the most dreadful enemies of the Commonwealth. Until Frederick the Great entered the scene, Polish-German antagonism was hardly observable. And yet, as we shall see, Lelewel found some pretext to comment upon it.

As already discussed, Lelewel was highly critical of the Piast monarchy, for he saw it as a period of decline for the alleged primordial Slavic equality and popular liberties, which yielded both to the pressure of the rising monarchical prerogatives and the emerging aristocracy. Thus, he welcomed the Jagiellonian epoch and the formation of noble democracy with much enthusiasm: in his view, it marked a "triumph of the national spirit" and a "turn toward Slavic principles," which he associated with religious tolerance and the ideas of brotherhood and equality of the nobles. Unfortunately, the situation changed with the beginning of the seventeenth century. This is the time when "alien and contradictory forces prevail": the Jesuits and Counterreformation, German Lutheranism, and the oligarchic-monarchical spirit. All these, he reasons, were "foreign elements . . . colluding against the national republicanism."[103] Of course, he supports his argument by pointing at the foreign monarchs, priests, and courtiers; its essence, however, is based on the assumption that democracy alone suited the Polish national character, and therefore all pretensions of the monarchy or aristocracy for primacy in the Commonwealth represented a foreign factor.

Finally, as far as the Germans are concerned, Lelewel uses the opportunity to scold his fellow historians who argued that some of the Commonwealth's problems originated in the weakness of the third estate, that is, the cities. Lelewel reasons that this idea is based on a false analogy with the West, along with the false notion that Poland should copy Western patterns. First, he argues, such an analogy is unreasonable, for Poland's path of historical development was essentially different: the country had not been a Roman province, it had never fully adopted feudalism, it had not participated in the crusades, and it lacked other experiences fundamental to creating the identity of western Europe. Second, the majority of burghers in Poland were ethnically or culturally German, and thus the rise of cities would continue with increased pressure from German culture, "threatening the principles and the spirit of the Commonwealth and the Polish nationality with annihilation."[104] Interestingly, some eighty years later a parallel argument was developed by Johannes Haller regarding German unity in the late medieval epoch. Haller criticized, and indeed mocked, his colleagues who believed that the Empire might have defended itself against political fragmentation had the emperors sought an alliance with the cities against feudal aristocracy. This was an idea that only bourgeois historians could have promoted, he claims; in fact, however, the cities were egoistic, greedy, and cosmopolitan and preferred international alliances (such as the Hanseatic and the Rhine unions) over German national interests.[105]

As far as morality is concerned, however, Polish historians wholeheartedly agreed with their German colleagues: demoralization came from abroad, and enthusiasm for French fashion equaled the corruption of manners. Thus, their attitude toward the Enlightenment and the widespread dispersal of French ideas that the Polish elites of the time embraced was ambivalent. "These tendencies were highly useful and beneficent for Poland," Tadeusz Korzon reasons, "but their source was not patriotism, which the philosophers of that time disrespected, having the progress of humankind in its entirety in mind."[106] Others explore the problem in detail, offering their readers some spicy images. Schmitt argues, "The plague of libertinism, which devastated the higher strata of western European society . . . , accompanied fashion that became popular among richer nobles, particularly before the first partition."[107] Szujski adds the popularity of gambling to the list, and Smoleński presents us with a still more colorful analysis: "The higher educated strata were infected with debauchery, for which the decline of religious feelings paved the way. Frivolity of the French aristocracy was embraced by the king and all the most outstanding figures, including women. Disrespect for family values, separations, and divorces became notoriously common."[108]

Still, expressing their disgust and contempt for the corrupted manners of the Enlightenment, Polish historians faced a dilemma that was more confusing than the parallel German one. In both countries the Enlightenment, undeniably inspired by foreign ideas, was a powerful impulse for educational, intellectual, and artistic activities that profoundly changed the mentality of the educated youth. This was more than fine for our historians: as demonstrated, although some of them were suspicious about foreign inspiration for cultural advancement, they all appreciated rationalism, idealism, and modern patriotism that were supposed to have risen from the movement. We shall have a closer look at these analyses in the next chapter, which deals with brighter aspects of the epoch.

However, Polish historians unanimously agreed that the period of national revival had begun earlier, almost immediately after the Enlightenment ideas, French fashion, and libertinism became popular in the country with the ascendance to the throne of Stanislaus August Poniatowski in 1764. As we shall see, the new schools, poetry, and patriotism, which our historians enthusiastically cherished, blossomed, especially in reaction to the shocking effect of the first partition of 1772. Thus, it was particularly difficult for them to draw a coherent image of the epoch: the fact that the most spectacular epoch of national revival owed a lot to the bewigged, perfumed men who spoke French with their married mistresses was more than embarrassing. A figure that symbolizes this embarrassment is Poniatowski, the last king and grand duke and one of the most controversial figures in Polish history.[109] We shall return to him in the next chapter; here it should suffice to say that his role, as an emblematic persona of the entire epoch, seems parallel to that of Frederick the Great in German history. They were both highly immoral personalities and outstanding minds that represented welcome political programs, and they therefore epitomize the paradoxical nature of German and Polish Enlightenment—or, more precisely, the confusion it caused among historians of the next century. However, Frederick was also a good soldier and an embodiment of spectacular success achieved by dubious means.[110] Stanislaus August, though he symbolized no less ambitious aspirations and hopes, nevertheless ended up a political failure. The obvious lesson from the stories of their reigns was dramatically different: Would Frederick have achieved so much, and would Stanislaus August have achieved more, had they been more morally principled?

The Jesuits and the Lawyers

The devil, despite his outstanding personal powers, needs accomplices. In the nineteenth-century German and Polish historical narratives, his role was played by the French kings and the Russian tsars, and the historians were horrified with the number of Germans and Poles these secular demons had seduced, bribed, and misguided. However, our historians were also univocally disgusted with the superstitions and prejudices of the baroque era, which they viewed as resulting from the religious fanaticism and irrationalism of the time. These regrettable tendencies, they believed, were in a way natural for premodern times, and yet they were also purposefully inspired and perpetuated by identifiable people and institutions. The organization that was most frequently accused of these demonic activities was the Society of Jesus: the Jesuit order. Astonishingly, perhaps, this idea appears to be more consistently and intensively advocated by Polish historians. One can speculate that German Protestant historians did not need to emphasize the issue that much, since their readers' negative opinion of the Jesuits was already firmly grounded.

Historians who attempted a defense of the Jesuits were rare. An illustrative example of the narrative skillfully undermining standard accusations against them is *History of the German People since the End of Medieval Age*, by Johannes Janssen. Upon republishing the book in 1878, the author was well aware that "the results [of his research] do not confirm the vulgar image of the glorious epoch and provoked astonishment of numerous readers." His strategy consists of two elements. First, he carefully analyzes the educational and charitable activities of the Jesuits, emphasizing their spectacular achievements. Second, he stresses that the Jesuits had been under attack from Protestant propagandists since the time of the order's founding, and he quotes numerous anti-Jesuit pamphlets at length. In his view, the scale and passionate fury of these attacks on one hand simply testify to the efficiency and successes of the Jesuits. On the other hand, he elaborates on the anti-Jesuit literature to compromise it, demonstrating its fanatical approach and fantastic elements.[111] Clearly, this is a classical rhetorical strategy: by quoting the sixteenth- and seventeenth-century theologians, who claimed that the Jesuits were descendants of the devil himself, and that refusing to hate them equaled hating God, Janssen attempts to ridicule any critique of the order, including that formulated from a modern, secular position.

Indeed, a comparison of the image of the Jesuits in German and Polish nineteenth-century narratives suggesting that the latter was more dreadful, may be illustrative. This is because the Polish historians' approach to the issue was marked by an attitude of superiority owing to their more "progressive" minds, hence the appearance that their criticism may seem to reflect standard anticlericalism. Most typically, Polish historians scolded the Jesuits as promoters of superstitions, prejudices, and ignorance. Eventually, German historians regarded them with more respect, as they believed the order to have been a powerful and dangerous enemy of the Germans, their identity, and all things German. Except for the French, the German national spirit supposedly had no more perfidious opponent than the Jesuits.

Heyck, for example, claims that the Jesuit colleges were "citadels of the foreign supremacy" over Germany and trained young Germans to put foreign ideas into practice and promote their political goals. Another factor he emphasizes is the allegedly demonic impact of the Jesuits as courtiers, especially in the case of Emperor Charles VI. Finally, Heyck identifies the baroque style in architecture as a destructive tool of Jesuit cosmopolitanism. Charles VI, he claims, could not have erected a better monument to his rule than the Karlskirche of Vienna, being "the papal Rome epitomized."[112] This is also a skillful rhetorical strategy, based on the supremacy of visual imagination over analysis. Focusing on the buildings that dominated the landscape of a number of German cities in the baroque epoch, the historian suggests they resembled fortresses of a foreign army occupying Germany. On one hand the impressive buildings symbolized Catholic domination over Germany, whereas on the other their walls screened the Jesuit conspirators from the eyes of the people while they concocted their plans to seize even more power.

Indeed, some historians located the Jesuits within the framework of Catholic obscurantism, bigotry, and backwardness. This went along with depressing images of the depravity and corruption that allegedly characterized numerous German ecclesiastical states, whose subjects, as Menzel argues, were "totally uneducated, stupid, and bigoted," whereas "monks and nuns feasted on the sweat of the people."[113] More typically, however, Protestant German historians believed that Jesuits had been powerful and highly successful enemies of their religion and the German national spirit. Counterreformation, they admitted, gave Catholicism a new impetus and revealed remarkable weaknesses of Protestantism, which, as Heyck argues, appeared "tired of theology" and of Luther himself.[114] Häusser reasons that by the 1660s the initial "spiritual and intellectual" energy of Protestantism seemed exhausted theologically because of the brutal rivalry between Lutherans and Calvinists, whereas Catholics regained much vigor and self-confidence. This was possible mostly due to the efforts of the Jesuits in the previous decades. Naturally, the historian emphasizes that the Jesuit order was a foreign agent, and its activities had nothing to do with German national interests. Finally, he concludes with satisfaction that the Jesuits' loyalty to the papacy and ostentatious cosmopolitanism led them into conflict against the "modern state" in the next century, leading to their downfall.[115] Before this happened, however, the Jesuit impact was most obvious at the imperial court. Their preponderant influence was regarded as responsible for the internal policies of a number of rulers, most notably Rudolf II and Charles VI.[116] This was possible due to their perfidy, as well as a sort of ideological vacuum resulting from the Thirty Years' War, which ripened the Empire in its ideological foundations. Eventually, Protestant historians argue, the Empire ceased to represent German interests. Its powers, however, were far from being exhausted; the Jesuits provided it with new objectives and methods.[117] As Jäger suggests, these methods, detestable as they were, soon proved counterproductive too and were, among other things, the cause of the anti-Habsburg uprising in Hungary during the Empire's conflict against the Ottomans. On the other hand, he also condemns the role played by "fanatical pastors" inspiring religious conflicts among the Protestant Germans.[118]

Remarkably, the baroque era is also the period when the Habsburgs finally earn their reputation as German renegades, at least among Protestant historians. This was a gradual process, to be sure, reaching back far into the medieval epoch. However, the emperors of the past who had favored their dynastic interests over those of the nation simply failed to meet the nineteenth-century standards. They were a collective disappointment. Charles V was still expected to have understood what a great opportunity for Germany the Reformation would be, but he was eventually unable to do so because he was actually more Spanish than German. The post-1648 emperors were not even expected to act as Germany's leaders, for Protestant historians did not regard them as German anymore. All that was expected from them in that time was for them to demonstrate dynastic egoism and vain pride, as well as to represent the interests of Catholicism, the anti-German religion.

───

The Jesuits had an invariably bad reputation among Polish historians. The only differences among the historians' attitudes toward the order related to the mood in which their reproaches were formulated: the pious Szujski employed melancholy and regret, whereas the anticlerical Smoleński attacked with anger and fury. The evolution, perhaps, was from the morally principled criticism resembling that of the Protestant pamphlets in the first half of the nineteenth century toward a more rationalist-positivist position in the second half, when the Jesuits were typically considered defenders of backwardness and irrationalism. The criticism, however, is related to timing. When Jesuits appear in Poland-Lithuania in the late sixteenth century, they are viewed as impressively, or perhaps devilishly, efficient. When they leave the scene in the second half of the eighteenth century, they are but a pitiful party of defenders of anachronism in all spheres of life, and their unceasing popularity confuses our historians, who regard their objectives as doomed.

Let us illustrate this evolution with a few examples. Lelewel was highly critical of Jesuits because of their dubious, cunning, and perfidious methods. In his opinion, "*Restrictiones mentales* justified all methods: none of them was forbidden, and all ways were allowed to achieve their goal. Dressed in scholarly garments, they attempted to seduce the higher strata of society. Consequently, they soon won numerous talented and educated people for their congregation."[119] Lelewel had even less sympathy for the Protestants than did the other Polish historians, for he considered Lutheranism to be a German religion that constituted a threat to Polish cultural identity. Still, like all his colleagues, he deplored the decline of religious liberty and tolerance in the age of the Counterreformation, when "all non-Catholics were regarded as foreign intruders" (though, he adds, there were some reasons for this belief). The intolerance of the seventeenth and eighteenth centuries ran against nineteenth-century ideals, and, no less importantly, it insulted the memory of the Polish-Lithuanian golden age, when the Commonwealth had guaranteed more religious freedom than any other country in Europe. The people to blame for the ruination of this ideal, according to Lelewel, were the Jesuits and Sigismund III of Vasa, their most powerful protector, or the monarch who most evidently adapted his policies according to their advice.[120] These policies, of course, best serve papal objectives. However, Lelewel adds proudly (I suppose) that the Polish-Lithuanian clergy did not obey all instructions from Rome, and thus, for example, the practice of religious intermarriage continued.[121]

Lelewel's ideological opponents arrived at similar conclusions. According to Karol Boromeusz Hoffman, "that generation, educated by the almighty Order having but the interests of the Church in mind, did not yet understand the benefits of religious tolerance."[122] Bobrzyński analyzes Jesuit impact on Polish history more carefully, skillfully integrating it into his general image. In his view, the initial phase of their activities should be appreciated. They appear when the Reformation "had already lost its case, failed to play a positive role, and was now becoming an anarchic factor, undermining the country's unity." And yet, the Jesuits quickly emancipate themselves from their original role of propagandists and teachers and enter politics, "which needs to be criticized severely by a Polish historian." Their goal was to use the resources of the Commonwealth for regaining neighboring territory and population—that of northern Germany, Sweden, and eventually also Russia—for the Catholic cause. In short, Bobrzyński, like the German Protestant authors, viewed the Jesuits as an instrument of a foreign policy. Of course, in his view the papacy was not a deadly enemy of Poland-Lithuania by definition, and the interests of the two might have been reconciled. The problem was that the Jesuits were not content with reconquering the Commonwealth for Catholicism; they abused its hospitality and were largely responsible for the conflicts with Sweden and Russia that effectively ruined the country.[123]

This was, however, but one element of the miseries they caused, according to Bobrzyński. Again, he views their political impact favorably in the first decades of their activity in the Commonwealth, when they focused on education and anti-Protestant propaganda under the umbrella of royal authority of Stephen Báthory and Sigismund III. This, he notices, caused much suspicion among the nobles, who were seemingly allergic to all attempts, real and imagined, at consolidating royal power; the opposition spread rumors about Jesuits as supporters of absolutism and, afraid of attacking the king directly, demanded their expulsion from the country. Alarmed by their rapidly declining popularity, the Jesuits responded with a radical shift: "They claim they never supported the monarchy and pose as the most dedicated enthusiasts of noble liberties, free elections, and unanimity of voting. They start advocating the idea that the Catholic Church is the best friend of anarchy and that the 'golden liberty' and Catholicism are two identical concepts!"[124] Obviously, Bobrzyński, as the advocate of strong monarchy and the most radical critic of the golden liberty, disapproved of this swift change.

Still, what the Polish historians criticized the most passionately about the Jesuits was their impact on education. Of course, the issue was closely related to religious intolerance, the cult of the golden liberty, and the nobility's egoistic and chauvinist mentality in general. In Schmitt's opinion, Jesuit education caused the ruination of "public opinion" and "virtue" and is therefore to be regarded as "responsible for the increasing depravity of our society and consequently for all the subsequent miseries of the Commonwealth."[125] Szujski bitterly elaborates on this, also emphasizing that originally the Jesuits promoted "piety and purity of manners." Thus, in the sixteenth century "they were still Poles," whereas later they specialized in flattering the magnates with their "panegyrics for immoral senators" and in promoting "superficial and pedantic education" and "Pharisaic religiosity." Therefore, he concludes, "we have to regard them as one of the causes of the moral downfall that preceded the political one."[126] Bobrzyński stresses as paradoxical that the cosmopolitan order became the most powerful supporter of obscurantism and parochialism and so managed to achieve an almost perfect monopoly in the Catholic education of nobles in the seventeenth and early eighteenth centuries. In his view, however, Jesuit education "has rightly been cursed by future generations," as it was a parody of what education ought to be: it discouraged the noble youth from "individual thinking" and the "true knowledge," simply consolidating and solidifying their class prejudices, false pride, chauvinism, and religious fanaticism, as well as producing innumerable ignorant sycophants who specialized in vain rhetorical apologia for their sponsors.[127] Smoleński identifies the entire "religious spirit" in the "Jesuit epoch" with obscurantism, prejudices, superstitions, and ignorance.[128] Korzon sums up: "We have arrived at the conclusion that ignorance was the first and the main cause of the downfall of the Commonwealth."[129]

And yet, the depravity caused by the Jesuits was supposed to have reached even deeper. The pious Szujski and the anticlerical Smoleński argue similarly in this respect. What the Jesuits promoted was the corruption of not only citizens but also their souls, by a "false religiosity." The Polish-Lithuanian religiosity of the baroque era, both historians believed, was dominated by "fanaticism," which they identified on one hand with a growing intolerance of non-Catholics and on the other hand with immoral superficiality. Ostentatious celebrations of religious festivities and feasts, as well as generosity for the Church and the monasteries, resulted in a "corruption of the consciousness," suggesting that sins might be forgiven and souls redeemed all too easily, particularly for the rich.[130] Smoleński offers a semipsychoanalytical take on the nature of baroque religiosity. In his opinion, "it seems that the moral economy of the contemporaries was fixed upon compensation through religious formalism," especially ostentatious penitential practices. Thus, "it was the dogma itself that inspired them to sin, for they could be redeemed by prayer and atonement." A sinful experience guaranteed a spectacular penance, which was viewed as the most respectable mark of piety and which people practiced with much enthusiasm.[131]

Historians of the neo-Romantic generation attempted a relative rehabilitation of the nobility, as well as of Jesuit education. This tendency may be seen in the series of papers published in 1918 as *Causes of the Downfall of the Commonwealth*. Their approach consists mainly in emphasizing the international context and stressing that what the modern historians viewed as prejudices, ignorance, and demoralization were phenomena typical of the time. Konopczyński, for example, claims that political corruption in the eighteenth-century Commonwealth was still not comparable with the situation in England or Sweden. Such practices, and many other alleged vices of the period, simply did not go against their moral standards. "If they were sinful," he argues, "it was because of their wicked ideas rather than because of the depravity of their characters." Kallenbach observes that although the curricula of the Jesuit gymnasia were "antiquated" by the mid-eighteenth century, when the society was formally dissolved in 1773 and its schools were secularized by the Commission for National Education (discussed in the next chapter), many of the former Jesuits were hired as teachers again, which, in his opinion, testifies to their professional skills.[132] Finally, Antoni Chołoniewski, the most radical enthusiast of the legacy of the Commonwealth among our historians, dismisses all accusations against the Jesuits and Counterreformation as exaggerated. In his view, both the Reformation and Counterreformation were marginal and short-lived and cannot seriously damage the bright image of the national past.[133]

One of the popular beliefs regarding the Day of Judgment is that it will be full of the outcry of sinners terrified by the prospect of the everlasting inferno. A similar outcry was produced by lawyers in August 1806, in the Holy Roman Empire's last hour, Eduard Heyck informs us. The lawyers, "who made the Empire suffer so much throughout the ages," debated whether Emperor Francis might have dissolved the Empire officially or should have simply abdicated, leaving its throne vacant.[134] Analogically, the Polish historians univocally emphasize that the last Polish-Lithuanian Sejm in 1793 approved the second partition of the Commonwealth in silence. The deputies (except for those who had been arrested) were actually locked in the castle in Grodno, guarded by Russian soldiers, and supposed to stay there until they agreed to the terms of the partition treaty. When the speaker in the Sejm read the text, he did not ask the deputies to vote but simply asked if anyone objected; since no one responded, the treaty was considered to be approved.

Outcry and silence as strategies of resistance proved to be of no use and were therefore noted by historians as symbols of the two countries' defenselessness. The people who had the dubious honor of facilitating the countries' last hours were also their living symbols. The lawyers epitomized the Empire, just as the parliamentary deputies did the Commonwealth, and this was what German historians hated about them.

As already discussed, in the historians' unanimous opinion about the post-1648 situation, the Empire was but a legal fiction, with no actual political power. Still, this fiction supported a number of bureaucrats and lawyers who lived off its institutions, who served its parliament, courts, and other offices, and maintained its shadowy existence. Some German historians were disgusted that the Empire survived so long in this condition, which they considered insulting for a modern nation. The most passionate of them was perhaps Treitschke, who coined a famous metaphor comparing the Empire to "an antiquated gothic building" that was "wrapped in the mist of phrases and lies." He also argued that "there was no other country in which one lied so often officially."[135] In Wachsmuth's opinion, it was the lawyers who epitomized the worst features of the German character—sluggishness, languor, and "barbaric stupidity"—and whose vices involved corruption and perverting the German language.[136]

Obviously, such opinions should be viewed in the context of a supranational tradition of blaming the state administration for its invariably irritating, inefficient, and superficial way of operating, as well as of a literary stereotype of both the lawyer and the bureaucrat as people of dubious reputation, contrasted with that of a "man of action." However, the post-1648 era was indeed fertile soil for such lamentations. It was a time, after all, when modern bureaucracies quickly rose, establishing innumerable new regulations, taxes, and obligations that typically co-existed with the old ones, inherited after the demise of the estate institutions that had dominated the social landscape of the previous epoch. Moreover, this process, which is generally considered to be the rationalization and centralization of state power, was particularly complicated in Germany, divided as it was into more than two thousand sovereign territories. Ironically, as many observed, the apparent anarchy that governed the Empire was gradually disappearing as it traveled down the social hierarchy. While political life in Germany was chaotic, the lives of the people were becoming more and more orderly as pressure from the state apparatus was growing. As mentioned, German historians drew a sad, and occasionally scandalous, picture of social relations in that time, emphasizing the oppression and exploitation of the poor by the rich and powerful. Regrettable as these conditions were, they belonged to the archaic social order and testified to the backwardness of the Empire, with its feudal character. The new bureaucratic and enlightened order that was emerging under some energetic German princes was not much easier to live under, however. The legal-administrative "tyranny" of the modern state that was born in that epoch did not go unnoticed by historians either, and it was diagnosed as a particularly German phenomenon.

"The systematic love for detail, characteristic of the German," Menzel argues, "gave rise to that artificial bureaucracy and supremacy of the clerk's office, which, under the name of the strictest justice, perhaps proved the most oppressive of tyrannies."[137] Wachsmuth bitterly observes that the immense growth of the princely administration and its prerogatives was only possible due to the soldiers, lawyers, and priests, who never questioned the authorities' policies and never supported the poor against the rich.[138] Almost a century later Haller reasoned that absolutism of the petty German states of that epoch resulted in unconditional obedience, the lack of political debate, and the absence of any political opposition, which the author identified as a specific trait of German political life.[139] Such observations, to be sure, were not typical for the German historians of the time. Nevertheless, they seem remarkably modern, both in the context of German history of the nineteenth and twentieth century and in the development of historiography in general.

CHAPTER FOUR

It Is Never Too Late

This last narrative chapter tells the story of national reconstruction, a process that is ideally full of pride in the past and inspiration for the future. Except for a number of malcontents and outsiders, our historians of the final decay and fall of the Holy Empire and Poland-Lithuania capped their narratives with a happy—or at least a promising—ending. At first glance this statement may seem incoherent, or at least paradoxical, so we begin with an explanation of why this chapter has been included in this book at all.

My book examines the parallels in the German and Polish narratives on their respective national histories. Thus, it would be regrettable to omit a chapter in which the analogy is at its most striking, particularly insofar as the dynamic of the story is concerned. In the final phase of the histories of the Holy Empire and Poland-Lithuania, the emphasis clearly switches from the state to the nation—a change that was to be expected, as the nation has actually been the main protagonist of our story from the very beginning. This is a fortunate and promising change of perspective, for nations, as the nineteenth-century historians viewed them, are eternal, and the law of perpetual decline and fall does not apply to them. The blissful transformation is also an occasion to present readers with a moral message, as is typical in dramas written to enlighten an audience—and many of the authors discussed herein took advantage of the opportunity to do so. The rise of Prussia under the Great Elector, the reforms of Frederick William, and the conquests of Frederick the Great introduced a moral and political order into the hitherto chaotic and depressing German history. As such, they were analogous to the reforms of Stanislaus August Poniatowski, the Great Diet, and the Constitution of May 3, 1791, which together reorganized the direction of Polish history. After centuries of heading toward a catastrophe, both nations regained a sense of their destiny and began a long journey that left the old political structures behind.

Second, it is time to critically reassess the thesis regarding the parallels between the German and Polish historians' approach to their old states. Readers may already have sensed the essential differences, and in this final chapter those differences will become even more obvious. All Polish historians agreed that the Kingdom of Poland and the Commonwealth were the true embodiment and home of the national Polish community, which expressed its unique aspirations and character. The majority claimed that at a certain moment this state had become dysfunctional and that the political culture of the Commonwealth in its last phase was full of calamitous abuses for which the entire nobility was responsible. The so-called "Saxon period" epitomized what they considered to be despicable and shameful aspects of this culture. And yet, that recognition had virtually no impact on their assessment of the partitions of Poland-Lithuania: they viewed them as a national tragedy and a deep wound in the Polish body politic. The Poles might have had it coming and they might have deserved it, but the sense of loss was nevertheless tremendous and painful. National history became a form of mourning lost political independence, and one of its crucial tasks was to remind the compatriots of their bygone fortunes.

The formal liquidation of the Holy Roman Empire in 1806, during the Napoleonic turmoil, was not a comparable shock to the Germans, and neither was the Congress of Vienna, despite its being a remarkable disappointment for many who had hoped for a unified Germany. It was the rise of Romanticism that inspired popular longing for the lost Empire, which was most popularly symbolized by the glorious epoch of the Staufen dynasty. However, quite in contrast to the Polish case, the German historians of the second half of the century put much effort into undermining this sentiment. Generally, in their view neither the history of the German kingdom nor of the Reich or the Holy Roman Empire was identifiable with German history. They were growing apart through centuries. Heinrich von Sybel, as noted, accused the Empire of having abused true German interests as early as during the time of the Ottonian dynasty. In his opinion, Henry the Fowler was the only actual patriot among the medieval emperors and the only one of them who understood these interests properly and acted accordingly.

The majority of Protestant historians placed the split between the national destiny and the history of the Empire after the Habsburgs' rise to power, arguing that the country, ruled by "foreigners" and the Roman Catholic Church, was unprepared for the "most German event in history"—the Reformation. This reasoning is best seen in the passages concerning the lack of national unity, a particularly German deficiency and the eternal problem well known to the nineteenth-century Germans from their own experience. On one hand, this was precisely what prevented the Empire from becoming the true Germany, which was unthinkable while the country was disunited. On the other hand, as the story advanced in time, the Protestant historians' sympathy for the ever more independent, united, and absolutist territorial duchies and principalities becomes evident. Eventually, these states were to protect Protestantism—and Germany—against the power of the Habsburgs and Rome.

The Protestant discourse responded positively to a popular German sentiment for the *Heimat*, for the celebrated German cultural and political variety and decentralization. Still, the idea of unity and power returned a number of times in later epochs. If only Charles V had converted to Protestantism, if only Gustav Adolph had lived a little longer, and so on, Germany could have been united, powerful, and Protestant. In 1629 and 1635, when the Catholic party was prevailing and triumphant, the idea of unity reappears—but as a nightmare.

And yet the Catholics were systematically excluded from the truly German history, and in the narratives concerning the period following the Peace of Westphalia they were presented as agents of the "foreign" Habsburgs and Rome. The union of Austria with Bohemia and Hungary, as well as Habsburg rule in Italy and in the Catholic Netherlands, demonstrated that the Empire had become not only spiritually but also politically and ethnically non-German. The Catholic courts, administration, and armies were permeated with foreign influences and dominated by non-Germans. The sadly repeated diagnosis that the Empire had ceased to exist after 1648 confirmed the political status quo and the impotence of the imperial institutions, and it suggested that the Empire was non-German—it was as alien as it was anachronistic. And, finally, the German territorial states also alienated themselves from a national destiny by their cosmopolitanism and their yielding to the demonizing French influence, as well as by the egoism and vanity of their rulers, who had no national consciousness but plenty of aristocratic sycophants and promiscuous mistresses.

This was the time when the Prussia of the Great Elector (as Frederick William [r. 1640–88] was popularly known) entered the scene, dominated it, and captured the attention of German historians, most strikingly those of the Prussian school. As the only state that resisted cosmopolitanism and the French influence, Prussia epitomized true Germandom. German history and the history of the Empire finally split apart, and so Prussian history came to effectively dominate many narratives on the late seventeenth and the eighteenth century, while the rest of Germany attracted marginal attention. "The entire modern German history since the Peace of Westphalia," Ludwig Stacke declared, "is but the history of the struggle and triumph of Brandenburg-Prussia."[1] Some historians realized that this was an ambiguous narrative strategy. Eduard Heyck, for example, admitted that he might have overemphasized Prussian history in his *German History*, while in fact in the seventeenth century Prussia had still been a provincial state of relatively minor importance. However, he explained that "our task was not to follow the traits that led nowhere as far as the development of Germany is concerned, but to focus on those that determined it."[2]

The Awakening

Before turning to politics, let us first have a look at the literature and culture of the Enlightenment, which, as German and Polish historians univocally believed, was the soil from which modern patriotism blossomed in both countries. Indeed, German historians emphasized the rise of Prussia as the factor that was to inspire the birth of a modern national consciousness, whereas the Polish historians pointed to the reforms under the last Polish king, Stanislaus August Poniatowski. At the same time, the opinion prevailed that the role of literature in the national awakening was of primary importance and that modern patriotism developed regardless of, or even despite, the regrettable political conditions of the time.

An illustrative example of such reasoning can be found in the essay "The Golden Times of Weimar," by Heinrich von Treitschke. The historian, still remembered today as the emblematic figure of German chauvinism and militarism, emphasized that the writings of Schiller, Klopstock, Goethe, or August von Kotzebue, which he valued highly for their patriotism, were products of a sort of political vacuum existing in the "apolitical epoch." These authors, he insisted, "were pure givers, receiving little more than nothing from their people." What the Germans received from the poets and dramatists of Weimar, he believed, was one of their principal virtues: German idealism. The striking contrast between the political misery and the spiritual perfection of eighteenth-century Germany led him to reflect on a Greek analogy. "Like Hellas had been between Persia and Macedonia ages before," he claimed, "so were the Germans sunk deep in their thoughts between France and Austria." Obviously, in his opinion Germany's neighbors had virtually nothing to offer as cultural achievements to inspire or indeed to compete with those of the Germans. France, he insisted, was just rising from barbarism toward culture in the time of Pierre-Simon Laplace. Interestingly, and perhaps ironically, however, he highly valued the patriotic enthusiasm that echoed Schiller's verses on Joan of Arc. Treitschke's essay concludes with a declaration that may seem surprising coming from the pen of an avowed admirer of the Prussian sword: Schiller understood that the triumphs of Kant and Goethe mattered more than Napoleon's victory at Marengo![3]

Treitschke's argument was typical of the nineteenth-century German historians' assessment of the legacy of *Sturm und Drang* literature: its main merit, which they enthusiastically admired, was the impulse it provided for modern patriotism, emerging from the ruins of the Empire that fell apart under the burden of cosmopolitanism and moral decay. The minority opinions suggesting that German literature and language had also been affected by the degeneration of the epoch, and particularly by foreign influences, have already been discussed in the previous chapter. The most optimistic authors, in contrast, emphasized that the national and political awakening was not limited to the literary production of a few Weimar poets. Wilhelm Wachsmuth, for example, claimed that the excesses of monarchical absolutism in the second half of the eighteenth century were already tamed by public opinion, invigorated by ever-more critical and emancipated literature.[4] Others pointed out the emancipation of modern scholarship, and naturally the role of the new Protestant universities and pietism was stressed, as were the birth of modern philology and the rising interest in history.[5] All these developments were viewed positively as marks of progress and especially as powerful stimuli for the rise of a national consciousness among Germans.

The image of the Enlightenment in Polish historiography is essentially similar, even though it differs in being less dramatic and less focused on a few great individuals and great artists. Its descriptions were also full of metaphors about the awakening, a renaissance, and the new light, but its firmament was different due to being inhabited by a large number of authors, scholars, and pedagogues, rather than by a few geniuses. It was only during the fervor of Romanticism that the cult of "poets as the nation's greatest sons" was to arrive to Poland; the Enlightenment was considered a time of hardworking, educated, and idealistic social activists. Its poets were applauded for the pedagogical aspects of their verses rather than their artistic value. Of course it was greatly appreciated that these verses were finally written in modern Polish, without the long excursuses in Latin that had been typical for baroque literature. It was, however, but one element of the new and essentially modern values being promoted by the enlightened authors—values that were to produce citizens full of patriotic sentiment and liberated from the class prejudices, religious fanaticism, and irrationalism of the previous century.

In other words, Polish historians held a higher opinion of society as a whole, but a lower opinion of its individual members, than their German colleagues, at least with respect to the educated strata willing to accept the new spirit of the Enlightenment. No other epoch provoked fewer controversies among Polish historians: it was a time of systematic, if limited, progress and of gradual growth rather than spectacular achievements. The initial phase, which actually occurred under the rule of Augustus III of the Wettin dynasty, was marked by the publication of a few books that were, as Józef Szujski put it, "encouraging the public opinion for the good cause."[6] These works, which critically assessed the status quo and promoted political reforms and rationalism in public life, included *The Free Voice Reassuring Liberty*, by Stanislaus Leszczyński (himself deprived of the Polish throne by the Wettins), and *On Effective Advice*, by Father Konarski. This was followed by a broad literary and artistic movement, largely sponsored by Stanislaus August Poniatowski, which, as the historians saw it, demonstrated that "the nation awoke and started thinking" or that "rationality was growing and acquiring self-confidence."[7] As Polish historians argued in unison, the crucial moment in the Polish Enlightenment was the establishment of the National Commission for Education in 1773, whose task was to reorganize and modernize the national network of secondary schools and academies, hitherto dominated by the Jesuit order, which had been dissolved by the pope the same year. The commission—whose activities involved producing new curricula and textbooks in Polish, as well as the promotion of rationalism and patriotism—was probably the single most appreciated institution in Polish history. As Michał Bobrzyński put it, as a result of these activities "it was not individuals anymore but the entire generation of educated youth that had to abandon the concepts and sentiments that had caused the decadence of the country and its society."[8]

The ubiquitous and uncritical admiration of Polish historians for the commission (whose achievements in fact did not constitute such a radical shift, as it had to employ numerous former Jesuits simply because of the lack of educated secular pedagogues) seems telling insofar as their image of social change is concerned. A centralized institution supervising the national education system was, in their view, a perfect instrument of such change, for they believed that rationalism, scientific progress, and modern patriotism went together. The wicked dysfunctionality of the Polish political institutions was, in their view, a by-product of the ignorance of the nobility, and familiarizing them with science and rational thinking was enough to make them abandon religious superstitions and class egoism alike, and to transform them into modern, patriotic citizens.

The Snuff and the Bayonets

What was so exciting and inspiring about Prussian history for German historians? It would be all too easy to answer this question by reminding the reader of what seemed obvious from a post-1871 perspective: that it was the Hohenzollerns' Prussia that many Germans expected to unite the country by 1848 and that these hopes were finally realized. Indeed, such was the perspective adopted by a number of German historians who narrated their national history as if Prussia had been predestined to unify the country since time immemorial. Methodological and ideological standards of the age suggested dating any respectable history as far back as possible, and so Prussian history, as narrated by Ranke or Droysen, began a long time before the Hohenzollerns became the Electors of Brandenburg. However, the actual period of Prussian exceptionalism and its "German mission" was typically associated with the reign of Frederick William, the Great Elector. And yet at that time Prussia's mission was far from accomplished, as was still the case in 1813, and uncovering the prospects of the Hohenzollerns' future greatness demanded a great deal of imagination and rhetorical skills. This is what we are going to examine more closely.

Droysen formulated the problem in grandiose schemes and phrased it accordingly. It is not easy to decipher the meaning of some of his concepts, in which the ideas of the "old" and the "new" world were crucial. The latter, as he interpreted it, tallied with "the truth that always prevails," and "writes history." According to the Hegelian paradigm, rewritten in the historicist manner, the modern spirit, being essentially one, takes various shapes in different countries. In the United States, Droysen argued, it was the war for independence; in France, it was the revolution; and in Germany, it was the slowest but in fact the most profound process of the formation of the Prussian state. The "moment of truth" in German history that corresponded to and preceded the analogous developments in the United States and France, he claimed with evident satisfaction, was Frederick the Great's ascendance to the throne.[9] Nevertheless, formulating that truth was a process that lasted about three hundred years: from the Reformation up to the so-called wars of liberation against Napoleon in 1813–15.

Let us look back for a moment at the state of affairs that Droysen labeled the "old medieval-feudal system," which the Romantics, as he sarcastically noted, imagined as the "Christian-Germanic order." It was, he claimed, the same system in Germany, in monarchical France, in liberal England, or in oligarchic Poland: a system of "easy government." Legislation and jurisdiction were controlled by the same people; administration was slow and dysfunctional; the court was plagued by cliques and the magnates' clientele; and the church was united with the state. All that, he summarized, was a strange combination of monarchy, aristocracy, and democracy: a life of illusions, being a contradiction of "the truth." This picturesque, albeit unclear, declaration comes from his *History of Prussian Politics*, which he wrote "in order to demonstrate that it has been Austria's destiny for ages to draw back from the Reich, whereas it has been natural for Prussia to surpass it in order to become the Reich."[10] Friedrich Meinecke emphasized that Droysen, when working on the book, was disappointed and embittered with Prussia's actual failure to meet his expectations, and this was why "there was something apocalyptic" in his words.[11] Yet, let us also have a look at the image Droysen drew in his *History of the Wars of Liberation*, which he wrote with a full sense of optimism. With the Reformation, he argued, "a struggle of the new order against the old one began: the struggle for legitimization based on faith instead of hierarchy, for sovereignty against the estates. The idea of the universal monarchy of the Ottonian and Hohenstaufen emperors has been replaced with the idea of the contemporary, territorial state, united, assured in its self-identity and its being the source of all authority." In the reasoning typical of Protestant historians, he specified that the state could enjoy this status because its authority was no longer sanctioned by the Church or by a compromise between the estates, or by election, but by God's grace alone.[12]

The actual struggle for such a state, however, was not initiated until the Grand

Elector did so, as he "recognized the vital trends" of his time: he then eliminated the privileges of the estates, founded a modern fiscal administration and army, introduced religious tolerance and "Evangelic liberty," and, finally, in the wake of his military and diplomatic successes, uplifted German dignity from the miserable condition to which it had sunk after the Thirty Years' War.[13] In the same vein, Stacke claimed that the Great Elector had captured the leadership of German affairs from the Habsburgs, who turned out to have been cosmopolitan rulers incapable of defense or even of understanding German national interests. The Great Elector, in contrast, "reoriented German life toward the national soil" and began construction of the "new Empire," even though, given the political conditions of his time, this task had to be limited to the consolidation of his own power.[14]

Johann Jastrow offered other explanations of what was revolutionary about the Great Elector's policies and what made Prussia's interests "almost identical" to those of Germany, in contrast to all other German states of the seventeenth century and particularly the "mixture of Slovenes, Magyars, Czechs, and Germans governed by the emperor and conforming to Italian-Spanish etiquette." These interests were not represented by the "European congress," as he mockingly termed the Reichstag in Regensburg. The Hohenzollerns' secret was their consistent policy of undermining and subsequently removing all intermediary instances separating the throne from the people: the autonomous institutions of the estates—the aristocracy, the nobility, and the cities. The policy was successfully inaugurated by the Great Elector, who managed to unite his lands into a centralized state, breaking the powers of the local, traditionally autonomous provincial institutions.[15]

Oskar Jäger made a telling comparison between the Great Elector and Louis XIV and concluded, like Droysen (although employing other arguments), that despite some evident similarities the legacies of the two rulers were strikingly different. Notably, none of the German historians referred to the French king as "the Great," and some of them observed with satisfaction that none of the Habsburg rulers earned such a label either, whereas two of the Hohenzollerns did. In sharp contrast to Droysen, Jäger emphasized what was common to both Frederick William and Louis in their centralizing, fiscal, and military policies that marked a decisive departure from the characteristics of a feudal monarchy. The essential difference, he believed, rested upon the fact that Louis was "a limited bigot," whereas Frederick William was a tolerant and imaginative ruler. He welcomed the Huguenot refugees from France and actively opposed religious persecution in his realm. He was also a great modernizer, one who planned the founding of a Prussian colony in Africa and the establishment of a suprareligious academy of sciences in Berlin, but he eventually "had to admit that the age was yet not ready for this ideal."[16]

Eduard Heyck took a more nuanced stance toward the person of the Great Elector, while still respecting his legacy. In his view, Frederick William did not realize what the "Prussian mission" actually was. Heyck also considered him a poor political strategist who provoked a number of painful failures due to his own miscalculations. It is from the timely distance of centuries, Heyck argued, that one can see that the Great Elector's political course toward a unitary, centralized, and militaristic state had to result in Prussian leadership in the Empire. He was the one, the historian concluded, "whom we do not perceive as the conscious unifier of Germany, but the one who prepared Prussia for this mission by defining its direction, if not its goal."[17]

The work of the Great Elector was continued by his successors, most notably his grandson Frederick William I, who inherited the royal title of "King in Prussia" after his father Frederick and whose crown, as Jäger formulated it, was made of a much better metal than the Polish crown of the Saxon Wettins.[18] He earned his excellent reputation among the German historians by a series of administrative and fiscal reforms that resulted in the formation of a formidable army and bureaucracy. According to Ranke, Frederick William was the one who actually surpassed Louis XIV in the "systematic reorganization" of his state and the concentration of his personal power to an extent that had been unimaginable in the history of the Germanic and Romanic peoples before him.[19] It was under his rule that the Prussian monarchy became what the Protestant historians considered ideal, and clearly superior to the contemporary French or Austrian absolutist monarchies: a rationally organized hierarchical structure and, at its apex, a king, one whose will was no longer disturbed by any of the traditional groups of influencers, such as the local assemblies or aristocratic cliques, and who, last but not least, had a large army at his disposal.

In this context the superiority of the Prussian monarchy over the French and the Austrian ones rested upon its fully centralized and efficient administration, its control over the churches, and, remarkably, the minor importance of the royal court—a nest of intrigues and moral degeneration. Jäger emphasized that Frederick William was a hardworking and pious enemy of luxury and frivolity; the only public pleasures he allowed himself were beer and snuff, consumed "in a decent burgher-like manner," and hunting, which "in no way hampered his public obligations." The only regrettable decision during his reign, in the historian's opinion, was the persecution of Catholics that he undertook as a response to the policies of Emperor Charles, as well as the deportation of a number of Catholic priests, among them the philosopher Christian Wolff, of which "he will have been probably ashamed." The number of new taxes, Jäger argued, constituted a necessity, as the king was building up his army, and, in addition, the burden they imposed certainly did not exceed the troubles caused by the chaos of the various older fees and regulations. In consequence, he concluded, Prussia quickly achieved and surpassed the level of economic development accomplished by the populous and fertile Habsburg lands that had been impoverished by their miserable administration.[20]

However, the majority of Protestant historians claimed that the most remarkable consequence of the reforms that gave the Prussian monarchs virtually unlimited power in their realm was the bringing of "humanism and Enlightenment" to their subjects, inspiring their national consciousness and patriotism. This idea was perhaps most radically formulated by Jastrow, who argued that the principles of equality and liberty, which are typically associated with the French Revolution, had in fact first been implemented by Frederick William with the introduction of compulsory military service.[21] An analogous (and equally paradoxical, from today's perspective) argument was developed by Johannes Haller, who chose antiquity rather than modern France as his point of reference. His eventual goal was to reassure his readers that the popular prejudice against Prussia as a militaristic power was erroneous. What is wrongly interpreted as militarism, he declared, was in fact the idea of universal service to the state, which involved the ruler as the "first servant of the state" and all his subjects, as in ancient Sparta and Rome.[22] Prussia was the first modern state that reinvigorated this essentially democratic principle and, as Ranke also emphasized, the first truly German great power (i.e., the first German state capable of challenging the aggressive neighbors of the Empire).[23]

Finally, Prussia's role in German history was defined by Frederick the Great, who, as Droysen phrased it, gave the Germans what they so desperately needed and what they actually did not expect anymore: a sense of power and greatness, self-respect, and respect from the other nations in Europe. Moreover, Frederick made all Germans—and by Germans Droysen meant Protestants, as he considered German Catholics to be denationalized cosmopolitans—regard Prussia as their true representative.[24] This aspect was stressed by all the Protestant historians, who believed that Frederick's military triumphs inspired a patriotic upheaval throughout Germany, and emphasized that Germans from all corners of the Empire volunteered for his army. Prussia's German mission, which had been made possible by Frederick's predecessors on the Prussian throne, now became real, and so too did the unity of Prussian and German histories.

However, the history of Frederick's rule in a sense exceeds the framework of Brandenburg-Prussia's struggle to dominate Germany and substitute the Empire as the actual subject of German history. With Frederick's ascendance to the throne, the tendency to personalize German history in a heroic manner, and thus to reduce it to the actions of a few great rulers, culminates in an apologia that cannot be reduced to the "Prussia's German mission" scheme. If historians disagreed as to whether the Great Elector truly recognized the sense of this mission or whether his rule can be seen as a factor that made it materialize, in Frederick's case they unanimously claimed that his legacy was unique and incomparable to any other in German or even world history. In the narratives of Protestant historians, the Prussian monarchs were the most eminent, influential, and independent actors in German history, and their impact dwarfed that of any potential rival, except perhaps Martin Luther's, deep in the medieval age. All the others simply played their roles, dictated by their epoch, by circumstances, or by a destiny that can annihilate the noblest intentions. Barbarossa, Maximilian, and Charles V faced realities and developments they did not necessarily understand, and so their choices were debatable and their legacies ambiguous. The Prussian monarchs acted as if they knew the verdict of destiny, and they contributed, step by step, to its gradual fulfillment.

Frederick's rule, like the Reformation, was exceptional in its being autotelic: its purpose was to realize and demonstrate the personality, charisma, and talents of the monarch. As Haller phrased it, Frederick was simply a genius whose will changed the laws of history. A historian, he claims, can only describe the ruler's actions and express his admiration for him.[25] The purpose of his reign was, in addition to contributing to the rise of Prussia with the conquest of Silesia, simply to write an outstanding chapter in world history, full of fantastic victories, pride, and glory. Frederick was comparable only to Alexander the Great and Napoleon, whose legacies were more universal than national. Ranke claimed that his great achievement, which he shared with the greatest writers of the time, was providing Germans with inspiration and "liberating their spirit."[26] Of course these apologetics were also intended to make sense out of the bloody chaos of Frederick's wars, which were hard to glorify without referring to mysticism.

This accumulation of apologetic heroism in the narratives about Frederick, best seen in the fragments concerning details from his personal life, also had a magnificent narrative advantage: it prepared the readers for a bitter pill—his less talented successors. It was unthinkable that any of them could surpass his achievements, and so the audience was prepared for the idea of an inevitable decline. The perfect harmony between the state and its monarch, which had been achieved by Frederick William, was untenable under Frederick the Great, who, despite being the "first servant" of his state, in fact used it for his own purposes, even if they were simply to immortalize his name and garnered fame. Having achieved exceptional greatness under Frederick, Prussia was ripe for the political, moral, and military breakdown it was to suffer twenty years after his death due to the impact of another "genius"—Napoleon.

The criticism of the apologetics on behalf of Prussia and her alleged mission were timid and limited. One did not have to find the Hohenzollerns' genius amiable to recognize that they managed to build up a strong state with an efficient administration and powerful army. What the critics could note was that the rise of Prussia marked the end of German unity, or the illusions thereof, and doomed

Germany to a Prussian-Austrian antagonism. Some authors added bitter remarks on the Great Elector's alliance with France and Frederick the Great's love for French culture, which has been discussed in the previous chapter. Finally, some observed with melancholy that the latter's war had spilled a lot of German blood.

Finally, and perhaps paradoxically, the German historians agreed that Germans owed their national unification, particularly in the spiritual sense, to their archenemy, Napoleon. In the universal opinion of German historians, resistance against the tyrant, the brutality of the French occupation, the experience of conscription to the French army and participation in its campaigns, and, most importantly, the so-called liberation wars of 1813–15 all contributed to a fundamental change in German mentality and national self-consciousness. The time of corruption, demoralization, and apathy was replaced, as Heyck put it, with a "new epoch of increased political consciousness."[27]

However, controversies arose over the extent to which the epoch was actually exceptional and singular. Jastrow, for example, argued that a similar patriotic upheaval and sense of unity had already happened twice in German history: the first time in consequence of the joint effort to conquer and control Italy, and the second time during the Reformation. Nevertheless, in his view all these cases brought unsatisfactory results, as the national unification had deteriorated into cosmopolitanism: in the first instance the Germans had been seduced by the idea of their primacy in the Christian world and their role in defending it against Islam and in the Reformation because, although it gave birth to the national Protestant churches, it soon became internationalized and lost its uniquely German character. Finally, while the resistance against Napoleon indeed inspired a patriotic upheaval and hope for unification, what followed, however, was a German sacrifice for European peace and a great disappointment for the youthful national movement.[28] Germany remained divided and controlled in large part by the Habsburgs and other insufficiently nationalist rulers.

The Protestant admirers of Prussia insisted that the only situation in German history comparable to the wars of liberation had been the Reformation, when all German patriots had stood united against the enemy. Haller argued that the nation's resistance against the French was possible only because of Prussian military tradition, the remembrance of its past glories, and the German Protestants' universal belief in Prussia's primacy in Germany.[29] Obviously, this reasoning was supported by claims that it was Prussia that suffered most from the Napoleonic domination and that sacrificed the most during the liberation wars, when, as Stacke put it, "Prussia and Germany became almost identical." Finally, this argumentation was accompanied by apologetics concerning the reforms undertaken by Heinrich von Stein and Karl August von Hardenberg after the humiliation of Prussia in the years 1805–7, when "duty and honor were forgotten."[30] After Napoleon, the Germans were ready for unification, and Prussia alone among the German states was ready to respond to this longing.

The Renaissance in Decline

The Polish nineteenth-century historians neither idealized Polish monarchs, as their Protestant-German colleagues did when narrating the history of the Hohenzollerns, nor did they overestimate the impact of the Polish rulers on the course of their history. None of the Polish rulers ever earned the reputation of a genius in the way Frederick the Great did. The Polish monarchs' intentions and actions, if appreciated at all, were regularly confronted with the resistance of public opinion and other centers of power, which effectively hampered their impact. Generally speaking, this was the evaluation of the majority of the Polish historians as to the reigns of Stephen Bátory, Vladislaus, John Casimir of Vasa, and, most notably, John III Sobieski, particularly praised for his victories against the Ottomans. They lacked either determination, or diplomatic skills, or time to implement the necessary reforms that could have saved the Commonwealth from political and moral deterioration. Although a number of our historians, particularly those from the so-called Cracovian school, are typically labeled as monarchists, because they saw the only chance for survival of the Commonwealth in building up a strong monarchy, eventually none of the monarchs embodied these hopes.

Moreover, historians with radically different ideological approaches, such as Lelewel and Bobrzyński, accused Polish monarchs of having misunderstood public opinion and of failing to grasp the true challenges of their time. The reign of Stanislaus August Poniatowski was an exception in this context, as it typically provoked profound embarrassment on the part of authors commenting on his reign. Historians of various ideological backgrounds, such as Schmitt and Walerian Kalinka, agreed that "his ideas and intentions were amiable, but he lacked the necessary character."[31] They also argued that his political program was excellent, but he was personally unfit to implement it. Despite his "superior qualities of various kinds," as Bobrzyński noted, and his undeniable political talents, he was unable to overcome serious resistance, and when he confronted it, he wavered, despaired, or betrayed his original allies and goals.[32] Szujski concluded that "he was unfit for the dignity of the monarch . . . , and his miserable conduct compromised the ideas of progress he himself promoted."[33]

This ambivalence about Poniatowski as a ruler and his legacy have already been discussed in the previous chapter. Two comments, however, need to be added. First, it is precisely because Poniatowski was so exceptional, and because he was the last king and grand duke as well as the unintentional sexton of the Commonwealth, that the history of his rule stands apart from Polish history no less than Frederick the Great's did from German history. No matter how dear were the institutions of the Commonwealth to the Polish historians, the history they narrated was not intended to end with them, nor with the image of the king passively watching the Warsaw insurrection of 1794, or gloomily sledging toward St. Petersburg to meet his destiny two years later. It was inconceivable to the historians that Poland could come to an end with the demise of its king, so under Poniatowski's reign the history of the nation and that of the Commonwealth gradually separate. Second, the king's ambivalence, which paralyzed the historians' capacity to pass perfect judgments, corresponded to their inability to reach agreement concerning the legacy of his reign. As in the case of the union with Lithuania, their opinions on this subject were radically contradictory.

The history of the eighteenth-century reforms, culminating in the Constitution of May 1791, met with apologetic reactions on the part of numerous Polish authors, who presented them as a process of full and irreproachable recovery from all the maladies of the Commonwealth and as reforms that actually made Poland the most progressive European nation of the era. Generally speaking, this narrative has dominated Polish textbooks since the country regained its independence in 1918. And yet, among historians whose writings are analyzed in this book, a more critical and equivocal opinion has prevailed. They acknowledge that the obstacles were many and the success, relative. Smoleński, for example, noted that conservatism of the nobility and "the constitution imposed and guaranteed" by foreign powers to support the "Polish anarchy" eventually minimized the effects of the "ambitious and purposeful" reforms, at least until the so-called Great Parliament of 1788–92.[34]

The most apologetic interpretations of the reforms were authored by historians of the so-called neo-Romantic generation of the late nineteenth and early twentieth centuries. Their uncritical evaluation primarily concerned the long-term consequences of the reforms and what they saw as the suprahistorical value of the reforms and the constitution as a moral point of reference for Polish society under the partitions. They viewed the constitution as a monumental achievement worthy of being hailed as an inspiration for the oppressed nation, rather than as a product of particular historical processes in the second half of the eighteenth century, when the Commonwealth still existed. Thus, Stanisław Kutrzeba claimed that as a result of the reforms implemented by the Great Parliament, "Polish statehood equaled and surpassed the standards of other countries in continental Europe. . . . Having achieved the advantages of the absolutist government, she avoided its dark sides: the oppression of the population deprived of any rights and fully dependent on the caprices of the authorities."[35] What is striking in this interpretation is the abstract concept of the "quality of statehood." Indeed, the Constitution of May

1791 perfectly suited such evaluations, as it was hardly implemented in practice at all: the Russian invasion under the pretext of extinguishing "the revolution" began just a year after its acclamation. It remained a declaration, or perhaps a vision of the reformist party, rather than the foundation of any real political order, and thus it was more apt for analyses by legal than political or social historians.

Well aware of this, Oswald Balzer emphasized the conciliatory nature of the Constitution of May 1791, which had provoked some criticism from more progressive authors, such as Lelewel, who argued that it was a product of the "mutual compromise of the rivalrous forces": the aristocracy, the nobility, and the burghers. His lack of enthusiasm was clearly motivated by his uncompromising democratic principles, which made him complain that the agreement did not serve the needs of the peasants.[36] In addition, he suggested that the constitution must have been flawed, as it had not saved the country from foreign aggression. He labeled the peasants "the most powerful class" of society because he believed that securing their support was the only way to make the new political order durable. Balzer, in contrast, believed that the flaws of the constitution were actually the source of its potentially lasting and smooth functioning. "A constitution has to mirror given social and political conditions," he argued, "and this one had to adapt to the circumstances of the time too. And it was perfect exactly due to its flaws, because the quality of constitutions should not be estimated according to the excellence of their principles, but the means of executing them."[37]

This thesis, paradoxical as it was in case of a constitution that had no chance to prove its efficiency, was supported with the claim that despite its innovations, the constitution was actually rooted in the "national spirit." Balzer stressed with pride that "the introduction of a number of Western solutions, which might have been superior but had been unfamiliar to the Poles, was cautious and respected the conditions of Polish society." As a consequence, he viewed it as the cumulative effect of the reforms of the previous three decades and "a great social and political renaissance of the nation, which was to give it a new life. It was one of the rare moments with which nations are blessed by God, and which need to be remembered for ages."[38] The constitution was supposed to have been both conservative, as it saved what was valuable in the Polish tradition, and revolutionary, as it removed all its deficiencies (or was intended to do so).

Let us note once again the emphasis that this reasoning places on the future: it is the legacy of the Constitution of May 1791 for the generations to come, rather than its actual impact in the conditions of its time, that is most vigorously praised. The declining Commonwealth was just the background for this immortal achievement. Such was the color of the interpretation by Bobrzyński, who was highly critical of the Great Parliament and its policies but still claimed that the constitution "was an ambitiously progressive program that led the nation toward modern developments."[39] In short, the Constitution of May 1791 began a different story than that of the Commonwealth. Its significance was more symbolic than practical; its role was to inspire future generations rather than to save the state for which it was designed.

On the other hand, the neo-Romantic historians also tended to underestimate the political carelessness and inexperience of the constitution's founding fathers. In their view, and particularly according to Szymon Askenazy—probably the most popular Polish historian of the first decades of the twentieth century—it was not a risky political adventure at all. The failure of the 1792 campaign to defend it was the result of the lack of determination of some leading politicians (most notably the king) and a series of unfortunate coincidences, and not poor planning, unreliable alliances, or the lack of any serious military preparations by supporters of the reforms.[40] Patriotic pride did not allow them to consider whether it had been wise of the Great Parliament to show overt hostility toward Russia and to denounce its position as a *protectrice* of the status quo in Poland, as guaranteed by a number of earlier treaties, without having organized an army to defend this brave policy in advance.

The opinion of historians who viewed the eighteenth-century reforms not as a moral message for future generations but as the final stage in the history of the Commonwealth was much less enthusiastic. To be sure, the general trends were highly appreciated, and the "transformation of the moral and political conditions was emphasized."[41] So too were a number of administrative and political reforms, particularly those concerning the legal status of the cities, their economic situation, and political rights.[42] Nevertheless, several aspects of the reformist movement were subjected to considerable criticism. Historians of the so-called Warsaw school, whose attitude was quite apologetic in general, stressed the lack of political imagination among the reformers, who, as Smoleński put it, did not take steps "to secure the country against foreign intervention."[43] Korzon points out that the reformers neglected "the two most important and urgent issues: the establishment of a strong central government, and a powerful army." In his view these omissions, which proved fatal in the face of Russian aggression, were consequences of the traditional distrust of the central government, new taxes, and public debt.[44]

The Cracovian historians, Kalinka and Bobrzyński, were quite enthusiastic about the initial phase of the reforms, initiated after the first partition in 1772 under the auspices of the newly established Permanent Council—the first modern government in Polish history. At that time, Kalinka argued, "the country received all administrative institutions that are indispensable for a modern state."[45] That, Bobrzyński added, marked relative progress "in comparison with the devastating anarchy and decline of the former period."[46] However, their opinion regarding the activities of the Great Parliament of 1788–92, popularly considered the splendid coronation of the movement's aspirations, was openly critical. "The traditional hatred against the king and the government" motivated the parliament to remove the Permanent Council, which had been compromised by the "painful and humiliating" Russian influence but was, after all, the only government Poland had. The parliament was also obsessed with the idea of limiting the king's prerogatives and thus postponed the reorganization of the army, viewing it as a potential tool of royal power. Finally, the parliament's activities, as Kalinka and Bobrzyński saw them, were "astonishingly naïve in international matters."[47] In addition, its sessions were dominated by lengthy, chaotic, and inefficient debates and the spectacle of vain speeches "whose direct consequences were of no avail, or indeed negative for the country."[48]

Having demonstrated the nature of the problems facing the country, they claimed that the idealized "national awakening" and alleged "transformation of the nobility" mentality were superficial and incomplete. "The first partition," Bobrzyński argued, "shocking as it was, had limited impact on the nation's moral and political views. The past was not abandoned at once." In his opinion the much-admired activities of the National Commission for Education also had theirs flaws: "it improved the moral and intellectual standards but did not inspire the political sense of the Poles, which had been ruined for centuries."[49] Kalinka believed that Polish society of the era fell apart and then split into two separate groups. The larger group was dominated "by the traditional apathy and anarchic instincts, and the lack of healthy political concepts and patriotism," whereas the other—the new generation, being a product of the National Commission's schools—was characterized by "a noble and immature patriotism."[50] Still, a closer look at Kalinka's narrative regarding the Great Parliament indicates that he actually found many traditional shortcomings of the Polish nobility in the young generation as well.

Clearly, these critiques, though insightful, were based on two assumptions that were not fully consistent. First, they rejected the apologetic approach that saw the entire period of 1772–92 as one that featured a total transformation of society and the country, basically removing all the flaws and defects of the old political order, and that presented the Constitution of May 1791 as the beginning of an entirely new political entity. Such an interpretation ignored a number of facts, and, more importantly, it was simply ahistorical, as societies do not abandon their past so easily. And yet, what the Cracovian historians criticized about the Polish Enlightenment was exactly that such a transformation did not occur. The reformers, they believed, aimed at an undeniable improvement of the old political order and the mentality it had produced: the noble democracy was to be cured of its anarchist elements, and the noble liberty was to embrace other strata of the society. Generally speaking, this was in line with the traditional ideal of the Polish nobility of building a perfect republic and had little to do with the absolutist *raison d'*état, in which the central government aimed at controlling the population and levying taxes in order to sustain an army large enough to confront potential rivals. The Cracovian historians believed that the articles of the 1791 constitution might well have been beneficial, but they could not ignore the fact that the deputies to the Great Parliament had spent four years discussing numerous minor political arrangements and compromises while the Russian and Prussian armies were assembling across the borders. And this ran against the famous *bon mot* of a Romantic poet: "It is no time to care for the roses when the forest is burning."

Finally, let us take a look at the unique opinion of Joachim Lelewel, who heavily criticized the Great Parliament and the Constitution of May 1791 using radically different premises as his point of departure. Eventually Lelewel, a historian who specialized in the medieval age and referred mostly to secondary sources when writing about recent developments, hesitated on the subject and gave an enthusiastic account of the eighteenth-century reforms in his book on Stanislaus Poniatowski's reign. However, in his 1828 *An Image of Polish History*, he took a radically different position, one based on his admiration for the alleged ancient virtues and values of the Polish nobility. Although he appreciated the idea of sharing the political and economic privileges of the nobility with the burghers, as well as the disputed effort to "get rid of the shameful foreign impact," the political arrangements set forth in the constitution deeply disappointed him. The hereditary throne, voting by majority rather than acclamation, the limitation of the prerogatives of the local diet members, royal authority over the military, and finally the revocation of the electoral rights of the poorest nobles—in all this he saw a horrendous subversion of what he considered the most precious achievements of previous generations, originating in the primordial Slavic values. In sharp contrast to all other authors whose writings have been analyzed in this book, Lelewel, the most prominent historian of the Romantic generation, did not regard the Constitution of May 1791 as a (potential or actual) abandonment of the vices of the noble democracy. Neither did he consider the reformers as naïve idealists with little practical sense. In his opinion, the new political order that the constitution postulated but never created was simply an aberration and a denial of what was unique and admirable in the Polish historical legacy. If Poland broke down, it was no coincidence that it happened exactly at the time the nation denied its most precious values.[51]

CONCLUSION

It is commonly acknowledged that nineteenth-century historians, and particularly central European ones, were nationalists. The terms "nationalism" and "nation" are so ubiquitous in the modern literature on the problem that one may get confused regarding their actual analytical sense: they refer to the ideological attitudes, methodological approaches, and rhetorical strategies of historians of the time, who indeed constantly appealed to the national sentiments of their readers. As far as ideology is concerned, nationalism, even though it certainly dominated the picture, is clearly a term employed too broadly and one that suggests an all too easy answer to the problem of the multiplicity of contemporary political sentiments. The nineteenth-century historians' views of what the nation ought to be like (or more precisely, what *their* nation ought to be like) were certainly too multifaceted, complicated, and contradictory to be embraced in one word.

If we regard two fundamental concepts—that of the nation as the only legitimate source of sovereignty, and that of a nation's inherent antipathy toward other nations—we can see that our historians' opinions and beliefs varied significantly in this respect (and were often incoherent). Few of them combined these two ideas and worshiped the nakedly chauvinist version of nationalism, based on the idea of the national interests and the "my country, right or wrong" principle. In the end, however, their nationalism, vehement as it was, was clearly mitigated by a number of other concepts: religion and Providence, civilization and culture, liberty and tolerance, or—in the German case—loyalty to the dynasty. Of course, one could argue that whatever other ideas these historians valued, they were just ornaments, and the result was easily predictable: they saw their nation as their embodiment and employed all other values as rhetorical weapons for the national cause. This would not be entirely wrong, but I believe it would be fairer to say they tried to combine two or more loyalties. One cannot be sure that Johann Gustav Droysen would have written his apologetics for Prussia if it had represented the Catholic cause, or that Joachim Lelewel would have been so sentimental about the Commonwealth if he had not been a democrat.

I also suppose that one of the main differences between historians of the nineteenth and the twenty-first centuries is that the former were in principle openly, unscrupulously, and manifestly proud of their origins, whether in nationality, confession, or the noble *von* implying a warrior (or an ambitious merchant) ancestor. The purpose of writing history was eventually to strengthen, rather than to question, the intuitive idea of ancestry, and in this sense it was indeed a nation-building project. However, one consequence of this attitude taken by the majority of our historians was their half-conscious elitism. Even though they saw continuity between the semimythical ancestors throughout the ages and the modern Germans and Poles as representatives of one cultural-political community, the nation—the axis of this continuity—was actually thin, or even symbolic. There were decades, or perhaps centuries, of national history in which there was scarcely anyone who represented what being a German or a Pole ought to have been according to a given author. Scarcely any of our historians considered the peasants of past ages to have been true Germans or Poles. On the other hand, few of them denied the right of outstanding individuals of foreign origin to become part of the nation, if only he or she embraced the values Germany and Poland represented.

Methodologically, all our historians were devout nationalists, as they wrote about the nation and for the nation. However, methodological limitations made the majority of our authors identify the subject of their national histories with the political-territorial frameworks of the Holy Empire and the Poland-Lithuania Commonwealth, respectively. In the nineteenth century German historians still cared little for the ethnic Germans of Transylvania or the Baltics, and Polish historians adopted the same attitude toward the Poles of Silesia and Pomerania, since both regions ceased to be parts of the Kingdom of Poland after its rebirth around 1300. In their view the nation was inseparable from the political institutions that embodied it. It was not the masses of peasants—who were supposed to work hard and sing cheerful songs like all other peasants—but the political constitution and national mentality that determined the nation's uniqueness, even though those aspects were believed to have been products of the "national character." In fact the national character was reconstructed from the political institutions and the culture they shaped. The majority of our historians realized it had been the functioning of institutions that formed the political culture they labeled as the "life of the nation," and yet at the same time they believed there was a sort of national spirit that existed independently, as a factor that was in dialogue with all material and ideological factors determining the course of national history.

Seen as a part of the nation-building project, all the efforts of our historians may be viewed as a campaign to construct the image of a "respectable nation." As discussed in the introduction, such an image had to involve some standard, some internationally recognizable ingredients. A respectable nation must have had a continuous history reaching as far into the past as possible. A semimythical original epoch, in which indigenous virtues flourished, was indispensable. It must have contributed to the progress of Western civilization with a number of constitutional, spiritual, and military achievements that were comparable with those of other nations and, in a way, superior to them. A number of perfidious foreign enemies, forming a powerful military threat and stubbornly conspiring for the ruination of the original harmony of the native society, was obligatory. Corrupted and arrogant aristocrats, decadent monarchs, their greedy sycophants and mistresses, and diabolical advisors (preferably Jesuit), filled up the necessary list of internal troublemakers. A sort of historical mission or destiny, conducted in the name of Providence or civilization and carrying heavy costs, was highly recommended.

However, as I have tried to demonstrate, German and Polish histories were more complicated than that, because of the sense of loss and failure that our historians had to deal with. This is the moment to reconsider the national exceptionalism they proclaimed, as well as the limitations of the parallels between them which this book has explored.

Truth and Method

Perhaps the most striking aspect of the narratives of our historians is the ambiguous status of the past they represent: a past that is both irretrievable and, at the same time, intimately related to the present by a number of continuities that shape the subject of national history—the idea of the "timeless nation" itself. A number of factors that were considered to have determined its nature were traced back to remarkably distant epochs; the national character was believed to have been formed at the beginning of the nation's "story" or even to have preceded it. For example, the national mission was dated back to the time of the Saxon emperors in the German case, and to Bolesław, the first king of Poland, in the Polish case. Despite our historians' sensitivity toward the unique standards and realities of past epochs, the nature of their relationship to the present in this respect was not genetic and cannot be reduced to a genetic explanation: it was a true continuity of essentially identical phenomena, which took different forms in different circumstances. To be sure, our historians emphasized that the actions of the past agents they discussed and analyzed were determined by the realities and mentality of their own time. Nonetheless, they expected them to meet the standards they regarded as timeless and to pursue objectives and policies that did not belong to any particular epoch (although in fact they may have originated in the nineteenth-century imagination). One can observe this tendency in, for example, the investigations of German historians into the problem of national consciousness in the past. Many of them claim that the German nation still did not exist in the eighteenth century, as the Germans of that time lacked any sense of national unity. At the same time, however, all the hallmarks of national consciousness, both during that time and in earlier epochs, are carefully noted as indicators of the processes that would appear in the future. The principle, as one of our historians claimed, was to trace the past developments that lead to the present. As a consequence, the past agents appear as tragic figures, trapped by the intellectual limitations of their time but still expected to meet the expectations of a future they could not imagine.

Most nineteenth-century historians were aware of the questionable nature of this kind of reasoning. The dilemma was most famously exposed in the so-called Sybel-Ficker controversy concerning the policies of the medieval emperors. Sybel, perhaps provocatively but still seriously, advocated the idea of evaluating past events and characters from the point of view of the historian's own values and standards, as he believed that the historian's role is to discover universal principles applicable to all epochs. The result of the debate that followed was inconclusive. Sybel's radical, or perhaps too open, attitude made his position vulnerable to attacks emphasizing that the historian is precisely the person who cannot simply ignore past realities and mentalities in the name of his or her own ideological principles. On the other hand, Sybel's principles were dear to many a German historian of his time, and his claims, although compromised by charges of being unprofessional, were still popularly accepted, albeit in a less overt form.

The most complex criticism of this kind of approach, which is called presentism, was formulated seventy years later by Herbert Butterfield in his book *The Whig Interpretation of History*, which discussed the dominant views on British history in the nineteenth and early twentieth centuries. What Butterfield criticized was the "pathetic fallacy" in "the practice of abstracting things from their historical context and judging them apart from their context—estimating them and organizing the historical story by a system of direct references to the present." The idea behind the practice that Butterfield criticized was to demonstrate that Whigs and Protestants were "perennial allies" of progress and liberty, "while Catholics and Tories have perpetually formed obstruction" against these values. The result, which Butterfield emphasized, was the "overdramatization" of history, which artificially stressed differences between past agents, such as Protestants and Catholics, and minimized differences between them and us, their heirs.[1]

Butterfield's criticism, undertaken in the name of impartiality and true historical understanding, may seem readily applicable to the works of our German and Polish historians. However, one serious caveat needs to be made. In sharp contrast to the British Whig historians (or, say, the French liberal historians), our German and Polish historians, except for the representatives of the Borussian school, did not see their favorite principles marching victoriously throughout the ages. There was no timeless principle they could worship that organized the past developments. Quite to the contrary, history disturbed the progress of their ideals many a time, and the overall results for the Germans before 1871, and the Poles before

1918, were highly unsatisfactory. Of course, this was no reason for them to revisit their principles. Their main ideological and interpretive goal was rather to identify the causes that prevented these principles from successfully organizing the course of each respective national history, as well as determining those who were to blame for this failure.

Another common solution adopted to mitigate the sense of frustration and disappointment that characterized the main body of our historians' narratives was great numbers of counterfactual hypotheses and scenarios. Their image of history was full of "turning points" that led to a division of the respective national histories into epochs when everything was still going right and the undesirable tendencies were still controllable and reversible versus those when the final catastrophe was unavoidable. These turning points provided fertile soil for departures into counterfactual scenarios that *could have* reversed the undesirable developments. If only the national dynasties had not died out; if only the emperors had abandoned their theocratic policies or converted to Protestantism; if only an agreement with the Cossacks could have been reached, or if Gustav Adolph had lived longer; if only Ducal Prussia had been reunited with Royal Prussia before the Hohenzollerns managed to get their rule firmly established in the province; if only Sigismund III of Vasa had given up his fatal dream of reconquering Sweden—German and Polish historical narratives are full of Pyrrhic victories of the imagination, departures from the past as it actually was. This certainly makes our discourse seem more intriguing and equivocal than the Whig-like interpretation of history, although counterfactual scenarios are in principle no less teleological than the "fallacy" of the constant rise and development of progress and liberty. They are not based on a reconsideration of what was actually probable in given circumstances but on what would have been desirable from the point of view of their authors. As a matter of fact, the idea of turning points or decisive moments, apart from its narrative and rhetoric potential, is itself closely related to counterfactual theorizing and, therefore, wishful thinking. It is based on the assumption that things might have gone very differently, which may seem imaginative and ambitious, but what it eventually offers is melancholy or resentment, which inevitably appears as soon as we realize things did not turn out that way. If you need an inspiring example, consider the idea, advocated by some unorthodox conservatives, that the Roman Empire might have survived till our times had Julian the Apostate lived longer and managed to suppress Christianity.

It may seem that the ideas of national unity and efficient government—the two missing factors deemed to explain the fall of the Empire and the Commonwealth, respectively, that is, preventing them from evolving into "normal" nation-states— were broad enough for our historians to rise above ideological divisions and party affiliations. One may indeed see this approach in some of the counterfactual hypotheses they formulated: that it would have been better for the unity of the Empire if any one of the parties involved in the religious conflicts of the sixteenth and seventeenth centuries had prevailed or that, since the Polish-Lithuanian nobility hated the idea of monarchical power so much, it would have been desirable to have had it limited, if only the parliament had been capable of governing the Commonwealth efficiently. However, it was more common for our historians to stubbornly defend their positions throughout the centuries: the anti-Catholic and anti-Habsburg one in Germany, or the republican or monarchical one in Poland. Obviously, the dogma pursued most assiduously proclaimed the poisonous impact of foreigners and foreign culture and the perfect character of the original national virtues, which were under constant attack from cosmopolitanism, decadence, and moral corruption. In sharp contrast to the optimistic interpretations of the past based on a belief in the constancy of progress, the incessant topicality of national history in Germany and Poland was bidirectional and depressing: on one hand, it was about the continuity of the strenuous struggle for implementation of timeless political and moral ideals and, on the other, it was about the alarming if monotonous repetition of failures of the representatives of those ideals.

Therefore, the problem of an unbiased, impartial knowledge and approach, which Butterfield and the majority of modern theoreticians of history regarded as the actual objective of history, was of relatively little importance for our historians. Leopold von Ranke, who was no less biased than a number of his colleagues in his actual interpretations, was quite exceptional in his declarations that historians should just narrate history "as it actually was," leaving "a higher standpoint" for philosophers, and that the only tendency they should yield to is that of "total non-tendentiousness."[2] The majority of historians viewed their craft as a service to their country and nation.

Moreover, it was popularly believed that history was predestined for this cause like no other field of scholarship. As Karl Rotteck argued, "Only history can shape a reasonable and lively public opinion, and provide it with practical aims," because "it is most gifted for the guidance of all who love their country and liberty, which are invariably interrelated."[3] A number of our historians, such as Droysen or Józef Szujski, as discussed in chapter 3, openly declared that the goal of historians is to decipher the decrees of Providence.[4] Indeed, some authors emphasized that this idea was inherent in the historicist paradigm: the historian's task was, as Jörn Rüsen defined Ranke's self-image, "a rational service to God."[5] This task and service included working for the particular brand of patriotism, morality, and political ideology that was dear to the given author, as well as identifying and demonizing the mistakes and misconceptions of the past.

To be sure, there was enough room for professionalism, methodological rigidity, and factual accuracy in this scheme. Service to the nation and professional standards were viewed as interrelated: the search for the truth was a patriotic activity, for it made it possible to develop a credible diagnosis of national maladies. Such was the essence of the subsequent generational conflicts between the Polish schools of history. The so-called Cracovian school attacked Romantic historiography under the banner of professionalism and their "scientific methods." Indeed, the Cracovian historians' approach to their sources, and to quantifiable methods, was certainly more advanced than that of some of their older colleagues. However, the idea behind their attack on the older generation was to reveal the true causes of the decline and fall of the Commonwealth, which the Romantic historians could not see because they were blinded by the "republican-revolutionary" doctrine, which, as Michał Bobrzyński formulated it, "had fatal results for our national work," that is, for the political awakening of the nation.[6] The Cracovian historians were in turn criticized by their younger colleagues, typically known as adherents of the Varsovian school of history, for their lack of professionalism. They were alleged to have overemphasized political and constitutional history and neglected social history in their analyses of the causes of the decline of the Commonwealth. However, this criticism was again anchored in truly pedagogical reasoning: the Cracovian school historians' conclusions were as methodologically imperfect as they were discouraging for the oppressed, disoriented nation. The actual reason for this criticism was the alleged "pessimism" of the Cracovian historians, who did not stress the bright sides of the national history enough, thus disappointing readers who longed for past greatness and glory. "It would be more reasonable," Władysław Smoleński argued, "to focus on the moral legacy of the nation that saved its existence and culture, instead of exploring all aspects of its downfall."[7] In other words, the alleged methodological shortcomings of the Cracovian historians were of secondary importance, even though emphasizing them was rhetorically useful; it was their ideological fallacy that truly mattered for their critics.

Analogical motifs inspired the historians of the Borussian school. As Ludwig Häusser claimed in 1841, its goal was to promote "vital history," as opposed to the democratic-liberal historians, who engaged in dilettantism and had an inclination for moralizing, and unlike Ranke and other narrow professionals, who were obsessed with accuracy, precision, and archival investigations. Fifteen years later, the same arguments were repeated by Sybel, who accused Ranke of legitimizing the contemporary political status quo—because of his refusal to insert history in political conflicts—and criticized the liberals for being too idealistic. In Sybel's view, the latter position was represented by Schlosser, whose popularity irritated him and who, Sybel declared, "will be totally forgotten as soon as Germans acquire an appropriate approach to their state."[8] Again, methodology was regarded as a way of obtaining the ideologically desirable results, and being biased was seen as a necessary prerequisite of writing history.

The idea of an ideologically autonomous historical inquiry, discovering the past for its own sake and independent of contemporary sociopolitical realities, became the subject of the famous *Methodenstreit* in the last decade of the nineteenth century. In this dispute over methods in 1896, Karl Lamprecht attacked Ranke and his legacy for his alleged personal bias and his metaphysical assumptions, which had more to do with religion and individual values than with a critical and unprejudiced analysis of sources. This provoked a fierce controversy among German historians, in which Lamprecht remained isolated and his postulates were rejected by the majority of his colleagues. The opinion prevailed that history cannot and indeed should not be isolated from politics or, no less importantly, from metaphysics, which is necessary for historical understanding.[9] As Friedrich Meinecke formulated it, "The metaphysical-transcendental origins of Ranke's ideas are located much deeper than Lamprecht can imagine: it is life itself that springs from them."[10]

Of course—as I hope has been demonstrated in the previous chapters of this book—Lamprecht's own historical narrative hardly met his ideal of unprejudiced and unbiased historical inquiry. Neither did that of his younger colleague Max Lenz, who also believed that he approached the past without any preliminary assumptions yet still took pride in the fact that the University of Berlin, where he taught, was "a spiritual regiment of the House of Hohenzollern."[11] The distinction made by Wacław Sobieski in his 1912 essay "History and Legend" seems equally disingenuous, as he claimed that history, in contrast to legend, "respects only the truth, and not beauty [and] seeks the truth exclusively, regardless of the impact it may have on popular morality."[12] This is not to say that nineteenth-century historians were in principle any more prejudiced and politically oriented than their successors. If there is any conclusion to be drawn from this brief overview, it is rather that the historians' bias, and their striving for ideological (or, as they would probably have said it, moral) impact can clearly be seen in their narratives regardless of their theoretical declarations. On the other hand, it can also surely be claimed that the growing emphasis on professionalism and critical analysis of sources did change the rhetorical strategies of our historians in the course of the nineteenth century. Over time, the way they argued became more and more distinctively historical and presented more and more facts, numbers, and technical concepts. The political message, however, was still there, clearly visible for all those who wished to see it.

However, this conclusion deserves one caveat. The narratives analyzed in this book are invariably syntheses of national history or essays concerning general and controversial topics. This kind of writing dominated the historical discourses in Germany and Poland for the major part of the nineteenth century. Nevertheless, over time a growing number of specialized monograph studies in local, economic, and cultural history were published. Obviously, these kinds of studies rarely found their way to the general public, but they certainly changed the way syntheses of national history were written. The authors of such synthetic studies had more and more specialized studies at their disposal and did not need to rely upon their own research. Some authors believe that by the turn of the twentieth century a new epoch had begun in the history of historiography in both countries: one of more detailed, monographic studies and of historical subdisciplines, which were to replace grand narratives and political history.[13]

Unfortunately, in this work I was unable to represent, let alone to cover, the entire variety of historical production in the two countries before World War I. Moreover, my choice of the texts analyzed in this book does not include the era's growing number of studies that focused on the more "recent" developments in German and Polish history, that is, after the fall of the Empire and the Commonwealth. Still, I believe that the analysis of the texts included allows for the conclusion that interest in political history, as well as the perceived need for grand narratives that presented a holistic image of the national past, was not fading at all in the last decades before the Great War. The humiliation of Germany and the independence of Poland brought about by the war provided a new and powerful impetus for this interest, which calls for a separate study.

Indeed, a shift toward a more nationalist, triumphant, mystical, and—in the German case—racist synthesis of the national history may certainly be observed in the first years of the twentieth century. The most illustrative example of this tendency was the program of the radically nationalist *Alldeutscher Verband*, supporting both German imperialism and *völkisch* nationalism. Among our historians, Felix Dahn, Karl Lamprecht, and Eduard Heyck joined this organization, becoming colleagues of Max Weber, Georg von Below, and Heinrich von Treitschke's most famous student, Dietrich Schäfer. As one of the authors of the organization's journal, *Alldeutsche Blätter*, argued, the new goal of twentieth-century German historians ought to be "the cognitive and political Germanization, and the strengthening of Germandom and German consciousness."[14] This fascination with German might, and a new racist redefinition of German identity, as projected onto national history by the generation that grew up in the unified German Empire, brings about the true end to our German-Polish parallel in both nations' images of their past, which was again confirmed by the reconfiguration of perspectives in 1918.

The Scholarly Battle of Königgrätz

The comparative approach adopted by this book prefers synchronic over diachronic analyses of the nineteenth-century German and Polish historical narratives. Although I tried to signal some aspects of the dynamics of both approaches to national history, some of them certainly remained underemphasized. One of them was the profound impact of the unification of Germany, the establishment of the new German Empire, and the chauvinist enthusiasm that followed.

This change may be represented by the events that accompanied the death of Georg Gottfried Gervinus, author of the pioneering *History of the National German Literature*. Gervinus was a member of the "Göttingen seven"—a group of professors expelled from the University of Göttingen because of their protest against the unconstitutional policies of the prince of Hannover; he was a member of the 1848 Frankfurt Parliament and vehemently opposed to Bismarck and the Borussian historians. He remained an "old-fashioned liberal" until his death in March 1871 or, more precisely, posthumously as well, as his last polemics reached his Leipzig publisher after his death. During his funeral, as his biographer Jonathan F. Wagner informs us, any mention of political controversies surrounding his activities was tactfully omitted. He received his portion of patriotic outrage, however, in the obituaries. According to Wagner, the elderly Ranke was the most merciful, simply suggesting that "recent developments" had surpassed him: he was unable to grasp the greatness of Bismarck's achievement. His other colleagues attacked him more openly. Georg Besseler reminded readers that Gervinus had been a man to whom the whole of Germany listened carefully before he fell into oblivion, whereas Richard Grosche claimed that "an abyss" grew between Gervinus and the reality of German history.[15] After the German victories at Königgrätz and Sedan, there was no more room for any variety in attitudes toward national history. German patriotic opinion gave its verdict: the Borussian historians were right, and their opponents were wrong (even if they were right in some details).

The Borussian school emerged triumphant in the contest for the interpretation of national history, reaching a status close to that enjoyed by the Whig interpretation in Britain.[16] The whole of German history was now seen as a path toward its unification by Hohenzollern Prussia, and the values it represented were projected far back into the past and viewed as factors that had paved the way for unification. Of course, there was still some room for discussion about the definition of truly German virtues; however, the preponderance of Prussia unequivocally indicated militarism and discipline plus bureaucracy and education as pillars of German society. What used to be the Borussian interpretation of German history at the end of the century merged with the Rankean approach to politics as a combination of *Geist und Macht*, and this truly national interpretation of history was gradually absorbing more and more elements of pan-German chauvinism. These tendencies reached their apogee in the writings of the so-called neo-Rankean historians, such as Max Lenz and Erich Marcks. The amalgamated approach to the national past may be symbolized by the latter's claim, expressed in his essay "Goethe and Bismarck," that the two great Germans' legacies were actually complementary and their essential goals identical.[17]

This process of pan-German standardization of the images of the national past in the decades preceding World War I often escapes the attention of modern historians. Except for the authors active in the socialist German Democratic Republic, who emphasized the combination of imperialist and racist tendencies in late Wilhelmine historical writing, post–World War II German specialists in the history of historiography have focused on the growing specialization of history at that time or on the number of great names: Max Weber, Karl Lamprecht, or Jakob Burckhardt. Quite to the contrary, contemporary historians—such as Eduard Fueter, Georg von Below, or Walter Goetz—have observed with satisfaction this evolution of historical discourse in Germany toward a unification of perspectives before the Great War. In their view, national history, having survived the period of turbulence and fierce conflicts before the unification of 1871, was rapidly achieving a state of "normalcy." As Goetz argued, the main controversies had been "silenced and solved," which opened the floor for an impartial and unbiased discussion based on the national compromise and the steady progress of research.[18]

What matters most, from the position this book takes, is that the point of origin for German national history changed. Germany was no longer frustrated and in search of its identity, because it had ceased to be disunited and incapable of building a national state of its own, so the pressure to explain these problems historically was radically reduced. To be sure, they did not disappear from the catalog of particularly German historical dilemmas. If there is any theoretical conclusion to this book, it is that historical discourse is like a snowball: moving down the hill of time, it absorbs elements of all discussions and controversies that once shaped it. No important historical question has ever been answered or any dilemma resolved, and the old ones, long buried under layers of fresher inquiries, are rediscovered when the snowball splits apart after hitting some wall, as happened in Germany in 1945. Still, after 1871 the snowball certainly changed direction: German historical discourse began evolving toward British or French standards, with the present day as the glorious culmination of the national history. This was in contrast to the Polish scheme, in which the culmination had taken place in the past and was expected to be resurrected once again in the future. The German strategy was no longer rebellious but legitimizing, for it seemed that German history ended satisfactorily. This was so, not because all its peculiarities and divergences from the "standard" Western way of development appeared to have straightened out but because the German "special way" was now considered the road to spectacular success. One might even argue that this enthusiasm was inflated by the fact that Bismarck's "solution to the German problem" came so late and was so unexpected, which infused German history with an exciting sense of drama. As it turned out, it was the future that was to be the source of German disappointment.

This evolution of the German attitude toward its national past may be symbolized by the history of Droysen's *History of Prussian Politics*. The famous historian worked on this project for thirty years, abandoning it a number of times for more urgent challenges, and finally left his magnum opus unfinished. The idea behind that project was for it to be an apologia for the "German mission of Prussia" or, as Dieter Hertz-Eichenrode termed it, "a scholarly battle of Königgrätz" that would eliminate Austria from the contest for primacy in Germany.[19] When Droysen began his work, he was deeply disappointed with Prussia's conciliatory attitude toward Austria and the results of the 1848–49 revolution, in which he participated as a parliamentary deputy. His frustration with politics at this time motivated him to engage in historical research, which he saw as a substitute for political activity or perhaps as the field in which the unfinished battle ought to be continued. His biographies typically emphasize that the reason for his ultimate failure to complete his *History of Prussian Politics* was simply its monumental size, as was the case with Ranke's *Universal History*, which the historian actually undertook at an advanced age.[20] However, taking into consideration Droysen's political motivations, it seems that the progress of his work might also have been hampered by actual political developments. Bismarck's astonishing successes surprised both his opponents and his adherents, and after the Battles of Königgrätz and Sedan had been won, the idea of conquering the minds of Germans and instilling in them the idea of Prussian primacy simply lost its relevance. Thus, it seems reasonable to assume that, after the German unification, Droysen, unable to abandon his project completely, focused on editing archival materials and bibliographical supplements to his work, providing it with an impressive stamp of professionalism and authority but adding little to its rhetorical potential.

One conclusion to this story would be that the interpretation of national history by Droysen and other Borussian historians was directly dictated by their political views, in other words, that it was the scholarly version of Bismarck's "blood and iron" policies. This in turn would take us to the standard critiques of German historicism, and its epistemological foundations, as an intellectual formation that idealized, or indeed idolized, state and power as God's instruments on earth—an idea that went back to Lutheran ethics, based on the epistle to the Romans by the Apostle Paul (13:1–7). Obviously, the nature of this criticism—apparently most profoundly formulated by Georg Iggers in *The German Conception of History*—after World War II was in line with other attempts to discover the intellectual roots of German militarism and Nazism, and it was more moral than epistemological. The most controversial idea that historians like Ranke or Droysen worshiped, and inherited after Hegel, was that God always supports the winners and thus the striving for political and military might in principle be moral, but only if crowned with success, which is viewed as divine sanction. Of course, Iggers and other authors also point out a number of logical inconsistencies in the historicist approach, for example, numerous exemptions from its own dogma of *Antinormativität* and *Antibegrifflichkeit* (non-normativity and non-conceptualism) for the sake of metaphysical idealization of the state, nation, and tradition.[21] Remarkably, analogous inconsistencies are emphasized by recent studies in order to *deny* the idea that historicism was a scholarly justification of militarism and authoritarianism.[22] Indeed, one might observe that the German historicist authors had it coming, for while their idolatry of the decrees of Providence made their interpretation of national history prevail after the unification of Germany under Prussian leadership in 1871, the catastrophe of German militarism and expansionism up to 1945 compromised it for generations.

Again, one more caveat needs to be made regarding the works analyzed in this book. Apart from the Borussian historians' dedication to certain epistemological and moral principles, their interpretation of German history was also determined by a number of professional or, if you like, factual factors. The main idea that animated German reconsiderations of their national history before 1871, regardless of the political preferences of their authors, was that the lamentable lack of national unity was a German tragedy, as well as the source of German historical exceptionalism. It was no wonder, then, that some authors turned their attention toward Prussia, the only German state that seemed to offer a solution to this problem, or at least the only solution other than the one offered by Austria, which was unacceptable for German Protestants because it was Catholic, cosmopolitan, and quite unpromising as far as the problem of actual unification was concerned. However, Hohenzollern Prussia was indeed a unique state in early modern Europe: professional historians could not deny that what made it exceptional was its militarism, expansionism, bureaucratic centralism, and diplomacy, as well as its revolutionary indifference toward traditional alliances, privileges, loyalties, and hierarchies within the Empire. Having chosen Prussia as their object of admiration, Borussian historians had no choice but to praise the Hohenzollerns' extraordinary striving for territorial expansion, their military successes, and, finally, their strategy of undermining the shaky structures of the Empire. Generally speaking, in doing so they did not depart from the standards of the academic historical writing of their time; quite to the contrary, some of them earned international fame for their accuracy, erudition, and innovative methods of research.

To be sure, there are moments in which the Borussian historians' apologetics for the Hohenzollerns must seem obsessive to us. For example, Treitschke purposefully limited his research to the Prussian archives in order to avoid dealing with documents that would present the Hohenzollerns' case unfavorably. One might also be astonished by Droysen's choice of Yorck von Wartenburg as his favorite national hero because of the general's decision to betray Napoleon immediately after the latter's first great failure in Russia. This was not radically different, however, from the practices of historians of all nationalities and ideological loyalties at that time (or perhaps in all times), who tended to justify and glorify in all circumstances the representatives of the cause they supported. The best one could expect from historians dedicated to their national cause, when they encountered moments in which their conationals breached some ethical standards, was a melancholic resignation and authorial accuracy, like the one present in the apocalyptic description of the bloody Polish victory over the Cossacks at Berestechko in 1651: "People forgot about their humanity, and everyone was murdered: the elderly, infants, and women."[23] The truly maleficent potential of the Borussian interpretation of history was hardly observable so long as it fought for a lost cause. It was only revealed after the unification of Germany, when its triumphant version became the official national interpretation of the past. So if there should be a general conclusion to this story, it would be that history writing may also result in an excessive triumphalism if its theses are paralleled by actual developments.

Trends, Typicality, and Anomalies

This book has illustrated a variety of examples of parallels between German and Polish attitudes toward their national histories. I believe it would make little sense to attempt a complete synthetical presentation of these parallels, because historical interpretations make sense only in a given context: rhetorical, ideological, and factual. To reach a satisfying conclusion, however, let us once again revisit some of the fundamental problems our historians encountered while narrating their interpretations of their respective national histories. One such problem was the contrast between the idea of national exceptionalness and some of the general trends or tendencies in European history—trends that were rarely perceived as historical laws by our authors but certainly possessed the power to set standards that were instrumental in making international comparisons. The nature of this contrast is in a way paradoxical, for it was commonly assumed that national histories are in principle exceptional and, at the same time, that they ought to correspond to these standards. Of course, some of our historians were aware that the two principles were barely reconcilable, but they still tried. Adam Szelągowski argued, "Having no criterion to assess the developments of national history, we compare it with others, with the entirety of universal developments. . . . The swerves from the general trends are regarded as anomalies, regression, or reaction, whereas the analogies should be considered as progress. . . . Nevertheless, one should also take into consideration the variations in a given historical process, and the individual character of all nations and races, which are not related to any general developments or progress."[24]

However, this approach also gave rise to a number of problems encountered by our historians while narrating their national histories. Some of them were caused by inner inconsistencies and some by the historians' resistance to evidence they had at their disposal. In contrast to Ranke's famous idea of *Primat der Aussenpolitik* (a focus on foreign policy and diplomacy), our historians' main interpretive efforts concerned internal political and constitutional developments, and their assessments in this respect were mostly determined by inclinations toward continual international comparisons. What preoccupied them when analyzing all stages of both German and Polish history was precisely the comparing of sociopolitical, institutional, and constitutional developments in the Empire and the Commonwealth and in other European countries, especially those of their powerful neighbors. Moreover, in sharp contrast to the respect the historians declared for the idea of national exceptionalism, these comparisons quite often worried them.

German historians were invariably worried that their country did not already follow the path of dynastic centralism that France, England, and Spain did in the time of the allegedly brilliant triumphs of the Empire, in the medieval era. When they discussed the late medieval and early modern periods, their comments in this regard became alarmist and were coupled with lamentable comparisons with Poland and Italy. Further unfavorable international comparisons followed with respect to the time of religious conflicts. Finally, these laments were replaced with triumphalism when the Great Elector of Brandenburg-Prussia entered the scene: the Prussian monarchs not only successfully selected the best from the foreign patterns and copied them but also surpassed other countries (particularly France and Austria) in building up a centralized, absolutist state. To be sure, voices could also be heard praising German exceptionalism, particularly the variety in German cultural life due to its political fragmentation. As was discussed in chapter 2, the expansion of the Empire was also praised for its alleged uniqueness. Over time, however, and especially after the unification of 1871, these opinions were effectively silenced by the standard interpretation, according to which German uniqueness had been a source of constant frustration, troubles, and, in the final analysis, had led to the downfall of the Empire.

Polish historians' opinions in this regard were manifestly more ambivalent. Many of our authors proudly emphasized the exceptional character of Poland's constitutional arrangements, particularly its alleged primacy in the universal striving toward the rights of the individual and democracy. In this case, however, the comparison was untimely: Poland-Lithuania was praised for its originality but not for its actual uniqueness; it was the triumph of democracy in the West that confirmed the genius of the Polish-Lithuanian experiment. However, the deficiencies of the political order of the Commonwealth, as revealed by the crisis of the seventeenth century, were univocally regarded as fatal in comparison to developments in the neighboring countries, which evolved in the opposite direction, that is, toward centralized, absolutist, and powerful monarchies. Eventually, the enthusiasm of the majority of Polish historians regarding the reforms of the Enlighten-ment, and especially the Constitution of May 1791, was replaced by a comparative approach. In the end, the Commonwealth was urged to abandon its wicked po-litical dogmas and join the family of healthy, well-organized, and well-governed countries. In the final analysis, Poland's exceptionalism was as much detested as it was praised by Polish historians, and the attempt to correct it in the Common-wealth's last hour was greeted with relief and ambiguously self-congratulatory re-marks, as if the country were safely returning from a dangerous expedition, only to die the following day.

One explanation for this trend may be similar to that offered by Arnaldo Momi-gliano on the analogous trends in Greco-Roman historical writings. Momigliano argues that when discussing the problems of the decadence and the fall of Empires, the ancient historians focused on constitutional factors, neglecting such aspects as wars and foreign invasions, because they considered the former to be rationally determined and the latter to be natural phenomena occurring randomly, like earth-quakes and tempests. Thus, constitutional arrangements belonged to history, and discussing them was viewed as intellectually and pedagogically inspiring. Violence was regarded as part of the natural order, and there was no point in informing an-cient readers that each country should expect an attack from its neighbors or ra-pacious barbarian intruders at any time.[25] Analogically, our nineteenth-century authors considered the rivalry and military clashes between states as obvious, and despite the fact that they devoted a great deal of space to narrative representations of such episodes, their analytical efforts focused on constitutional matters and the internal sociopolitical developments that shaped them. It is no coincidence that German historians abandoned these issues when narrating the history of the Empire after the Peace of Westphalia. They did so because of the opinion that the constitution of the Empire at that time had been determined by a fatal draw of the conflicted parties and foreign influences, and its evolution was no longer possible.

This leads us to the conclusion that our historians viewed the past primarily as a sphere of decisions and choices, thus relegating social, mental, and economic issues to the background of their image of the past. While it is true that this im-age evolved over the course of the nineteenth century—as economic and cultural history was gaining more attention and becoming more methodologically sophis-ticated—nevertheless the problem of the voluntary decisions of past agents and the historians' evaluation of them was never marginalized. They never ceased to constitute one of the main interpretive challenges for our authors, even though over time the number of factors that were considered to have been determinative of these decisions was growing, due to the availability of new evidence and meth-ods, as well as the existing interpretations that could not be ignored—making the problem of their assessment ever more complicated.

At the same time, the problem of the relationship of the two national histories to the standard European path of development that all countries were expected to follow, without it offending their own exceptionalness, was always seen in the context of relations with neighbors in their actual, diachronic development. Although following the mythical standard path was always desirable, copying the actual foreign patterns was regarded as suspicious, if not regrettable. As discussed in chapter 1, German and Polish historians idealized the earliest epochs of their respective national histories, when both national cultures were deemed to represent the ideal of pure originality, unpolluted by foreign influences, and mirroring the inherent virtues of the two races. However, in the process of the formation of state structures and fundamental political institutions, they were immediately faced with the foreign influences that unavoidably accompanied modernization, whether endogenic or imported. This problem appeared repeatedly in subsequent epochs. German historians unanimously sided with the medieval emperors in their conflicts against the papacy, while Joachim Lelewel and his followers passionately traced the alleged resistance of medieval Polish society to foreign feudal patterns. German historians were devastated by the scale of French cultural influences in their country, whereas Polish historians lamented the Jesuits' impact on the Commonwealth. The problem of expansion into the ethnically alien territories, as discussed in chapter 2, provoked fierce debates: Did it testify to the strength and vitality of the national political culture, or did it pervert the healthy original path of development and national character?

Membership in the Western cultural and political hemisphere, and the ongoing process of international cultural transfer it entailed, constituted a challenge to our historians. They constantly vacillated between the idea that each nation should follow its own way and find its own destiny, in concert with the splendid isolation in each nation's perfect condition that would allow it to cultivate its original virtues and values, versus the idea of competition and rivalry, which unavoidably involved transfers in actual history and comparisons in the historical narrative. The perfect solution to this dilemma, which preserved national pride and the idea of endogenous virtues without ignoring the fact of the ongoing transfers between the national culture and its neighbors, was to celebrate those cases of actual or alleged cultural exports or other achievements in which the national polity was supposed to represent the entire Western community. Thus, the Germans focused on the Reformation and the Poles on religious tolerance and the peaceful character of the Polish-Lithuanian union, and both the German and Polish historians emphasized their nations' contributions to rescuing Europe from the menace of Islam. Questions regarding the exportation of the Hohenzollern political model or that of Poland's noble democracy were not discussed in detail, even though the former was supposed to have surpassed the general European standards of enlightened absolutism and the latter to have left other countries behind in their longing for democracy.

Such interpretations may of course be viewed as emanations of the national complexes inherent in adjacent countries, whose historians are forced to negotiate their respect for the cultural trendsetters and recognition of the actual scale of foreign impact with their assertions of the superiority of their culture and their national pride. Again, in this respect the German-Polish parallel quickly evaporates in the decades after Bismarck accomplishes the unification, when Germany rapidly overcame its standing as a relatively poor and schizophrenic member of the European family, hesitating between Prussia and Austria, and became a new, self-proclaimed trendsetter, intoxicated with the sense of its newfound might. However, and no less importantly, the same tendencies may be viewed as inherent inconsistencies in the historicist paradigm that dominated nineteenth-century historical writing, caught between the ideals of exceptionality, national destiny, and repetitive reincarnations of the spirit of time.

As John Stuart Mill argued, there are two basic analytical reasons for making comparisons.[26] First, they may be used to emphasize the uniqueness of the case in question by contrasting it with an apparently analogous case or phenomenon and then demonstrating that the alleged analogy is actually false. This kind of argumentation, as Reinhart Koselleck observed, dangerously borders on the vain rhetoric of a stereotype, because of the temptation to contrast the object of comparison—particularly if the object is our beloved idea, character, or nation—against its simple antitheses, representing obviously different qualities.[27] The second comparative strategy aims at grasping certain general features, or typical patterns of behavior, that would remain unobservable if the analysis were limited to one case only, or if one were to search for the explanations from the context and particularities of only this case.[28] The disadvantage of this strategy is exactly the tendency to underemphasize the individual context, which may be disregarded if we focus on commonalities or regularities that in fact may be superficial or of secondary importance.

Inasmuch as this book has focused on analogies between two cases, demonstrating their wide range and substantial variety, I suppose it falls into the second ideal type of comparison. However, the fact that German and Polish historians narrated their respective national histories by employing a number of shared concepts, rhetorical devices, stereotypes, and arguments does not lead to a conclusion that their narrative and interpretive strategies were universal or typical for their time. As I have argued, they represented a common attitude toward the past, determined by their profound dissatisfaction with its ultimate outcome, and their main effort was directed toward explaining what they believed *ought not* to have happened or what should have gone differently. Thus, I suppose it would be reasonable to assume that the approach they represented might have been typical for the historical writing of those nations that, at a given moment in their history, were forced to make an analogous use of their past to question the status quo rather than to legitimize it. Unfortunately, I am not qualified to make claims beyond the fact that the nineteenth-century German and Polish national discourses were strikingly similar to each other in many respects. The question of whether they were essentially similar to other national discourses of that time awaits a separate study.

Of course, our German and Polish historians did much more than answer the question of what had gone wrong with the Empire and the Commonwealth, respectively. National history writing is part of the identity-building project, and the ability to think critically occupies a marginal position in building national identities. Clearly, our historians had to answer the question of who was to blame for the mistakes of the past, as well as what should have been done in order to avoid them in the future, but they were also supposed to identify sources of pride and satisfaction in national history, which are crucial for the process of constructing or, more precisely, constantly *reconstructing* national identities by rewriting and reinterpreting national histories. I suppose that our historians were not very unique in their claims for the originality and purity of their national cultures, the excellence of their national virtues, the exceptionalness of their nations' achievements, and the perfidy of their enemies. But still, in sharp contrast to the historians of happier nations, they had to be careful in their choice of the moments and characters they wished their readers to consider as sources of positive self-identification, for behind each battle won by their ancestors lay the painful presence of the disappointing finality, not very well hidden, and there were doubts as to whether each monarch or statesman of the past had served his national cause wisely or whether he had, in the final analysis, contributed to the country's troubles in the future.

The nineteenth century is popularly called the "age of history," and Jörn Rüsen rightly called it "the last religion of the educated."[29] That statement suggests the profundity of contemporary interest in history and its importance for self-identification. I am not inclined to speculate as to what kinds of subconscious needs our historians satisfied in the minds of their readers. Regarding their enthusiasm and indulgence for the contemporary custom of producing multivolume historical narratives, these needs must have been remarkable. This, however, is no longer the case, so now is the time to conclude this work.

TIMELINE

Poland / Commonwealth

Mid-tenth century	various Slavic tribes united under the Piast dynasty.
966	Mesco accepts Christianity; in 1025 his son Boleslaus is crowned the first king of Poland.
979–1034	series of wars against eastern German princes, occasionally supported by the Holy Empire.
1030s	popular rebellion, presumably antifeudal and anti-Christian, suppressed with the aid of the Empire.
1138–1300	political fragmentation under various Piast rulers.
1340s	Casimir the Great annexes Red Ruthenia.
1386	Poland united with the freshly baptized Lithuania under the Jagiellon dynasty.
1409–1466	Teutonic knights crushed in a series of wars; Royal Prussia reunited with Poland.
1505	parliament (the Sejm) secures its control over legislation and taxation.
1569	final union with Lithuania; the Commonwealth is established.
1572–1573	after the death of the last Jagiellon, the first constitution (Henrician Articles) regulates the election and prerogatives of monarchs and secures religious tolerance.
1605	first *rokosz*, or formal rebellion against the king.
1648–1665	Cossack, Swedish, Prussian, and Russian invasions devastate the Commonwealth.

1652	*liberum veto* first used in the parliament.
1683	John III Sobieski helps to save Vienna from the Ottoman invaders.
1699–1763	the Saxon dynasty; Poland-Lithuania, defeated by Sweden, becomes a Russian protectorate in 1717.
1763	Stanislaus Poniatowski, a protégé of Catherine II, elected to the throne; he initiates a program of enlightened reforms.
1772	first partition of the Commonwealth by Austria, Prussia, and Russia.
1788–92	Great Parliament and the Constitution of May 1791 overrun by the Confederation of Targowica and the Russian invasion.
1793–95	Kościuszko's uprising and the last two partitions.

Germany / Empire

843	Kingdom of East Franks emerges on the ruins of the Carolingian Empire; its throne becomes elective in 911.
962	Otto I of the Saxon dynasty crowned as emperor in Rome; the Kaiserzeit begins.
1024–1250	Salian and Staufen dynasties; the crusades, the peak of the Empire's territorial expansion and of its conflict with the papacy, followed by the period of internal conflicts and decline of the royal-imperial power.
1356–1512	formation of the political constitution and the main institutions of the Empire; adoption of the name Holy Roman Empire of the German Nation.
After 1452	Habsburgs monopolize the imperial throne; in 1516 they become kings of Spain and, in 1526–27, of Bohemia and Hungary.
1512–1555	Protestant Reformation and subsequent religious wars, ending with a truce between Catholics and Lutherans.
1618–1648	Thirty Years' War. The Peace of Westphalia makes the emperor's authority over the princes purely formal; Calvinism recognized as the third official religion of the Empire.

1650s	East Prussia emancipates itself from the formal sovereignty of Poland-Lithuania to fully combine with Brandenburg; it steadily develops into an absolutist monarchy.
1648–1766	Alsace and Lorraine gradually annexed by France; Habsburgs give up their claims for the Spanish throne in exchange for Naples, Milan, Sardinia, and the Spanish Netherlands.
1740–1763	wars between Prussia and Austria establish the Austro-Prussian dualism in Germany.
1792–1803	revolutionary France annexes the left bank of the Rhine; the number of the Empire's constituent territories is reduced.
1806	after the formation of the Confederation of the Rhine under Napoleon's domination, Emperor Francis declares the Holy Empire abolished.

Introduction

1. Tadeusz Cegielski, *Das Alte Reich und die erste Teilung Polens 1768–1774* (Stuttgart: Franz Steiner Verlag; Warszawa: PWN, 1988), 4–16.

2. Edmund Burke, *The Annual Register, or a View of the History, Politics, and Literature* (1773; London, 1784), 9; Karl Marx, *Secret Diplomatic History of the Eighteenth Century* (London: Swan Sonnenschein, 1895), 25; Edmund Sorel, *La question d'Orient au XVIIIe siècle: Le partage de Pologne et le traité de Kajnerdi* (Paris, 1889).

3. Antoine Guilland, *Modern Germany and Her Historians* (London: Jarrold and Sons, 1915), 191.

4. Michael G. Müller, "Republicanism versus Monarchy? Government by Estates in Poland-Lithuania and the Holy Roman Empire: Sixteenth to Eighteenth Centuries," in *Historical Concepts between Eastern and Western Europe*, ed. Manfred Hildemeier (New York: Berghahn Books, 2007), 36–47; *Zeitschrift für Ostmitteleuropaforschung* 53, no. 1 (2004) (for Bömelburg); Otto Hintze, *Staat und Verfassung: Gesammelte Abhandlungen zur allgemeinen Verfassungsgeschichte* (Göttingen: Vandenhoeck & Ruprecht, 1970); Cegielski, *Das Alte Reich*; Klaus Zernack, *Niemcy-Polska: Z dziejów trudnego dialogu historiograficznego* [Poland-Germany: History of the flawed historiographical dialogue], ed. H. Olszewski, trans. Łukasz Musiał (Poznań: Wyd. Poznańskie, 2006).

5. Joachim Whaley, *Germany and the Holy Roman Empire*, 2 vols. (Oxford: Oxford University Press, 2012), 2:xxiv. See also R. J. W. Evans, Michael Schaich, and Peter H. Wilson, eds., *The Holy Roman Empire, 1495–1806* (London: Oxford University Press, 2011); Hans Ottomeyer, Jutta Götzmann, Ansgar Reiss, Heinz Schilling, and Werner Heun, eds., *Heiliges Römisches Reich Deutscher Nation 962—1806: Altes Reich und neue Staaten 1495–1806*, 2 vols. (Dresden: Sandstein Verlag, 2006); Joachim Whaley, "The Old Reich in Modern Memory: Recent Controversies Concerning the Relevance of Early Modern German History," in *German Literature, History and the Nation*, ed. Christian Emden and David Midgley (Oxford: Peter Lang, 2004), 25–49.

6. Certeau wrote that historical interpretation is a construct "qui se donne le pouvoir de dire ce que l'autre signifié sans le savoir"—based on the interplay of citation and judgment. Michel de Certeau, *L'Écriture de l'histoire* (Paris: Gallimard, 1975), 111.

7. These include mainly the general histories of historiography, starting with G. P.

Gooch, *History and Historians in the Nineteenth Century* (London: Longmans, Green, 1913). For newer works, see Ernst Breisach, *Historiography: Ancient, Medieval, and Modern* (Chicago: University of Chicago Press, 1983); John Burrow, *A History of Histories* (New York: Allan Lane/Penguin Books, 2008); G. G. Iggers, Q. E. Wang, and S. Mukherjee, *A Global History of Modern Historiography* (New York: Routledge/Taylor & Francis, 2008); D. R. Woolf, *A Global History of History* (Cambridge: Cambridge University Press, 2011). Two recent multivolume, multiauthored works clearly aim at abandoning the national divisions: *The Oxford History of Historical Writing*, general editor Daniel Woolf, 5 vols. (Oxford: Oxford University Press, 2010–11); and *Writing the Nation: National Historiographies and the Making of Nation States in 19th and 20th Century Europe*, ed. Stefan Berger, Christoph Conrad, and Guy P. Marchal, 7 vols. (Basingstoke: Palgrave Macmillan, 2008–12). As far as monographs are concerned, a rare example of the comparative approach is Monika Baár, *Historians and Nationalism: East-Central Europe in the Nineteenth Century* (New York: Oxford University Press, 2010).

8. Hans Ulrich Thamer, "Das Heilige Römische Reich als politisches Argument im 19. und 20. Jahrhundert," in *Heiliges Römisches Reich Deutscher Nation 962 bis 1806: Essays*, ed. Hans Ottomeyer, Jutta Götzmann, Ansgar Reiss, Heinz Schilling, and Werner Heun (Dresden: Sandstein Verlag, 2006), 387.

9. Uwe Prüscher, "Reichsromantik: Erinnerungen an das Alte Reich zwischen den Freiheitskriegern von 1813–14 und den Revolutionen von 1848–49," in *Heiliges Römisches Reich Deutscher Nation 962 bis 1806*, ed. Ottomeyer et al., 320–22.

10. Michael G. Müller, "Koniec dwu republik: Rozbiory Polski i rozpad dawnej Rzeszy," in *Polacy i Niemcy: Historia, kultura, polityka*, ed. Andreas Lawaty and Hubert Orłowski (Poznań: Wyd. Poznańskie, 2003), 56–57.

11. Herbert Fisher, *The Medieval Empire* (London: Macmillan, 1898), 1:95–96.

12. Lutz Raphael and Ilaria Porciani, eds., *Atlas of European Historiography: The Making of a Profession, 1800–2005* (London: Palgrave Macmillan, 2010), 158–62.

13. Georg G. Iggers, "The Intellectual Foundations of Nineteenth-Century 'Scientific' History: The German Model," in *The Oxford History of Historical Writing*, vol. 4, ed. Stuart Macintyre, Juan Maiguashca, and Atilla Pók (Oxford: Oxford University Press, 2011), 41–58.

14. Zakrzewski quoted in Andrzej Feliks Grabski, "Die polnische und die deutsche Historiographie in die zweiten Hälfte des 19. Jahrhunderts," *Jahrbuch für Geschichte der sozialistischen Länder Europas* 32 (1988): 195.

15. Baár, *Historians and Nationalism*, 65 (original emphasis).

16. See Billie Melman, "Claiming the Nation's Past: The Invention of an Anglo-Saxon Tradition," *Journal of Contemporary History* 26, no. 3–4 (1991): 575–95.

17. Heinrich Leo, *Lehrbuch der Universalgeschichte*, 6 vols. (Halle: Eduard Anton, 1841–50), 2:591.

18. See Benedikt Stuchtey, "Literature, Liberty and the Life of the Nation: British

Historiography from Macaulay to Trevelyan"; and Ceri Crossley, "History as a Principle of Legitimation in France (1820–48)," both in *Writing National Histories: Western Europe since 1800*, ed. Stefan Berger, Mark Donovan, and Kevin Passmore, 30–46 and 49–56, respectively.

19. See Andrzej Feliks Grabski, *Dzieje historiografii*, with an introduction by Rafał Stobiecki (Poznań: Wyd. Poznańskie, 2003), 389–90.

20. Walter Goetz, *Die deutsche Geschichtsschreibung des letzten Jahrhunderts und die Nation* (Leipzig/Dresden: Teubner, 1919), 18–21; Günther List, "Historische Theorie und nationale Geschichte zwischen Frühliberalismus und Reischsgründung," in *Geschichtswissenschaft in Deutschland: Traditionelle Positionen und gegenwärtige Aufgaben*, ed. Bernd Faulenbach (München: Beck, 1974), 35–53.

21. See Andrzej Wierzbicki, *Historiografia polska doby romantyzmu* (Wrocław: Ossolineum, 1999), 375–80. For more on Lelewel, see Joan S. Skurnowicz, *Romantic Nationalism and Liberalism: Joachim Lelewel and the Polish National Idea* (New York: Columbia University Press, 1981); and Baár, *Historians and Nationalism*.

22. Andrzej Wierzbicki in his *Historiografia polska doby romantyzmu* includes the following among the epigones of Lelewel: W. A. Maciejewski, Adrian Krzyżanowski, Julian Bartoszewicza, Kazimierz Jarochowski, Władysław Syrokomla (Kondratowicz), and Walerian Koronowicz-Wróblewski.

23. See Grabski, "Die polnische und die deutsche Historiographie," 187–201.

24. See Andrzej F. Grabski, "Warszawska szkoła historyczna: Próba charakterystyki," in *Polska myśl filozoficzna i społeczna*, vol. 2, ed. Barbara Skarga (Warszawa: Książka i Wiedza, 1975), 456–534.

25. For more on historicism, see Ernst Troeltsch, *Historismus und seine Probleme* (Tübingen: Mohr, 1922), although this work is more theoretical consideration than historical analysis. See also Friedrich Meinecke, *Die Entstehung des Historismus*, 2 vols. (München: Oldenbourg, 1936); Friedrich Jaeger and Jörn Rüsen, *Geschichte des Historismus: Eine Einführung* (München: Beck, 1992); Annette Wittkau, *Historismus: Zur Geschichte des Begriffs und des Problems* (Göttingen: Vandenhoeck & Ruprecht, 1992); and Frederick C. Beiser, *The German Historicist Tradition* (New York: Oxford University Press, 2011).

26. Goetz, *Die deutsche Geschichtsschreibung des letzten Jahrhunderts und die Nation*, 10–14.

27. For the fullest recent synthesis of this process, see Ilaria Porciani and Jo Tollebeek, eds., *Setting the Standards: Institutions, Networks, and Communities of National Historiography* (Basingstoke: Palgrave Macmillan, 2012). This is the second work in the series Writing the Nation: National Historiographies and the Making of Nation States in 19th and 20th Century Europe, edited by Stefan Berger, Christoph Conrad, and Guy P. Murchal.

28. Erhard Wiersing, *Geschichte des historischen Denkens* (Paderborn: Schöningh, 2007), 385–88; Jerzy Maternicki, *Wielokształtność historii: Rozważania o kulturze historycznej i badaniach historiograficznych* (Warszawa: PWN, 1990), 113–14.

29. List, "Historische Theorie und nationale Geschichte," 35–53. For more on German historians' involvement in the 1848–49 revolution, see Niklas Lenhard-Schramm, *Konstrukteure der Nation: Geschichtsprofessoren als politische Akteure in Vormärz und Revolution 1848/49* (Münster: Waxmann, 2014).

30. Iggers, "Intellectual Foundations of Nineteenth-Century 'Scientific' History," 49.

31. List, "Historische Theorie und nationale Geschichte," 39–41.

32. Horst Walter Blanke, *Historiographiegeschichte als Historik* (Stuttgart: Bad Cannstatt, 1991), 207–20.

33. Władysław Smoleński, *Szkoły historyczne w Polsce: Główne kierunki poglądów na przeszłość*, ed. M. H. Serejski (Wrocław: Ossolineum, 1952).

34. Olgierd Górka, *Optymizm i pesymizm w historiografii polskiej: Odwrócenie pojęć* (Lwów: Ossolineum, 1936).

Prologue: A Note on Some Fundamental Historical Concepts

1. Alexander Demandt, "Zum Dekadenzproblem," in *Zeit und Unzeit: Geschichtphilosophische Essays* (Köln/Wien: Böhlau, 2002), 111–13.

2. Frank W. Walbank, "The Idea of Decline in Polybius," in *Niedergang: Studien zu einem geschichtlichen Thema*, ed. Reinhart Koselleck and Paul Widmer (Stuttgart: Klett-Cotta, 1980), 41–58.

3. See Arnold J. Toynbee, *The Study of History*, abridgement by D. C. Somervell (Oxford: Oxford University Press, 1947).

4. Peter Burke, "The Idea of Decline from Bruni to Gibbon," in *Edward Gibbon and the Decline and Fall of the Roman Empire*, ed. G. W. Browersock, John Clive, and Stephen R. Granbard (Cambridge, MA: Harvard University Press, 1977), 87–102.

5. See Violetta Julkowska, *Retoryka w narracji historycznej Joachima Lelewela* (Poznań: Wyd. UAM, 1998), 127; M. Cytowska and H. Szelest, *Literatura grecka i rzymska w zarysie* (Warszawa: Państw. Wydawn. Naukowe, 1983), 342–43.

6. Demandt, "Zum Dekadenzproblem," 115.

7. Pierre Chaunu, *Histoire et décadence* (Paris: Perrin, 1981), 67–72.

8. See John Burrow, *A History of Histories* (New York: Allan Lane/Penguin Books, 2008), 80–82; and Ernst Breisach, *Historiography: Ancient, Medieval, and Modern* (Chicago: University of Chicago Press, 1983), 66–67.

9. Niccolò Machiavelli, *History of Florence and of the Affairs of Italy*, Project Gutenberg, accessed 20 August 2016, http://www.gutenberg.org/files/2464/2464-h/2464-h.htm.

10. Edward Gibbon, *The History of the Decline and Fall of the Roman Empire*, vol. 6 (London: Strahan & Cadell, 1788), 385.

11. Montesquieu, *Considerations on the Causes of the Greatness of the Romans and Their Decline*, trans. David Lowenthal, with notes and introduction (New York: Free Press; London: Collier-Macmillan, 1965), chap. XVIII, retrieved from the Constitution Society, accessed 22 August 2016, http://www.constitution.org/cm/ccgrd_l.htm.

12. See Andrzej Feliks Grabski, *Dzieje historiografii* (Poznań: Wyd. Poznańskie, 2003), 349–51.

13. English translation from C. F. Volney, *The Ruins: Or a Survey of the Revolutions of Empires* [1789], chap. VIII (first quote), chap. XIII (second quote), retrieved from the Online Library of Liberty, accessed 21 August 2016, http://oll.libertyfund.org/titles/volney-the-ruins-or-a-survery-of-the-revolutions-of-Empires.

14. Burke, "Idea of Decline."

15. Burke, "Idea of Decline."

16. Joachim Lelewel, *Historyka tudzież o łatwem i pozytecznem nauczaniu historii* (Wilno: Żółtkowski, 1815), 196–97.

17. Juliusz Słowacki, *Jan Bielecki*, in *Wiersze i poematy* (Warszawa: Państwowy Instytut Wydawniczy, 1974), 105.

18. Hegel, *Elements of the Philosophy of Right*, ed. Allen W. Wood, trans. H. B. Nisbet, (Cambridge: Cambridge University Press, 1991), 373.

19. Regarding criticism of German historicism's stance, according to Frederick C. Breiser (*The German Historicist Tradition* [New York: Oxford University Press, 2011], 265), Karl Lamprecht was first to put forward this accusation, doing so in his *Alte und neuer Richtungen in der Geschichtswissenschaft* (Berlin: Gaertner, 1896), 34, 38, 44, 48.

20. See Georg G. Iggers, *The German Conception of History* (Middletown: Wesleyan University Press, 1968), 8–10.

21. See Wolfgang Schivelbusch, *Die Kultur der Niederlage* (Berlin: Alexander Fest, 2001), 11–13.

22. Reinhart Koselleck, "Erfahrungswandel und Methodenwechsel: Eine historisch-anthropologische Skizze," in *Historische Methode*, ed. Christian Meier and Jörn Rüsen (Munich: Deutscher Taschenbuch, 1988), 60.

23. Schivelbusch, *Die Kultur der Niederlage*, 24–40.

24. See Patrick Bahners, "National Unification and Narrative Unity: The Case of Ranke's German History," in *Writing National Histories: Western Europe since 1800*, ed. Stefan Berger, Mark Donovan, and Kevin Passmore (New York: Routledge, 1999), 57–68.

25. Horst Walter Blanke, *Historiographiegeschichte als Historik* (Stuttgart: Bad Cannstatt, 1991), 207–21.

26. Among the many works on historicism, I consider the following fundamental: Ernst Troeltsch, *Historismus und seine Probleme* (Tübingen: Mohr, 1922), which has more emphasis on theoretical assumptions than historical analysis; Friedrich Meinecke, *Die Entstehung des Historismus*, 2 vols. (München: Oldenbourg 1936); Friedrich Jaeger and Jörn Rüsen, *Geschichte des Historismus: Eine Einfuehrung* (München: Beck, 1992); Annette Wittkau, *Historismus: Zur Geschichte des Begriffs und des Problems* (Göttingen: Vandenhoeck & Ruprecht, 1992); and Frederick C. Beiser, *The German Historicist Tradition* (New York: Oxford University Press, 2011).

27. Ernst Schulin, "Universalgeschichte und Nationalgeschichte bei Leopold von Ran-

ke," in *Leopold von Ranke und die moderne Geschichtswissenschaft*, ed. Wolfgang J. Mommsen (Stuttgart: Klett-Cotta, 1988), 48.

28. Droysen and Gervinus as cited in Wolfgang Mommsen, "Deutsche Geschichtsschreibung im 19. Jahrhundert," in *Geschichte und Geschichtswissenschaft in der Kultur Italiens und Deutschlands*, ed. Arnold Esch and Jens Petersen (Tübingen: Niemeyer, 1989), 82–83.

29. Georg G. Iggers, "The Intellectual Foundations of Nineteenth-Century 'Scientific' History: The German Model," in *The Oxford History of Historical Writing*, vol. 4, ed. Stuart Macintyre, Juan Maiguashca, and Atilla Pók (Oxford: Oxford University Press, 2011), 41–58.

30. Mommsen, "Deutsche Geschichtsschreibung," 81.

31. Werner quoted in Mommsen, "Deutsche Geschichtsschreibung," 102.

Chapter One. Nature and Nation

1. Georg Wilhelm Friedrich Hegel, *Vorlesungen über die Philosophie der Geschichte*, in *Hegel, Recht, Staat, Geschichte: Eine Auswahl aus seinen Werken*, ed. Friedrich Bülow, 5th ed. (Stuttgart: Kröner, 1955), 396.

2. See Immanuel Geiss, *Geschichte des Rassismus* (Frankfurt: Suhrkamp, 1988), 143–60; and Izabela Surynt, *Postęp, kultura i kolonializm: Polska a niemiecki projekt europejskiego Wschodu w dyskursach publicznych XIX wieku* (Wrocław: Atut, 2006), 40–42.

3. Julian Ursyn Niemcewicz, *Śpiewy historyczne* (Warszawa: Drukarnia Rządowa, 1819), 563.

4. Henryk Schmitt, *Dzieje narodu polskiego od najdawniejszych czasów, potocznie opowiedziane*, vol. 1 (Lwów: Ossolineum, 1863), 1–2.

5. Kurt Breysig, *Kulturgeschichte der Neuzeit*, 2 vols. (Berlin: Bondi, 1901), 2 (pt. 1):1.

6. Karl Lamprecht, *Deutsche Geschichte*, 4 vols. (Berlin/Freiburg: Heyfelder, 1902), 1:130–40.

7. Lamprecht, *Deutsche Geschichte*, 1:148.

8. Felix Dahn, *Deutsche Geschichte*, vol. 1 (Gotha: Pertes, 1883), 129–31.

9. Eduard Heyck, *Deutsche Geschichte* (Bielefeld/Leipzig: Velhagen & Klasing, 1906), 1:115–20; Ludwig Stacke, *Deutsche Geschichte* (Bielefeld/Leipzig: Velhagen & Klasing, 1880), 1:56–60.

10. Lamprecht, *Deutsche Geschichte*, 1:173–75.

11. Heyck, *Deutsche Geschichte*, 1:119–24.

12. Stacke, *Deutsche Geschichte*, 1:56–70.

13. See Reiner Kipper, *Der Germanenmythos im Deutschen Kaiserreich: Formen und Funktionen historischer Selbstthematisierung* (Göttingen: Vandenhoeck & Ruprecht, 2002), 12–13.

14. Dahn, *Deutsche Geschichte*, 1:132–40.

15. Oskar Jäger, *Deutsche Geschichte*, 2 vols. (München: Beck, 1909), 1:19–21.

16. The remark in question is: "Inesse quin etiam sanctua aliquid et providum putant, nec aut consilia earum asperantur aut response neglegunt." Tacitus, *Germania* 8.3.

17. Heinrich Leo, *Vorlesungen über die Geschichte des deutschen Volkes und Reiches*, 5 vols. (Halle: Anton, 1854), 1:136–42.

18. Stacke, *Deutsche Geschichte*, 1:65.

19. Dahn, *Deutsche Geschichte*, 1:143–44.

20. Heyck, *Deutsche Geschichte*, 1:113.

21. Dahn, *Deutsche Geschichte*, 1:122–24.

22. C. A. Bonath, *Die deutsche Geschichte für Schulen und zum Selbstunterrichte* (Stendal: Franzen und Grosse, 1864), 5–7.

23. Lamprecht, *Deutsche Geschichte*, 1:315–22, 2:99–104.

24. Breysig, *Kulturgeschichte der Neuzeit*, 2 (pt. 1):686–703.

25. Jäger, *Deutsche Geschichte*, 1:48–54.

26. Kipper, *Der Germanenmythos*, 64–65.

27. Heinrich von Sybel, "Die christlich-germanische Staatslehre: Ihre Bedeutung in der Gegenwart, ihr Verhältnis zum historischen Christen- und Germanenthum," in Sybel, *Kleine historische Schriften* (Stuttgart: Cotta, 1880), 1:365–414.

28. Julius Ficker, "Das Deutsche Kaiserreich in seinen universalen und nationalen Beziehungen," in *Universalstaat oder Nationalstaat: Macht und Ende des ersten deutschen Reiches; Die Streitschriften von Heinrich von Sybel und Julius Ficker zur deutschen Kaiserpolitik des Mittelalters*, ed. Friedrich Schneider (Innsbruck: Univ. Verl. Wagner, 1941), 49–51.

29. Kipper, *Der Germanenmythos*, 62–63.

30. Leo, *Vorlesungen über die Geschichte*, 1:162–77.

31. Stacke, *Deutsche Geschichte*, 1:152–53.

32. Lamprecht, *Deutsche Geschichte*, 1:302–17.

33. Dahn, *Deutsche Geschichte*, 1:199–201.

34. Johann Jastrow, *Geschichte des deutschen Einheitstraumes und seiner Erfüllung* (Berlin: Allgemeiner Verein für deutsche Literatur, 1890), 15–16.

35. See Wolfgang Samtleben, *Die Idee einer altgermanischen Volksfreiheit im vormärzlichen deutschen Liberalismus* (Hamburg: Evert, 1935).

36. See Heinz Gollwitzer, "Zum politischen Germanismus des 19. Jahrhunderts," in *Festschrift für Hermann Heimpel zum 70. Geburtstag am 19. September 1971* (Göttingen: Max Planck Institut für Geschichte, 1971), 282–356; Klaus von See, *Deutsche Germanen-Ideologie: Vom Humanismus bis zur Gegenwart* (Frankfurt: Athenäum-Verl., 1970); and Léon Poliakov, *Der Arische Mythos: Zu den Quellen von Rassismus und Nationalismus* (Hamburg: Junius, 1993).

37. For an analysis of this myth in Polish literature, see Alina Witkowska, *Słowianie, my lubim sielanki* (Warszawa: PIW, 1972); and Maria Janion, *Niesamowita Słowiańszczyzna* (Kraków: Wyd. Literackie, 2006).

38. See Ludwig Krapf, *Germanenmythos und Reichsideologie: Frühhumanistische Rezep-

tionsweisen der Taciteischen "Germania" (Tübingen: Niemeyer, 1979); Horst Kirchner, *Das germanische Altertum in der deutschen Geschichtsschreibung des 18. Jahrhunderts* (Berlin: Ebering, 1938); Jan Malicki, *Mity narodowe: Lechiada* (Wrocław: Ossolineum, 1981); and Jan Maślanka, *Słowiańskie mity historyczne w literaturze polskiego Oświecenia* (Wrocław: Ossolineum, 1968).

39. See Tadeusz Ulewicz, *Świadomość słowiańska Jana Kochanowskiego: Z zagadnień psychiki polskiego renesansu* (Kraków: Seminarium Historii Literatury Polskiej UJ, 1948), 94–119; and Adam Naruszewicz, "List do króla Stanisława Augusta 20.IV.1777," in *Historycy o historii*, ed. Marian Henryk Serejski (Warszawa: PWN, 1963), 41–43.

40. *Greckie i łacińskie źródła do najstarszych dziejów Słowian*, vol. 1, *Do VIII wieku*, ed. Marian Plezia (Poznań: Pol. Tow. Ludoznawcze, 1952), 68, 91, 95.

41. Franciszek Bronowski, *Idea gminowładztwa w polskiej historiografii (Geneza i formowanie się syntezy republikańskiej Joachima Lelewela)* (Łódź: Łódzkie Tow. Naukowe, 1969), 82–83.

42. For more on Sarmatism, see Karin Friedrich, *The Other Prussia: Royal Prussia, Poland and Liberty, 1569–1772* (Cambridge: Cambridge University Press, 2000), 76–82.

43. Surowiecki quoted in F. Bronowski, "Wawrzyniec Surowiecki jako badacz dawnej Słowiańszczyzny," *Zeszyty Naukowe Uniwersytetu Łódzkiego* 1, no. 3 (1956): 92.

44. Surowiecki quoted Witkowska, *Sławianie*, 32.

45. Zorian Dołęga Chodakowski, *O Słowiańszczyźnie przed chrześcijaństwem oraz inne pisma i listy*, ed. Julian Maślanka (Warszawa: PWN, 1967); Ryszard Walicki, "Wacław Maciejowski i Zorian Dołęga Chodakowski: Studium z dziejów słowianofilstwa polskiego," *Archiwum Historii Filozofii i Myśli Społecznej* 13 (1967): 271–301.

46. Jerzy Jedlicki, *Jakiej cywilizacji Polacy potrzebują* (Warszawa: PIW, 2002), 63–73.

47. Józef Ignacy Kraszewski, *Stara baśń: Powieść z XI wieku*, with *Dopisek* and *Dziejowe legendy*, ed. Wincenty Danek (Wrocław: Ossolineum, 1975), 441.

48. See, for example, Joan S. Skurnowicz, *Romantic Nationalism and Liberalism: Joachim Lelewel and the Polish National Idea* (New York: Columbia University Press, 1981); and Monika Baár, *Historians and Nationalism: East-Central Europe in the Nineteenth Century* (New York: Oxford University Press, 2010)

49. Joachim Lelewel, *Uwagi nad dziejami Polski i ludu jej*, vol. 3 of *Polska, dzieje i rzeczy jej* (Poznań: Żupański, 1855), 45–54.

50. For more on this relative to Lelewel's most famous student, Mickiewicz, see Andreas Lawaty, "Zur romantischen Konzeption des Politischen: Polen und Deutsche unter fremder Herrschaft," in *Romantik und Geschichte: Polnisches Paradigma, europäischer Kontext, deutsch-polnische Perpektive*, ed. Alfred Gall, Thomas Grob, Andreas Lawaty, and German Ritz (Wiesbaden: Harrassowitz, 2007), 21–59.

51. See Marian Henryk Serejski, "Z zagadnień genezy państwa polskiego w historiografii (o tzw. teorii podboju)," *Kwartalnik Historyczny* 60, no. 3 (1953): 147–63.

52. Joachim Lelewel, Uprzednia myśl, czyli słowa do poszukiwań wstępne, vol. 3 of *Polska, dzieje i rzeczy jej*, 11.

53. Lelewel, *Uwagi nad dziejami Polski*, 73–86.

54. Joachim Lelewel, *Polska wieków średnich, czyli w dziejach narodowych polskich postrzeżenia*, vol. 2 (Poznań: Kamieński i Ska, 1847), 297.

55. See Walicki, "Wacław Maciejowski i Zorian Dołęga Chodakowski," 289; Juliusz Bardach, *Wacław Aleksander Maciejowski i jego współcześni* (Wrocław: Ossolineum, 1971); and Janion, *Niesamowita Słowiańszczyzna*, 92–106.

56. Lelewel, *Uwagi nad dziejami Polski*, 275–79.

57. Schmitt, *Dzieje narodu polskiego*, 1:8.

58. Schmitt, *Dzieje narodu polskiego*, 1:96–99.

59. Michał Bobrzyński, *Dzieje Polski w zarysie*, ed. Marian Henryk Serejski and Andrzej Feliks Grabski (Warszawa: PIW, 1986), 85, 94, 98.

60. Władysław Smoleński, *Dzieje narodu polskiego* (Warszawa: Gebethner i Wolff, 1904), 3–4.

61. Bobrzyński, *Dzieje Polski* (1986 ed.), 85–89; Józef Szujski, *Dzieje Polski*, 4 vols. (Lwów: Wild, 1862–66), 1:39–42; Smoleński, *Dzieje narodu polskiego*, 5.

62. Joachim Lelewel, *Dzieje Litwy i Rusi aż do unii z Polską w Lublinie 1569 zawartej* (Warszawa: PWN, 1969), 91–102.

63. Karol Boromeusz Hoffman, *Historia reform politycznych w dawnej Polsce*, ed. Andrzej Wierzbicki (Warszawa: PIW, 1988), p. 31.

64. Szujski, *Dzieje Polski*, 1:44.

65. Smoleński, *Dzieje narodu polskiego*, 8–10.

66. Lelewel, *Uwagi nad dziejami Polski*, 88–90, 178–83.

67. Schmitt, *Dzieje narodu polskiego*, 1:104, 167–71.

68. Karol Szajnocha, *Jadwiga i Jagiełło, 1374–1413: Opowiadanie historyczne*, ed. Stefan M. Kuczyński and Maria Bokszczanin, 4 vols. (Warszawa: PIW, 1974), 2:354–55.

69. Szujski, *Dzieje Polski*, 1:41, 111, 180.

70. Stanisław Kaczkowski, *Krzyżacy i Polska: Wspomnienie historyczne* (Poznań: Żupański, 1845), 8–15.

71. Bobrzyński, *Dzieje Polski* (1986 ed.), 97–100, 107, 125.

72. Bobrzyński, *Dzieje Polski* (1986 ed.), 163–67, 178.

73. Smoleński, *Dzieje narodu polskiego*, 14, 41, 57–58.

Chapter Two. The Zenith

1. Dionysius of Halicarnassus, *The Roman Antiquities*, trans. Edward Spelman (London, 1758), Book I, 11–14.

2. See Heinrich Hostenkamp, *Die mittelalterliche Kaiserpolitik in der deutschen Historiographie seit v. Sybel und Ficker* (Berlin: Ebering, 1934); Heinz Gollwitzer, "Zur Auffassung der mittelalterlichen Kaiserpolitik im 19. Jahrhundert: Eine ideologie- und wisseschaftgeschichtliche Nachlese," in *Dauer und Wandel der Geschichte: Aspekte europäischer Vergangenheit; Festgabe für Kurt Raumer*, ed. Rudolf Vierhaus and Manfred Botzenhart

(Münster, 1966), 483–512; and Thomas Brechenmacher, "Wie viel Gegenwar verträgt historisches Urteilen? Die Kontroverse zwischen Heinrich von Sybel und Julius Ficker über die Bewertung der Kaiserpolitik des Mittelalters (1859–1862)," in *Historische debatten und Kontroverse im 19. und 20. Jahrhundert*, ed. Jürgen Elvert and Susanne Kranz (Wiesbaden: Steiner, 2003), 34–54.

3. Wilhelm Giesebrecht, *Geschichte der deutschen Kaiserzeit*, 6 vols. (Leipzig: Duncker & Humblot, 1881), vol. 1, *Gründung des Kaiserthums*, vi–viii.

4. Wolfgang Menzel, *Germany from the Earliest Period*, trans. Mrs. George Horrocks (New York: P. F. Collier, 1900), 632.

5. August Friedrich Gfrörer, *Allgemeine Kirchengeschichte*, 4 vols. (Stuttgart: Krabbe, 1841–46); Constantin Höfler, *Kaiser Friedrich II: Ein Beitrag zur Berechtigung der Ansichten über den Sturz der Hohenstaufen* (München: Literarisch-artistische Anst., 1844).

6. Böhmer quoted in Thomas Brechenmacher, *Grossdeutsche Geschichtsschreibung im neunzehnten Jahrhundert: Die erste Generation (1830–1848)* (Berlin: Duncker & Humblot, 1996), 201–2.

7. Karol Szajnocha, *Jadwiga i Jagiełło, 1374–1413: Opowiadanie historyczne*, ed. Stefan M. Kuczyński and Maria Bokszczanin, 4 vols. (Warszawa: PIW, 1974), 1:79.

8. Tarnowski quoted in Władysław Konopczyński, "O idei jagiellońskiej," in Konopczyński, *O wartość naszej spuścizny dziejowej: Wybór pism*, ed. Piotr Biliński (Kraków: Ośrodek Myśli Politycznej, 2009), 317.

9. Henryk Schmitt, *Dzieje narodu polskiego od najdawniejszych czasów, potocznie opowiedziane*, vol. 1 (Lwów: Ossolineum, 1863), 389.

10. Joachim Lelewel, *Uwagi nad dziejami Polski i ludu jej*, vol. 3 of *Polska, dzieje i rzeczy jej* (Poznań: Żupański, 1855), 264–65; Lelewel, *Dzieje Litwy i Rusi aż do unii z Polską w Lublinie 1569 zawartej* (Warszawa: PWN, 1969), 160.

11. Antoni Chołoniewski, *Duch dziejów Polski* (1918; Warszawa: Ad astra, 2000), 57.

12. Julius Ficker, "Das Deutsche Kaiserreich in seinen universalen und nationalem Beziehungen," in *Universalstaat oder Nationalstaat: Macht und Ende des ersten deutschen Reiches; Die Streitschriften von Heinrich von Sybel und Julius Ficker zur deutschen Kaiserpolitik des Mittelalters*, ed. Friedrich Schneider (Innsbruck: Univ. Verl. Wagner, 1941), 73–75, 78–79, 83–85.

13. Ludwig Karl Aegidi, *Woher und Wohin? Ein Versuch die Geschichte Deutschlands zu verstehen* (Hamburg: Boyes & Geisler, 1866), 13.

14. Oskar von Wydenbrugk, *Die deutsche Nation und das Kaiserreich* (München: Fleischmann, 1862), 75.

15. Hans Prutz, *Staatengeschichte des Abendlandes im Mittelalter*, 2 vols. (Berlin: Grote, 1885–87), 2:4–6; Ferdinand Gregorovius, *Geschichte der Stadt Rom im Mittelalter*, 8 vols. (Dresden: Jess, 1926), 2:1402–3.

16. Höfler quoted in Brechenmacher, *Grossdeutsche Geschichtsschreibung*, 152.

17. Ficker, "Das Deutsche Kaiserreich," 116.

18. Wydenbrugk, *Die deutsche Nation und das Kaiserreich*, 36.

19. Aegidi, *Woher und Wohin?*, 11; Prutz, *Staatengeschichte des Abendlandes*, 2:3–4.

20. Lelewel, *Dzieje Litwy i Rusi*, 91; Szajnocha, *Jadwiga i Jagiełło*, 1:312.

21. Lelewel, *Dzieje Litwy i Rusi*, 186; Szajnocha, *Jadwiga i Jagiełło*, 4:481.

22. Władysław Smoleński, *Dzieje narodu polskiego* (Warszawa: Gebethner i Wolff, 1904), 68–69; Michał Bobrzyński, *Dzieje Polski w zarysie*, ed. Marian Henryk Serejski and Andrzej Feliks Grabski (Warszawa: PIW, 1986), 206.

23. Józef Szujski, "Z wykładów o dziejach cywilizacji polskiej," in *Dzieła*, ser. 2, vol. 7 (Kraków: published by the author, 1888), 5.

24. Józef Szujski, *Dzieje Polski*, 4 vols. (Lwów: Wild, 1862–66), 293.

25. Szujski, "Z wykładów o dziejach cywilizacji polskiej," in *Dzieła*, ser. 2, vol. 7, 1–20.

26. Stanisław Smolka, *Rok 1386: W pięciowiekową rocznicę* (Kraków: Żupański & Heumann, 1886), 41–45.

27. Smolka, *Rok 1386*, 117–20.

28. Smolka, *Rok 1386*, 62–77.

29. Oskar Jäger, *Deutsche Geschichte*, 2 vols. (München: Beck, 1909), 1:147–48.

30. Gustav Freytag, *Bilder aus der deutschen Vergangenheit*, 7 vols. (Leipzig: Hirzel, 1913–15), 1:507. As a side note, this edition of Freytag's work was the thirty-fifth.

31. Oskar Halecki, "Ekspansja i tolerancja," in *Przyczyny upadku Polski: Odczyty* (Kraków: Gebethner i Wolff, 1918), 50.

32. Bobrzyński, *Dzieje Polski* (1986 ed.), 453.

33. Heinrich von Sybel, "*Über die neueren Darstellungen der deutschen Kaiserzeit*," in *Universalstaat oder Nationalstaat*, ed. Schneider, 5–18.

34. Menzel, *Germany from the Earliest Period*, 634.

35. Heinrich von Treitschke, *Deutsche Geschichte im 19. Jahrhundert* (1928; Wiesbaden/Essen: Vollmer, Phaidon, 1997), 9–10; Hans Prutz, *Staatengeschichte des Abendlandes*, 2:3–9; Jäger, *Deutsche Geschichte*, 1:188–92.

36. August Friedrich Gfrörer, *Allgemeine Kirchengeschichte*, 4 vols. (Stuttgart: Krabbe, 1841–46), 3:1258–59, quoted in Brechenmacher, *Grossdeutsche Geschichtsschreibung*, 138.

37. Heinrich Leo, *Vorlesungen über die Geschichte des deutschen Volkes und Reiches*, 5 vols. (Halle: Anton, 1857), 2:417–20.

38. Jäger, *Deutsche Geschichte*, 1:269.

39. Walter Alison Phillips, James Wycliffe Headlam-Morley, and Arthur William Holland, *A Short History of Germany and Her Colonies (reproduced from the 11th edition of Encyclopædia Britannica)* (London: Encyclopædia Britannica, 1914), 8–9.

40. Prutz, *Staatengeschichte des Abendlandes*, 2:3–4; Wydenbrugk, *Die deutsche Nation und das Kaiserreich*, 76.

41. Ludwig Stacke, *Deutsche Geschichte*, 3 vols. (Bielefeld/Leipzig: Velhagen & Klasing, 1880–81), 1:298–99.

42. Wydenbrugk, *Die deutsche Nation und das Kaiserreich*, 64–65.

43. Aegidi, *Woher und Wohin?*, 10.

44. Prutz, *Staatengeschichte des Abendlandes*, 2:7–9.

45. Johann Jastrow, *Geschichte des deutschen Einheitstraumes und seiner Erfüllung* (Berlin: Allgemeiner Verein für deutsche Kultur, 1890), 37–38.

46. Leopold von Ranke, *Weltgeschichte*, 8 vols. (Munich and Leipzig: Duncker & Humblot, 1922), 6:151–52; James Bryce, *The Holy Roman Empire* (London: Macmillan, 1913), 130; Wydenbrugk, *Die deutsche Nation und das Kaiserreich*, 33–36.

47. Stacke, *Deutsche Geschichte*, 1:388–89.

48. Lamprecht, *Deutsche Geschichte*, 2:285–88, 411, 3:103–16.

49. Heinrich von Sybel, "Die deutsche Nation und das Kaiserreich," in *Universalstaat oder Nationalstaat*, ed. Schneider, 163–67.

50. Leopold von Ranke, *Deutsche Geschichte im Zeitalter der Reformation*, 5 vols. (Berlin: Duncker & Humblot, 1839–47), 1:13.

51. Ranke, *Deutsche Geschichte im Zeitalter der Reformation*, 1:18–27.

52. Johannes Haller, *Die Epochen der deutschen Geschichte* (München: Paul List, 1956), 35–66.

53. Julian Ursyn Niemcewicz, Śpiewy historyczne (Lwów: Jabłoński, 1849), 60–62.

54. Józef Szujski, *Historii polskiej treściwie opowiedzianych ksiąg dwanaście* (Warszawa: Berger, 1880), 78–88.

55. Szujski, "Kilka uwag o 'Dziejach Polski' w krótkim zarysie Michała Bobrzyńskiego," in *Dzieła* ser. 2, vol. 7, 154–209 (quote, 184).

56. Szujski, "O młodszości naszego cywilizacyjnego rozwoju szereg spostrzeżeń," in *Dzieła*, ser. 2, vol. 7, 370.

57. Oskar Halecki, Wacław Sobieski, Józef Gustaw Krajewski, and Władysław Konopczyński, *Historia polityczna Polski*, 2 vols. (Kraków, 1923), 2:526.

58. Bobrzyński, *Dzieje Polski* (1986 ed.), 453.

59. Eugène Starczewski, *L'Europe et la Pologne* (Paris: Perrin, 1913), 61–64; Konopczyński, in Halecki et al., *Historia polityczna Polski*, 2:196.

60. See Lelewel, *Uwagi nad dziejami Polski*, 167–68.

61. Stacke, *Deutsche Geschichte*, 1:298–99.

62. Menzel, *Germany from the Earliest Period*, 407.

63. Ranke, *Deutsche Geschichte im Zeitalter der Reformation*, 1:54–57.

64. Johann Gustav Droysen, *Geschichte der preussischen Politik*, 5 vols. (Berlin: Veit, 1857), 1:11.

65. Menzel, *Germany from the Earliest Period*, 806.

66. Johann von Döllinger, "The Relation of the City of Rome to Germany in the Middle Ages," in *Studies in European History*, trans. Margaret Warre (London, 1890), 58–79.

67. Chołoniewski, *Duch dziejów Polski*, 123–38.

68. Stanisław Kutrzeba, "Siły państwowe," in *Przyczyny upadku Polski: Odczyty* (Kraków: Gebethner i Wolff, 1918), 132–33.

69. Lelewel, *Uwagi nad dziejami Polski,* 173.

70. Szujski, *Dzieje Polski,* vol. 2, *Jagiellonowie,* 4–6.

71. Szujski, *Dzieje Polski,* 2:78–80.

72. Niemcewicz, Śpiewy historyczne (1849 ed.), 61–62.

73. Szujski, *Dzieje Polski,* 2:339.

74. Adam Szelągowski, *Wzrost państwa polskiego w XV i XVI wieku: Polska na przełomie wieków średnich* (Lwów/Warszawa: Połoniecki, Wende, 1904), 44–46.

75. Bobrzyński, *Dzieje Polski* (1986 ed.), 265–66.

76. Bobrzyński, *Dzieje Polski* (1986 ed.), 275–78.

77. Droysen, *Geschichte der preussischen Politik,* 1:4–18.

78. Droysen, *Geschichte der preussischen Politik,* 1:33–36.

79. Heyck, *Deutsche Geschichte,* 2:255–60.

80. Jäger, *Deutsche Geschichte,* 1:342–55.

81. Jäger, *Deutsche Geschichte,* 1:444–454.

82. Prutz, *Staatengeschichte des Abendlandes,* 1:695–97.

83. Haller, *Die Epochen der deutschen Geschichte,* 69–73, 103.

84. Heinrich Leo, *Lehrbuch der Universalgeschichte,* 6 vols. (Halle: Eduard Anton, 1851), 2:591.

85. Friedrich von Raumer, *Geschichte Europas seit dem Ende des fünfzehnten Jahrhunderts,* 8 vols. (Leipzig: Brockhaus, 1832), 1:195–96.

86. Lamprecht, *Deutsche Geschichte,* 4:114–27.

87. Lelewel, *Uwagi nad dziejami Polski,* 131–32, 154–55.

88. Lelewel, *Uwagi nad dziejami Polski,* 207–8.

89. Niemcewicz, Śpiewy historyczne (1819 ed.), 564–65.

90. Schmitt, *Dzieje narodu polskiego,* 1:661–67.

91. Szujski, *Dzieje Polski,* 2:164.

92. Bobrzyński, *Dzieje Polski* (1986 ed.), 156–57.

93. Bobrzyński, *Dzieje Polski* (1986 ed.), 212–15.

94. Fryderyk Papée, *Polska i Litwa na przełomie wieków średnich* (Kraków: AU, 1904), 1:20–21.

95. Schmitt, *Dzieje narodu polskiego,* 1:392.

96. Lelewel, *Uwagi nad dziejami Polski,* 210–11.

97. Lelewel, *Uwagi nad dziejami Polski,* 188–206; Bobrzyński, *Dzieje Polski* (1986 ed.), 275–77.

98. Smoleński, *Dzieje narodu,* 88–89.

99. Ranke, *Deutsche Geschichte im Zeitalter der Reformation,* 1:8–9, 44–45, 48–49.

100. Menzel, *Germany from the Earliest Period,* 646–47.

101. Ranke, *Deutsche Geschichte im Zeitalter der Reformation,* 1:63–77.

102. Droysen, *Geschichte der preussischen Politik*, 1:25–33.

103. Menzel, *Germany from the Earliest Period*, 634.

104. Raumer, *Geschichte Europas*, 1:195–96; Stacke, *Deutsche Geschichte*, 1:694–705.

105. Ranke, *Deutsche Geschichte im Zeitalter der Reformation*, 1:69; Droysen, *Geschichte der preussischen Politik*, 121–23.

106. Ludwig Häusser, *Deutsche Geschichte vom Tode Friedrichs des Grossen bis zur Gründung des Deutschen Bundes*, 4 vols. (Berlin: Weidmann, 1861–63), 1:5.

107. Lamprecht, *Deutsche Geschichte*, 4:7–10.

108. See Patrick Bahners, "National Unification and Narrative Unity: The Case of Ranke's German History," in *Writing National Histories: Western Europe since 1800*, ed. Stefan Berger, Mark Donovan, and Kevin Passmore (London: Routledge, 1999), 57–68; and Arthur G. Dickens, John M. Tonkin, and Kenneth Powell, *The Reformation in Historical Thought* (London: Blackwell, 1985), 170–73.

109. Jäger, *Deutsche Geschichte*, 1:563–75.

110. Wilhelm Wachsmuth, *Europäische Sittengeschichte vom Ursprunge volksthümlicher Gestaltungen bis auf unsere Zeit*, 6 vols. (Leipzig: Vogel, 1838), 5 (pt. 1):5–10.

111. Heyck, *Deutsche Geschichte*, 2:523.

112. Droysen, *Geschichte der preussischen Politik*, 3:363–65; 4:4–5.

113. Ludwig Häusser, *Geschichte des Zeitalters der Reformation 1517–1648*, ed. Wilhelm Oncken (Berlin: Weidmann, 1903), 107–15.

114. Wachsmuth, *Europäische Sittengeschichte*, 5 (pt. 1):198–99.

115. Raumer, *Geschichte Europas*, 1:379–82.

116. Heyck, *Deutsche Geschichte*, 2:560–61; Häusser, *Geschichte des Zeitalters der Reformation*, 107–8.

117. Jäger, *Deutsche Geschichte*, 1:504.

118. Haller, *Die Epochen der deutschen Geschichte*, 129–31.

119. This quotation is from a letter written by Johann Friedrich Böhmer in 1843, cited in Brechenmacher, *Grossdeutsche Geschichtsschreibung*, 205.

120. Johannes Janssen, *Geschichte des deutschen Volkes seit dem Ausgang des Mittelalters*, vol. 5, *Vorbereitung des dreissigjährigen Krieges* (Freiburg: Herder, 1924), 672.

121. Jäger, *Deutsche Geschichte*, 1:513.

122. Szujski, *Dzieje Polski*, 2:163.

123. Bobrzyński, *Dzieje Polski* (1986 ed.), 290–91.

124. Feliks Koneczny, *Dzieje Polski*, 2 vols. (Łódź: Rozwój, 1902), 2:88–89.

125. Schmitt, *Dzieje narodu polskiego*, 1:487–88.

126. Bobrzyński, *Dzieje Polski* (1986 ed.), 289.

127. Lelewel, *Uwagi nad dziejami Polski*, 295–96; Chołoniewski, *Duch dziejów Polski*, 82–90; Halecki, *Ekspansja i tolerancja*, 69–72.

128. Szelągowski, *Wzrost państwa polskiego w XV i XVI wieku*, 186–89.

129. Szujski, *Dzieje Polski*, 2:161, vol. 3, *Królowie wolno obrani*, 6.

130. Lelewel, *Uwagi nad dziejami Polski*, 187.

131. Lelewel, *Uwagi nad dziejami Polski*, 295–98.

132. Koneczny, *Dzieje Polski*, 2:88–89.

133. Bobrzyński, *Dzieje Polski* (1986 ed.), 287–89, 299–300.

134. Chołoniewski, *Duch dziejów Polski*, 90.

Chapter Three. The Decline and Fall

1. Ludwig Häusser, *Geschichte des Zeitalters der Reformation 1517–1648*, ed. Wilhelm Oncken (Berlin: Weidmann, 1903), 627–28.

2. Józef Szujski, *Dzieje Polski*, vol. 3, *Królowie wolno obrani* (Lwów: Wild, 1864), 309–10.

3. Ludwik Kubala, *Szkice historyczne*, vol. 3, *Wojna moskiewska 1654–55* (Warszawa: Gebethner i Wolff, 1910), 1.

4. Władysław Konopczyński, "Pierwszy rozbiór," in *Przyczyny upadku Polski: Odczyty* (Kraków: Gebethner i Wolff, 1918), 210.

5. Michał Bobrzyński, *Dzieje Polski w zarysie*, ed. Marian Henryk Serejski and Andrzej Feliks Grabski (Warszawa: PIW, 1986), 430.

6. Joachim Lelewel, *Uwagi nad dziejami Polski i ludu jej*, vol. 3 of *Polska, dzieje i rzeczy jej* (Poznań: Żupański, 1855), 448.

7. Szujski, *Dzieje Polski*, vol. 4, *Królowie wolno obrani* (Lwów: Wild, 1866), 315–16.

8. Bobrzyński, *Dzieje Polski* (1986 ed.), 429–30.

9. Friedrich von Raumer, *Geschichte Europas seit dem Ende des fünfzehnten Jahrhunderts*, 8 vols. (Leipzig: Brockhaus, 1832–50), 2:650–652.

10. Häusser, *Geschichte des Zeitalters der Reformation*, 619–20.

11. Ludwig Stacke, *Deutsche Geschichte*, 3 vols. (Bielefeld/Leipzig: Velhagen & Klasing, 1880–81), 3:295–96.

12. Henryk Schmitt, *Dzieje Polski XVIII i XIX wieku*, 4 vols. (Kraków: Czas, 1866), 1:10.

13. Häusser, *Geschichte des Zeitalters der Reformation*, 627–28.

14. Johann Gustav Droysen, *Vorlesungen über das Zeitalter der Freiheitskriege*, 2 vols. (Gotha: Perthes, 1886), 1:18.

15. Raumer, *Geschichte Europas*, 2:651.

16. Władysław Smoleński, *Dzieje narodu polskiego* (Warszawa: Gebethner i Wolff, 1904), 227.

17. Johann Jastrow, *Geschichte des deutschen Einheitstraumes und seiner Erfüllung* (Berlin: Allgemeiner Verein für deutsche Literatur, 1890), 62–64.

18. Häusser, *Geschichte des Zeitalters der Reformation*, 630.

19. Kevin Cramer, *The Thirty Years' War and German Memory in the Nineteenth Century* (Lincoln: University of Nebraska Press, 2007), 217–18.

20. Lelewel, *Uwagi nad dziejami Polski*, 307–17.

21. Schmitt, *Dzieje Polski XVIII i XIX wieku*, 1:159.

22. Stacke, *Deutsche Geschichte*, 3:288–91.

23. Raumer, *Geschichte Europas*, 2:596–613.

24. Eduard Heyck, *Deutsche Geschichte*, 3 vols. (Bielefeld/Leipzig: Velhagen & Klasing, 1906), 3:20–22.

25. Karl Grün, *Kulturgeschichte des siebzehnten Jahrhunderts*, 2 vols. (Leipzig: Barth, 1880), 278–83.

26. Franciszek Bujak, "Siły gospodarcze," in *Przyczyny upadku Polski*, 82.

27. Szujski, *Dzieje Polski*, 4:209–210.

28. Schmitt, *Dzieje Polski XVIII i XIX wieku*, 1:13.

29. Cramer, *Thirty Years' War*, 188.

30. Droysen, *Vorlesungen über das Zeitalter der Freiheitskriege*, 1:4–5.

31. Szujski, *Dzieje Polski*, 4:37–39.

32. Konopczyński, "Pierwszy rozbiór," 230–31.

33. Lelewel, *Uwagi nad dziejami Polski*, 238–39.

34. Józef Kallenbach, "Siły moralne i umysłowe," in *Przyczyny upadku Polski*, 169.

35. Tadeusz Korzon, *Historia Polski*, ed. Bolesław Bator (Kijów: Rada Okręgowa, 1918), 350.

36. Wilhelm Wachsmuth, *Europäische Sittengeschichte vom Ursprunge volksthümlicher Gestaltungen bis auf unsere Zeit*, 6 vols. (Leipzig: Vogel, 1838), 5 (pt. 1):492.

37. Lelewel, *Uwagi nad dziejami Polski*, 395–405.

38. Stanisław Kutrzeba, "Siły państwowe," in *Przyczyny upadku Polski*, 134.

39. Tadeusz Korzon, *Odrodzenie w upadku*, ed. Marian Henryk Serejski and Andrzej Feliks Grabski (Warszawa: PIW, 1975), 87–88.

40. Antoni Chołoniewski, *Duch dziejów Polski* (1918; Warszawa: Ad astra, 2000), 90.

41. Schmitt, *Dzieje Polski XVIII i XIX wieku*, 1:126.

42. Lelewel, *Uwagi nad dziejami Polski*, 462.

43. Józef Szujski, "Rzut oka na stanowisko Polski w historii powszechnej," in Szujski, *O fałszywej historii jako mistrzyni fałszywej polityki: Rozprawy i artykuły*, comp. and ed. Henryk Michalak (Warszawa: PIW, 1991), 60.

44. Szujski, *Dzieje Polski*, 3:1–3.

45. Droysen, *Vorlesungen über das Zeitalter der Freiheitskriege*, 1:7, 14–47.

46. Jastrow, *Geschichte des deutschen Einheitstraumes*, 57–58.

47. Wachsmuth, *Europäische Sittengeschichte*, 5 (pt.1):455–56.

48. Häusser, *Geschichte des Zeitalters der Reformation*, 620.

49. Häusser, *Geschichte des Zeitalters der Reformation*, 619.

50. Otto Hintze, *Der deutsche Staatsgedanke* (1924), 128–29, quoted in Bernd Faulenbach, *Die Ideologie des deutschen Weges: Die deutsche Geschichte in der Historiographie zwischen Kaiserreich und Nationalsozialismus* (München: Beck, 1980), 39.

51. Wachsmuth, *Europäische Sittengeschichte*, 5 (pt.1): 455.

52. Korzon, *Odrodzenie w upadku*, 47.

53. Droysen, *Vorlesungen über das Zeitalter der Freiheitskriege*, 1:107–26.

54. Stacke, *Deutsche Geschichte*, 2:293–94.

55. Heyck, *Deutsche Geschichte*, 3:334–36.

56. Lelewel, *Uwagi nad dziejami Polski*, 448–61.

57. Schmitt, *Dzieje Polski XVIII i XIX wieku*, 1:126, 160, 2:15–17.

58. Szujski, *Dzieje Polski*, 3:240, 485, 4:291, 366.

59. Smoleński, *Dzieje narodu polskiego*, 233.

60. Bujak, "Siły gospodarcze," 110–14.

61. Korzon, *Odrodzenie w upadku*, 45, 93–95.

62. Władysław Łoziński, *Życie polskie w dawnych wiekach*, ed. Janusz Tazbir (Warszawa: Iskry, 2006), 51–52.

63. Wolfgang Menzel, *Germany from the Earliest Period*, trans. Mrs. George Horrocks (New York: P. F. Collier, 1900), 3:1350–58.

64. Oskar Jäger, *Deutsche Geschichte*, 2 vols. (München: Beck, 1909–10), 2:159–60.

65. Stacke, *Deutsche Geschichte*, 2:291–92.

66. Wachsmuth, *Europäische Sittengeschichte*, 5 (pt. 1):498–99.

67. Grun, *Kulturgeschichte des siebzehnten Jahrhunderts*, 1:287–88.

68. Stacke, *Deutsche Geschichte*, 2:287–88.

69. Schmitt, *Dzieje Polski XVIII i XIX wieku*, 2:15–17.

70. Bujak, "Siły gospodarcze," 91.

71. Smoleński, *Dzieje narodu polskiego*, 179.

72. Korzon, *Odrodzenie w upadku*, 87–88, 322–24.

73. Chołoniewski, *Duch dziejów Polski*, 67.

74. Oskar Halecki, "Ekspansja i tolerancja," in *Przyczyny upadku Polski*, 69–70.

75. Feliks Koneczny, *Dzieje Polski*, 2 vols. (Łódź: Rozwój, 1902), 139.

76. Lelewel, *Uwagi nad dziejami Polski*, 330–49, 369, 395–408, 431–34.

77. Lelewel, *Uwagi nad dziejami Polski*, 370–78.

78. Bobrzyński, *Dzieje Polski* (1986 ed.), 388–89.

79. Grün, *Kulturgeschichte des siebzehnten Jahrhunderts*, 1:289.

80. Menzel, *Germany from the Earliest Period*, 3:1340.

81. Jäger, *Deutsche Geschichte*, 2:10, 45, 57, 83.

82. Raumer, *Geschichte Europas*, 2:572–73, 618–19.

83. Wachsmuth, *Europäische Sittengeschichte*, 5 (pt. 1):289–94.

84. Raumer, *Geschichte Europas*, 1:586.

85. Heyck, *Deutsche Geschichte*, 3:320–23.

86. Stacke, *Deutsche Geschichte*, 2:503–4.

87. Jäger, *Deutsche Geschichte*, 2:53, 94–97, 120–25, 151.

88. Droysen, *Vorlesungen über das Zeitalter der Freiheitskriege*, 1:24–25.

89. Wachsmuth, *Europäische Sittengeschichte*, 5 (pt. 1):465.

90. Heyck, *Deutsche Geschichte*, 3:319.

91. Grün, *Kulturgeschichte des siebzehnten Jahrhunderts*, 1:296.

92. Jäger, *Deutsche Geschichte*, 2:59–61.

93. Stacke, *Deutsche Geschichte*, 2:504–5, 554–56.

94. Wachsmuth, *Europäische Sittengeschichte*, 5 (pt. 1):503.

95. Jastrow, *Geschichte des deutschen Einheitstraumes*, 83–88.

96. See, for example, Trevor Aston, ed., *Crisis in Europe 1560–1660: Essays from Past and Present* (London: Routledge & Kegan Paul, 1965); Geoffrey Parker and Lesley M. Smith, *The General Crisis of the Seventeenth Century* (London: Routledge & Kegan Paul, 1978); and Peter Clark, ed., *The European Crisis of the 1590s* (London: Allen and Unwin, 1985).

97. Konopczyński, "Pierwszy rozbiór," 213–14.

98. Szujski, *Dzieje Polski*, 4:137–38.

99. For more on this matter, see Larry Wolff, *Inventing Eastern Europe: The Map of Civilization on the Mind of the Enlightenment* (Stanford: Stanford University Press, 1994).

100. Bujak, "Siły gospodarcze," 105–6.

101. Bobrzyński, *Dzieje Polski* (1986 ed.), 430.

102. Władysław Smoleński, *Wiara w życiu społeczeństwa polskiego w epoce jezuickiej*, ed. Bohdan Baranowski (Warszawa: Ludowa Spółdzielnia Wydawnicza, 1951), 75.

103. Lelewel, *Uwagi nad dziejami Polski*, 307–11.

104. Lelewel, *Uwagi nad dziejami Polski*, 434–37.

105. Johannes Haller, *Die Epochen der deutschen Geschichte* (München: Paul List, 1956), 80.

106. Korzon, *Historia Polski*, 351.

107. Schmitt, *Dzieje Polski XVIII i XIX wieku*, 4 vols. (Lwów: Maniecki, 1868), 4:7.

108. Szujski, *Dzieje Polski*, 4:139, 400; Smoleński, *Dzieje narodu polskiego*, 301.

109. For more on Poniatowski, see Andrzej Zahorski, *Spór o Stanisława Augusta* (Warszawa: PIW, 1988), 151–300.

110. See, for example, *Deutsche Reichsgeschichte: Eine Darstellung der Verfassung des deutschen Volkes und Reiches von den ältesten Zeiten bis zur Neugestaltung Deutschlands im Jahre 1849* (Leipzig: Matthes, 1849), 71.

111. Johannes Janssen, *Geschichte des deutschen Volkes seit dem Ausgang des Mittelalters*, vol. 5, *Vorbereitung des dreissigjährigen Krieges* (Freiburg: Herder, 1924), 191–216.

112. Heyck, *Deutsche Geschichte*, 3:16–17, 240, 322.

113. Menzel, *Germany from the Earliest Period*, 3:1351–54.

114. Heyck, *Deutsche Geschichte*, 3:17.

115. Häusser, *Geschichte des Zeitalters der Reformation*, 295–97, 453.

116. C. A. Bonath, *Die deutsche Geschichte für Schulen und zum Selbstunterrichte* (Stendal: Franzen und Grosse, 1864), 159–61.

117. *Deutsche Reichsgeschichte*, 60.

118. Jäger, *Deutsche Geschichte*, 2:5, 31.

119. Lelewel, *Uwagi nad dziejami Polski*, 299–300.

120. Joachim Lelewel, *Obraz dziejów polskich* (Poznań: Żupański, 1857), 60–68.

121. Lelewel, *Uwagi nad dziejami Polski*, 437–40.

122. Karol Boromeusz Hoffman, *Historia reform politycznych w dawnej Polsce*, ed. Andrzej Wierzbicki (Warszawa: PIW, 1988), 150.

123. Bobrzyński, *Dzieje Polski* (1986 ed.), 334–36, 346–47.

124. Bobrzyński, *Dzieje Polski* (1986 ed.), 359.

125. Henryk Schmitt, *Dzieje narodu polskiego od najdawniejszych czasów, potocznie opowiedziane*, vol. 1 (Lwów: Ossolineum, 1863), 668.

126. Szujski, *Dzieje Polski*, 3:88–89, 245–47.

127. Bobrzyński, *Dzieje Polski* (1986 ed.), 431–433.

128. Smoleński, *Dzieje narodu polskiego*, 227–29.

129. Tadeusz Korzon, "Zamknięcie dziejów wewnętrznych za St. Augusta," in Korzon, *Odrodzenie w upadku*, 302.

130. Szujski, *Dzieje Polski*, 4:271–73.

131. Smoleński, *Wiara w życiu społeczeństwa polskiego*, 59–70.

132. Konopczyński, "Pierwszy rozbiór," 218–19; Kallenbach, "Siły Moralne i Umysłowe," 158–62.

133. Chołoniewski, *Duch dziejów Polski*, 82–89.

134. Heyck, *Deutsche Geschichte*, 3:369.

135. Heinrich von Treitschke, *Deutsche Geschichte im 19. Jahrhundert* (1928; Wiesbaden/Essen: Vollmer, Phaidon, 1997), 12.

136. Wachsmuth, *Europäische Sittengeschichte*, 5 (pt. 1):296.

137. Menzel, *Germany from the Earliest Period*, 3:1358.

138. Wachsmuth, *Europäische Sittengeschichte*, 5 (pt. 1):486–89.

139. Haller, *Die Epochen der deutschen Geschichte*, 148–49.

Chapter Four. It Is Never Too Late

1. Ludwig Stacke, *Deutsche Geschichte*, 3 vols. (Bielefeld/Leipzig: Velhagen & Klasing, 1881), 2:299.

2. Eduard Heyck, *Deutsche Geschichte*, 3 vols. (Bielefeld/Leipzig: Velhagen & Klasing, 1906), 3:239.

3. Heinrich von Treitschke, "Die Goldenen Tage von Weimar," in Treitschke, *Bilder aus der deutschen Geschichte* (Leipzig: Hirzel, 1908), 2:1–26.

4. Wilhelm Wachsmuth, *Europäische Sittengeschichte vom Ursprunge volksthümlicher Gestaltungen bis auf unsere Zeit*, 6 vols. (Leipzig: Vogel, 1831–39), 5 (pt. 1):490–503.

5. Oskar Jäger, *Deutsche Geschichte*, 2 vols. (München: Beck, 1909–10), 2:53–57; Heyck, *Deutsche Geschichte*, 3:336–38.

6. Józef Szujski, *Dzieje Polski*, vol. 4, *Królowie wolno obrani* (Lwów: Wild, 1866), 375–77.

7. Michał Bobrzyński, *Dzieje Polski w zarysie*, 2 vols. (Jerozolima: W Drodze, 1944), 2:257; Joachim Lelewel, *Panowanie króla Stanisława Augusta Poniatowskiego obejmujące trzy dziesięciolecia usilności narodu podźwignięcia się, ocalenia bytu i niepodległości*, in *Dzieła*, vol. 8, ed. Józef Dutkiewicz, Marian Henryk Serejski, and Helena Więckowska (Warszawa: PWN, 1961), 348–49.

8. Bobrzyński, *Dzieje Polski* (1944 ed.), 2:259–60.

9. Johann Gustav Droysen, *Geschichte der preussischen Politik*, 5 vols. (Leipzig: Veit, 1874), 5:5.

10. Droysen, *Geschichte der preussischen Politik*, 5:7–11.

11. Friedrich Meinecke, "Johann Gustav Droysen: Sein Briefwechsel und seine Geschichtsschreibung," in Meinecke, *Zur Geschichte der Geschichtsschreibung*, ed. Eberhard Kessel (München: Oldenbourg, 1968), 150–57.

12. Johann Gustav Droysen, *Vorlesungen über das Zeitalter der Freiheitskriege*, 2 vols. (Gotha: Perthes, 1886), 1:6–7.

13. Johann Gustav Droysen, *Geschichte der preussischen Politik*, 5 vols. (Berlin/Leipzig: Veit, 1857–74), 4:4–10.

14. Stacke, *Deutsche Geschichte*, 2:313–14.

15. Johann Jastrow, *Geschichte des deutschen Einheitstraumes und seiner Erfüllung* (Berlin: Allgemeiner Verein für deutsche Literatur, 1890), 154–59.

16. Jäger, *Deutsche Geschichte*, 2:38–40, 51.

17. Heyck, *Deutsche Geschichte*, 3:184–86.

18. Jäger, *Deutsche Geschichte*, 2:47–48.

19. Leopold von Ranke, *Preussische Geschichte* (Hamburg/Leipzig: Hoffmann & Campe, [1934]), 442.

20. Jäger, *Deutsche Geschichte*, 2:96–98.

21. Jastrow, *Geschichte des deutschen Einheitstraumes*, 175.

22. Johannes Haller, *Die Epochen der deutschen Geschichte* (München: Paul List, 1956), 162–65.

23. Ranke, *Preussische Geschichte*, 450.

24. Droysen, *Geschichte der preussischen Politik*, 5:485.

25. Haller, *Die Epochen der deutschen Geschichte*, 163.

26. Leopold von Ranke, *Aus zwei Jahrtausenden deutscher Geschichte*, ed. Gustav Roloff (Leipzig: Langewiesche, 1924), 241

27. Heyck, *Deutsche Geschichte*, 3:354.

28. Jastrow, *Geschichte des deutschen Einheitstraumes*, 101–10.

29. Haller, *Die Epochen der deutschen Geschichte*, 178–93.

30. Stacke, *Deutsche Geschichte*, 2:560–62, 608.

31. Henryk Schmitt, *Dzieje Polski XVIII i XIX wieku* [published as vol. 2 of the series Dzieje narodu polskiego], 4 vols. (Kraków/Lwów: Czas/Maniecki, 1866–68), 3:41.

32. Bobrzyński, *Dzieje Polski* (1944 ed.), 2:254

33. Szujski, *Dzieje Polski*, 4:396–397.

34. Władysław Smoleński, *Dzieje narodu polskiego* (Warszawa: Gebethner i Wolff, 1904), 301.

35. Stanisław Kutrzeba, "Siły państwowe," in *Przyczyny upadku Polski: Odczyty* (Kraków: Gebethner i Wolff, 1918), 131–32.

36. Lelewel, *Panowanie króla Stanisława Augusta Poniatowskiego*, 420–21.

37. Oswald Balzer, *Reformy społeczne i polityczne Konstytucji 3 Maja* (Kraków: Spółka Wydawnicza Polska, 1901), 77.

38. Balzer, *Reformy społeczne i polityczne*, 76–77.

39. Bobrzyński, *Dzieje Polski* (1944 ed.), 2:270.

40. See Aleksander Bocheński, *Dzieje głupoty w Polsce* (Warszawa: Czytelnik, 1988), 213–75.

41. Szujski, *Dzieje Polski*, 4:375–77.

42. Tadeusz Korzon, *Odrodzenie w upadku*, ed. Marian Henryk Serejski and Andrzej Feliks Grabski (Warszawa: PIW, 1975), 241–43.

43. Smoleński, *Dzieje narodu polskiego*, 339.

44. Korzon, *Odrodzenie w upadku*, 243; Tadeusz Korzon, *Wewnętrzne dzieje Polski za Stanisława Augusta*, 6 vols. (Kraków: PAU, 1897), 3:349–50.

45. Walerian Kalinka, *Sejm Czteroletni*, 2 vols. (Lwów: Seyfarth & Czajkowski, 1884), 2:242.

46. Bobrzyński, *Dzieje Polski* (1944 ed.), 2:253.

47. Kalinka, *Sejm Czteroletni*, 1:665–75.

48. Bobrzyński, *Dzieje Polski* (1944 ed.), 2:263.

49. Bobrzyński, *Dzieje Polski* (1944 ed.), 2:253–54, 264.

50. Kalinka, *Sejm Czteroletni*, 1:664–67.

51. Joachim Lelewel, *Obraz dziejów polskich* (Poznań: Żupański, 1857), 80–81.

Conclusion

1. Herbert Butterfield, *The Whig Interpretation of History* (London: Bell & Sons, 1951), 12–13.

2. Leopold von Ranke, *Historische Meisterwerke*, 24 vols. (Hamburg/Wien: Gutenberg, 1930), 4:447.

3. Günther List, "Historische Theorie und nationale Geschichte zwischen Frühliberalismus und Reichsgründung," in *Geschichtswissenschaft in Deutschland: Traditionelle Positionen und gegenwärtige Aufgaben*, ed. Bernd Faulenbach (München: Beck, 1974), 36.

4. Andrzej Feliks Grabski, *Metodologiczne problemy tzw. krakowskiej szkoły historycznej*, in *Orientacje polskiej myśli historycznej* (Warszawa: PWN, 1972), 301–40.

5. Rüsen cited in Erhard Wiersing, *Geschichte des historischen Denkens* (Paderborn: Schöningh, 2007), 385–88.

6. Bobrzyński cited in Marian Henryk Serejski, *Historycy o historii: Od Adama Narusze-wicza do Stanisława Kętrzyńskiego*, vol. 1, *1775–1918* (Warszawa: PWN, 1963), 159.

7. Władysław Smoleński, *Szkoły historyczne w Polsce: Główne kierunki poglądów na prz-eszłość*, ed. Marian Henryk Serejski (Wrocław: Ossolineum, 1952), 145.

8. Sybel cited in List, *Historische Theorie und nationale Geschichte*, 38–41.

9. See Hans Schleier, "Die Ranke-Renaissance," in *Studien über die deutsche Ges-chichtswissenschaft von der Reichseinigung von oben bis zur Befreiung Deutschlands vom Fas-chismus*, ed. Joachim Streisand (Berlin: Akademie Verlag, 1965), 2:111–13.

10. Friedrich Meinecke, "Erwiderung," *Historische Zeitschrift* 77 (1896): 262.

11. Schleier, "Die Ranke-Renaissance," 105–7.

12. Wacław Sobieski, "Historia a legenda," in *Trybun ludu szlacheckiego: Pisma history-czne*, ed. Konstanty Grzybowski (Warszawa: PIW, 1978), 377.

13. See Jolanta Kolbuszewska, *Mutacja modernistyczna w historiografii polskiej (przełom XIX i XX wieku)* (Łódź: Ibidem, 2005); and Jörn Rüsen, "Johann Gustav Droysen," in *Deut-sche Historiker*, ed. Hans-Ulrich Wehler (Göttingen: Vandenhoeck & Ruprecht, 1971), 2:7–23.

14. Hans Krause, "Die alldeutsche Geschichtsschreibung vor dem Ersten Weltkrieg," in *Studien über die deutsche Geschichtswissenschaft von der Reichseinigung von oben bis zur Befreiung Deutschlands vom Faschismus*, ed. Joachim Streisand (Berlin: Akademie Verlag, 1965), 2:207.

15. Jonathan F. Wagner, *Germany's 19th Century Cassandra: The Liberal Federalist Georg Gottfried Gervinus* (New York: Peter Lang, 1995), xii–xiii, 179–82.

16. See Herbert Butterfield, *The Englishman and His History* (Cambridge: Cambridge University Press, 1944), 1–11.

17. Erich Marcks, "Goethe und Bismarck," in *Männer und Zeiten* (Leipzig: Quelle & Meyer, 1913), 2:13.

18. See Eduard Fueter, *Geschichte der neueren Historiographie* (Zürich: Orell Fussli, 1985); Walter Goetz, *Die deutsche Geschichtsschreibung des letzten Jahrhunderts und die Na-tion* (Leipzig/Dresden: Teubner, 1919), 21–26.

19. Dieter Hertz-Eichenrode, "Die 'Neuere Geschichte' an der Berliner Universität: Historiker und Geschichtsschreibung im 19./20. Jahrhundert," in *Geschichtswissenschaft in Berlin im 19. und 20. Jahrhundert*, ed. Reimer Hansen and Wolfgang Ribbe (Berlin: Walter de Gruyter, 1992), 272.

20. See Wilfried Nippel, *Droysen: Ein Leben zwischen Wissenschaft und Politik* (München: Beck, 2008); Rüsen, "Johann Gustav Droysen"; Otto Hintze, "Johann Gustav Droysen," in *Soziologie und Geschichte: Gesammelte Abhandlungen zur Soziologie, Politik und Theorie der Geschichte*, ed. Gerhard Oestreich (Göttingen: Vandenhoeck & Ruprecht, 1964), 453–99; Friedrich Meinecke, "Johann Gustav Droysen: Sein Briefwechsel und sei-ne Geschichtsschreibung," in *Zur Geschichte der Geschichtsschreibung*, ed. Eberhard Kessel (München: Oldenbourg, 1968), 125–67.

21. See Georg G. Iggers, *The German Conception of History* (Middletown, CT: Wesleyan University Press, 1968).

22. See Christian Simon, *Historiographie* (Stuttgart: Ulmer, 1996), 127–34. For more on historicism as an intellectual and epistemological trend, see Frederick C. Beiser, *The German Historicist Tradition* (New York: Oxford University Press, 2011).

23. Ludwik Kubala, *Szkice historyczne*, 6 vols. (Warszawa/Lwów: Gebethner i Wolff / Altenberg, 1901–22), 1:306.

24. Adam Szelągowski, *Wzrost państwa polskiego w XVi XVI wieku: Polska na przełomie wieków średnich* (Lwów/Warszawa: Połoniecki / Wende, 1904), 1–2.

25. Arnaldo Momigliano, "On Causes of War in Ancient Historiography," in Momigliano, *Studies in Historiography* (London: Weidenfeld & Nicolson, 1966), 112–26.

26. John Stuart Mill, *Philosophy of Scientific Method*, ed. Ernst Nagel (New York: Hafner, 1950), 211–33.

27. Koselleck cited in Heinz-Gerhard Haupt and Jürgen Kocka, *Historischer Vergleich: Methoden, Aufgaben, Probleme; Eine Einleitung*, in Haupt and Kocka, *Geschichte und Vergleich* (New York: Campus, 1996), 9–46.

28. See Charles Tilly, *Big Structures, Large Processes, Huge Comparisons* (New York: Russell Sage Foundation, 1984), 80.

29. Rüsen cited in Wiersing, *Geschichte des historischen Denkens*, 385–88.

SELECTED BIBLIOGRAPHY

Primary Sources

Aegidi, Ludwig Karl. *Woher und Wohin? Ein Versuch die Geschichte Deutschlands zu verstehen.* Hamburg: Boyes & Geisler, 1866.

Balzer, Oswald. *Reformy społeczne i polityczne Konstytucji 3 Maja.* Kraków: Spółka Wydawnicza Polska, 1901.

Bałaban, Józef. *Historya Polski.* Lwów: Altenberg, 1908.

Bobrzyński, Michał. *Dzieje Polski w zarysie.* 2 vols. Jerozolima: W Drodze, 1944.

Bobrzyński, Michał. *Dzieje Polski w zarysie.* Edited by Marian Henryk Serejski and Andrzej Feliks Grabski. Warszawa: PIW, 1986.

Bonath, C. A. *Die deutsche Geschichte für Schulen und zum Selbstunterrichte.* Stendal: Franzen und Grosse, 1864.

Breysig, Kurt. *Kulturgeschichte der Neuzeit.* 2 vols. Berlin: Bondi, 1900–1901.

Bryce, James. *The Holy Roman Empire.* London: Macmillan, 1913.

Brzeski, Tadeusz. "Teorya przyczyn upadku Polski." *Kwartalnik Historyczny* 32 (1918): 173–240.

Chodakowski, Zorian Dołęga. *O Słowiańszczyźnie przed chrześcijaństwem oraz inne pisma i listy.* Edited by Julian Maślanka. Warszawa: PWN, 1967.

Chołoniewski, Antoni. *Duch dziejów Polski.* 1918. Warszawa: Ad astra, 2000.

Dahn, Felix. *Deutsche Geschichte.* Volume 1. Gotha: Pertes, 1883.

Deutsche Reichsgeschichte: Eine Darstellung der Verfassung des deutschen Volkes und Reiches von den ältesten Zeiten bis zur Neugestaltung Deutschlands im Jahre 1849. Leipzig: Matthes, 1849.

Döllinger, Johann von. "The Relation of the City of Rome to Germany in the Middle Ages." In *Studies in European History,* 58–79. Translated by Margaret Warre. London: J. Murray, 1890.

Droysen, Johann Gustav. *Geschichte der preussischen Politik.* 5 vols. Berlin/Leipzig: Veit, 1857–74.

Droysen, Johann Gustav. *Vorlesungen über das Zeitalter der Freiheitskriege.* 2 vols. Gotha: Perthes, 1886.

Fisher, Herbert. *The Medieval Empire.* 2 vols. London: Macmillan, 1898.

Freytag, Gustav. *Bilder aus der deutschen Vergangenheit*. 7 vols. Leipzig: Hirzel, 1913–15.

Gfrörer, August Friedrich. *Allgemeine Kirchengeschichte*. 4 vols. Stuttgart: Krabbe, 1841–46.

Giesebrecht, Wilhelm. *Geschichte der deutschen Kaiserzeit*. 6 vols. Leipzig: Duncker & Humblot, 1877–95.

Grün, Karl. *Kulturgeschichte des siebzehnten Jahrhunderts*. 2 vols. Leipzig: Barth, 1880.

Haller, Johannes. *Die Epochen der deutschen Geschichte*. München: Paul List, 1956.

Häusser, Ludwig. *Deutsche Geschichte vom Tode Friedrichs des Grossen bis zur Gründung des Deutschen Bundes*. 4 vols. Berlin: Weidmann, 1861–63.

Häusser, Ludwig. *Geschichte des Zeitalters der Reformation 1517–1648*. Edited by Wilhelm Oncken. Berlin: Weidmann, 1903.

Heyck, Eduard. *Deutsche Geschichte*. 3 vols. Bielefeld/Leipzig: Velhagen & Klasing, 1906.

Hoffman, Karol Boromeusz. *Historia reform politycznych w dawnej Polsce*. Edited by Andrzej Wierzbicki. Warszawa: PIW, 1988.

Jäger, Oskar. *Deutsche Geschichte*. 2 vols. München: Beck, 1909–10.

Janssen, Johannes. *Geschichte des deutschen Volkes seit dem Ausgang des Mittelalters*. 6 vols. Freiburg: Herder, 1924.

Jastrow, Johann. *Geschichte des deutschen Einheitstraumes und seiner Erfüllung*. Berlin: Allgemeiner Verein für deutsche Literatur, 1890.

Kaczkowski, Stanisław. *Krzyżacy i Polska: Wspomnienie historyczne*. Poznań: Żupański, 1845.

Kalinka, Walerian. *Ostatnie lata panowania Stanisława Augusta*. Kraków: Spółka Wyd. Polska, 1891.

Kalinka, Walerian. *Sejm Czteroletni*. 2 vols. Lwów: Seyfarth & Czajkowski, 1884.

Klopp, Onno. *Die gothaische Auffassung der deutschen Geschichte und der Nationalverein*. Hannover: Klindworth, 1862.

Koneczny, Feliks. *Dzieje Polski*. 2 vols. Łódź: Rozwój, 1902.

Konopczyński, Władysław. "O idei jagiellońskiej." In Konopczyński, *O wartość naszej spuścizny dziejowej: Wybór pism*, edited by Piotr Biliński, 316–34. Kraków: Ośrodek Myśli Politycznej, 2009.

Korzon, Tadeusz. *Historia Polski*. Edited by Bolesław Bator. Kijów: Rada Okręgowa, 1918.

Korzon, Tadeusz. *Odrodzenie w upadku*. Edited by Marian Henryk Serejski and Andrzej Feliks Grabski. Warszawa: PIW, 1975.

Korzon, Tadeusz. *Wewnętrzne dzieje Polski za Stanisława Augusta*. 6 vols. Kraków: PAU, 1897–98.

Kraszewski, Józef Ignacy. *Stara baśń: Powieść z XI wieku*, with *Dopisek* and *Dziejowe legendy*. Edited by Wincenty Danek. Wrocław: Ossolineum, 1975.

Kubala, Ludwik. *Szkice historyczne*. 6 vols. Warszawa/Lwów: Gebethner i Wolff / Altenberg, 1901–22.

Lamprecht, Karl. *Deutsche Geschichte*. 4 vols. Berlin/Freiburg: Heyfelder, 1902–4.

Lelewel, Joachim. *Dzieje Litwy i Rusi aż do unii z Polską w Lublinie 1569 zawartej.* Warszawa: PWN, 1969.

Lelewel, Joachim. *Historyka tudzież o łatwem i pozytecznem nauczaniu historii.* Wilno: Żółtkowski, 1815.

Lelewel, Joachim. *Obraz dziejów polskich.* Poznań: Żupański, 1857.

Lelewel, Joachim. *Panowanie króla Stanisława Augusta Poniatowskiego obejmujące trzy dziesięciolecia usilności narodu podźwignięcia się, ocalenia bytu i niepodległości.* In *Dzieła,* vol. 8, edited by Józef Dutkiewicz, Marian Henryk Serejski, and Helena Więckowska, 265–424. Warszawa: PWN, 1961.

Lelewel, Joachim. *Polska wieków średnich, czyli w dziejach narodowych polskich postrzeżenia.* Volume 2. Poznań: Kamieński i Ska, 1847.

Lelewel. Joachim. *Uwagi nad dziejami Polski i ludu jej.* Volume 3 of *Polska, dzieje i rzeczy jej.* Poznań: Żupański, 1855.

Leo, Heinrich. *Lehrbuch der Universalgeschichte.* 6 vols. Halle: Eduard Anton, 1841–50.

Leo, Heinrich. *Vorlesungen über die Geschichte des deutschen Volkes und Reiches.* 5 vols. Halle: Anton, 1854–1868.

Menzel, Wolfgang. *Geschichte der Deutschen bis auf die neuesten Tage.* 3 vols. Stuttgart: Kröner, 1872. Published in English as *Germany from the Earliest Period.* Translated by Mrs. George Horrocks. New York: P. F. Collier, 1900.

Niemcewicz, Julian Ursyn. *Śpiewy historyczne.* Warszawa: Drukarnia Rządowa, 1819; Lwów: Jabłoński, 1849.

Papée, Fryderyk. *Polska i Litwa na przełomie wieków średnich.* 2 vols. Kraków: AU, 1904.

Phillips, Walter Alison, James Wycliffe Headlam-Morley, and Arthur William Holland. *A Short History of Germany and Her Colonies (reproduced from the 11th edition of Encyclopedia Britannica).* London: Encyclopædia Britannica, 1914.

Prutz, Hans. *Staatengeschichte des Abendlandes im Mittelalter von Karl dem Grossen bis auf Maximilian.* 2 vols. Berlin: Grote, 1885–87.

Przyczyny upadku Polski: Odczyty. Kraków: Gebethner i Wolff, 1918.

Ranke, Leopold von. *Aus zwei Jahrtausenden deutscher Geschichte.* Edited by Gustav Roloff. Leipzig: Langewiesche, 1924.

Ranke, Leopold von. *Deutsche Geschichte im Zeitalter der Reformation.* 5 vols. Berlin: Duncker & Humblot, 1839–47.

Ranke, Leopold von. *Preussische Geschichte.* 6 vols. Hamburg/Leipzig: Hoffmann & Campe, 1934.

Ranke, Leopold von. *Weltgeschichte.* 8 vols. München/Leipzig: Duncker & Humblot, 1922.

Raumer, Friedrich von. *Geschichte Europas seit dem Ende des fünfzehnten Jahrhunderts.* 8 vols. Leipzig: Brockhaus, 1832–50.

Schmitt, Henryk. *Dzieje narodu polskiego od najdawniejszych czasów, potocznie opowiedziane.* Volume 1. Lwów: Ossolineum, 1863.

Schmitt, Henryk. *Dzieje Polski XVIII i XIX wieku* [published as volume 2 of the series Dzieje narodu polskiego], 4 vols. Kraków/Lwów: Czas/Maniecki, 1866–68.

Smoleński, Władysław. *Dzieje narodu polskiego*. Warszawa: Gebethner i Wolff, 1904.

Smoleński, Władysław. *Wiara w życiu społeczeństwa polskiego w epoce jezuickie*. Edited by Bohdan Baranowski. Warszawa: Ludowa Spółdzielnia Wydawnicza, 1951.

Smolka, Stanisław. *Rok 1386:* W pięciowiekową rocznicę. Kraków: Żupański & Heumann, 1886.

Sobieski, Wacław. "Historia a legenda." In *Trybun ludu szlacheckiego: Pisma historyczne*, edited by Konstanty Grzybowski, 372–88. Warszawa: PIW, 1978.

Stacke, Ludwig. *Deutsche Geschichte*. 3 vols. Bielefeld/Leipzig: Velhagen & Klasing, 1880–81.

Starczewski, Eugène. *L'Europe et la Pologne*. Paris: Perrin, 1913.

Sybel, Heinrich von. "Die christlich-germanische Staatslehre: Ihre Bedeutung in der Gegenwart, ihr Verhältnis zum historischen Christen- und Germanenthum." In Sybel, *Kleine historische Schriften*, 1:365–414. Stuttgart: Cotta, 1880.

Szajnocha, Karol. *Jadwiga i Jagiełło, 1374–1413: Opowiadanie historyczne*. Edited by Stefan M. Kuczyński and Maria Bokszczanin. 4 vols. Warszawa: PIW, 1974.

Szelągowski, Adam. *Wzrost państwa polskiego w XV i XVI wieku: Polska na przełomie wieków średnich*. Lwów/Warszawa: Połoniecki, Wende, 1904.

Szujski, Józef. *Dzieje Polski*. 4 vols. Lwów: Wild, 1862–66.

Szujski, Józef. *Historii polskiej treściwie opowiedzianych ksiąg dwanaście*. Warszawa: Berger, 1880.

Szujski, Józef. *O fałszywej historii jako mistrzyni fałszywej polityki: Rozprawy i artykuły*. Compiled and edited by Henryk Michalak. Warszawa: PIW, 1991.

Szujski, Józef. *O młodszości naszego cywilizacyjnego rozwoju szereg spostrzeżeń*. In *Dzieła*, ser. 2, vol. 7, 361–73. Kraków: Nakładem rodziny, 1888.

Szujski, Józef. "Z wykładów o dziejach cywilizacji polskiej." In *Dzieła*, ser. 2, vol. 7, 1–20. Kraków: published by the author, 1888.

Treitschke, Heinrich von. *Bilder aus der deutschen Geschichte*. 2 vols. Leipzig: Hirzel, 1908.

Treitschke, Heinrich von. *Deutsche Geschichte im 19. Jahrhundert*. 1928. Wiesbaden/Essen: Vollmer, Phaidon, 1997.

Universalstaat oder Nationalstaat: Macht und Ende des ersten deutschen Reiches; Die Streitschriften von Heinrich von Sybel und Julius Ficker zur deutschen Kaiserpolitik des Mittelalters. Edited by Friedrich Schneider. Innsbruck: Univ. Verl. Wagner, 1941.

Wachsmuth, Wilhelm. *Europäische Sittengeschichte vom Ursprunge volksthümlicher Gestaltungen bis auf unsere Zeit*. 6 vols. Leipzig: Vogel, 1831–39.

Wydenbrugk, Oskar von. *Die deutsche Nation und das Kaiserreich*. München: Fleischmann, 1862.

Secondary Literature Published before 1920

Below, Georg von. *Die deutsche Geschichtsschreibung von den Befreiungskriegen bis zu unseren Tagen*. Leipzig: Quelle & Mayer, 1916.

Croce, Benedetto. *Zur Theorie und Geschichte der Historiographie*. Translated by Enrico Pizzo. Tübingen: Mohr, 1915.

Dembiński, Bronisław. *Szujski i jego synteza dziejów*. Kraków: Akademia Umiejętności, 1908.

Feldman, Wilhelm. *Dzieje polskiej myśli politycznej, 1864–1914*. Warszawa: Instytut Badania Najnowszej Historii Polski, 1933.

Fueter, Eduard. *Geschichte der neueren Historiographie*. Zürich: Orell Fussli, 1985.

Gibbon, Edward. *The History of the Decline and Fall of the Roman Empire*. Volume 6. London: Strahan & Cadell, 1788.

Goetz, Walter. *Die deutsche Geschichtsschreibung des letzten Jahrhunderts und die Nation*. Leipzig/Dresden: Teubner, 1919.

Gooch, G. P. *History and Historians in the Nineteenth Century*. London: Longmans, Green, 1913.

Gregorovius, Ferdinand. *Geschichte der Stadt Rom im Mittelalter*. 8 vols. Dresden: Jess, 1926.

Guilland, Antoine. *Modern Germany and Her Historians*. London: Harold and Sons, 1915.

Hegel, Georg Wilhelm. *The Philosophy of History*. Translated by J. Sibree. Kitchener: Batoche Books, 2001.

Herder, Johann Gottfried. *Outlines of a Philosophy of the History of Man*. Translated by T. Churchill. New York: Bergman, 1966.

Kochanowski, Jan Karol. *Le développement de l'historiographie polonaise dans la seconde moitié du XIXe siècle*. Roma: Accademia die Lincei, 1906.

Lamprecht, Karl. *Alte und neue Richtungen in der Geschichtswissenschaft*. Berlin: Gaertner, 1896.

Łoziński, Władysław. *Życie polskie w dawnych wiekach*. Edited by Janusz Tazbir. Warszawa: Iskry, 2006.

Smoleński, Władysław. *Szkoły historyczne w Polsce: Główne kierunki poglądów na przeszłość*. Edited by Marian Henryk Serejski. Wrocław: Ossolineum, 1952.

More Recent Secondary Literature

Adam Naruszewicz i historiografia Oświecenia. Edited by Kazimierz Bartkiewicz. Warszawa: Verbum, 1998.

Adamus, Jan. *Monarchizm i republikanizm w syntezie dziejów Polski*. Łódź: Ossolineum, 1961.

Adamus, Jan. *O syntezach historycznych Szujskiego: Szkic z dziejów polskiej myśli historycznej.* Warszawa: Komitet, 1938.

Aston, Trevor. *Crisis in Europe 1560–1660: Essays from Past and Present.* London: Routledge & Kegan Paul, 1965.

Baár, Monika. *Historians and Nationalism: East-Central Europe in the Nineteenth Century.* New York: Oxford University Press, 2010.

Bahners, Patrick. "National Unification and Narrative Unity: The Case of Ranke's German History." In *Writing National Histories: Western Europe since 1800,* edited by Stefan Berger, Mark Donovan, and Kevin Passmore, 57–68. New York: Routledge, 1999.

Beiser, Frederick C. *The German Historicist Tradition.* New York: Oxford University Press, 2011.

Berding, Helmut. "Leopold von Ranke." In *Deutsche Historiker,* volume 1, edited by Hans Ulrich Wehler, 7–24. Göttingen: Vandenhoeck & Ruprecht, 1971.

Blanke, Horst Walter. *Historiographiegeschichte als Historik.* Stuttgart: Bad Cannstatt, 1991.

Bobińska, Celina, ed. *Spór o historyczną szkołę krakowską.* Kraków: Wyd. Literackie, 1972.

Bocheński, Aleksander. *Dzieje głupoty w Polsce.* Warszawa: Czytelnik, 1988.

Bömelburg, Hans-Jürgen. "Die Tradition einer multinationalen Reichsgeschichte in Mitteleuropa: Historiographische Konzepte gegenüber Altem Reich und Polen-Litauen sowie komparatistische Perspektiven." *Zeitschrift für Ostmitteleuropaforschung* 53, no. 3 (2004): 318–50.

Bömelburg, Hans-Jürgen. "Oskar Halecki i historiografia niemieckojęzyczna." In *Oskar Halecki i jego wizja Europy,* edited by Małgorzata Dąbrowska, 208–22. Warszawa/ Łódź: IPN, 2012.

Bömelburg, Hans-Jürgen. *(Pierwsza) Rzesza & Rzeczpospolita (Obojga Narodów): Pochwała różnorodności i opowieść o upadku.* In *Polsko-niemieckie miejsca pamięci,* edited by Hans-Henning Hahn and Robert Traba, 25–40. Warszawa: Scholar, 2012.

Brechenmacher, Thomas. *Grossdeutsche Geschichtsschreibung im neunzehnten Jahrhundert: Die erste Generation (1830–1848).* Berlin: Duncker & Humblot, 1996.

Brechenmacher, Thomas. "Wie viel Gegenwart verträgt historisch urteilen? Die Kontroverse zwischen Heinrich von Sybel und Julius Ficker über die Bewertung der Kaiserpolitik des Mittelalters (1859–1862)." In *Historische Debatten und Kontroversen im 19. und 20. Jahrhundert,* edited by Jürgen Elvert and Susanne Kranz, 35–54. Wiesbaden: Steiner, 2003.

Breisach, Ernst. *Historiography: Ancient, Medieval, and Modern.* Chicago: University of Chicago Press, 1983.

Brock, Peter, John Stanley, and Piotr Wróbel, eds. *Nation and History: Polish Historians from Enlightenment to the Second World War.* Toronto: University of Toronto Press, 2006.

Bronowski, Franciszek. *Idea gminowładztwa w polskiej historiografii (Geneza i formowanie się syntezy republikańskiej Joachima Lelewela).* Łódź: Łódzkie Tow. Naukowe, 1969.

Burke, Peter. "The Idea of Decline from Bruni to Gibbon." In *Edward Gibbon and the Decline and Fall of the Roman Empire*, edited by G. W. Browersock, John Clive, and Stephen R. Granbard, 87–102. Cambridge, MA: Harvard University. Press, 1977.

Burrow, John. *A History of Histories*. New York: Allan Lane / Penguin Books, 2008.

Butterfield, Herbert. *The Englishman and His History*. Cambridge: Cambridge University Press, 1944.

Butterfield, Herbert. *The Whig Interpretation of History*. London: Bell & Sons, 1931.

Cegielski, Tadeusz. *Das Alte Reich und die erste Teilung Polens 1768–1774*. Edited by Karl Otmar Aretin. Translated by Włodzimierz Borodziej and Michael G. Müller. Stuttgart: Franz Steiner Verlag; Warszawa: PWN, 1988.

Certeau, Michel de. *L'Écriture de l'histoire*. Paris: Gallimard, 1975.

Chaunu, Pierre. *Histoire et décadence*. Paris: Perrin, 1981.

Chickering, Roger. *Karl Lamprecht: A German Academic Life (1856–1914)*. Atlantic Highlands, NJ: Humanities Press, 1993.

Chickering, Roger. *We Men Who Feel Most German: A Cultural Study of the Pan-German League (1886–1914)*. Boston: Allen & Unwin, 1984.

Clark, Peter, ed. *The European Crisis of the 1590s*. London: Allen and Unwin, 1985.

Crossley, Ceri. "History as a Principle of Legitimation in France (1820–48)." In *Writing National Histories: Western Europe since 1800*, edited by Stefan Berger, Mark Donovan, and Kevin Passmore, 49–56. New York: Routledge, 1999.

Deletant, Dennis, and Harry Hanak, eds. *Historians as Nation Builders in Central and South-Eastern Europe*. London: Macmillan, 1988.

Demandt, Alexander. *Zeit und Unzeit: Geschichtsphilosophische Essays*. Köln/Wien: Böhlau, 2002.

Dembiński, Bogusław, Oskar Halecki, and Marceli Handelsman. *L'historiographie polonaise du XIX-me et du XX-me siècle*. Varsovie, 1933.

Dickens, Arthur G., John M. Tonkin, and Kenneth Powell. *The Reformation in Historical Thought*. London: Blackwell, 1985.

Dutkiewicz, Józef. *Zarys historii historiografii polskiej*. Volume 3, *1900–1939*. Warszawa: PWN, 1959.

Faulenbach, Bernd. *Die Ideologie des deutschen Weges: Die deutsche Geschichte in der Historiographie zwischen Kaiserreich und Nationalsozialismus*. München: Beck, 1980.

Geiss, Immanuel. *Geschichte des Rassismus*. Frankfurt: Suhrkamp, 1988.

Gollwitzer, Heinz. "Zum politischen Germanismus des 19. Jahrhunderts." In *Festschrift für Hermann Heimpel zum 70. Geburtstag am 19. September 1971*, 282–356. Göttingen: Max Planck Institut für Geschichte, 1971.

Górka, Olgierd. *Optymizm i pesymizm w historiografii polskiej: Odwrócenie pojęć*. Lwów: Ossolineum, 1936.

Grabski, Andrzej Feliks. "Die polnische und die deutsche Historiographie in die zweiten Hälfte des 19. Jahrhunderts." *Jahrbuch für Geschichte der sozialistischen Länder Europas* 32 (1988): 187–201.

Grabski, Andrzej Feliks. *Dzieje historiografii.* With an introduction by Rafał Stobiecki. Poznań: Wyd. Poznańskie, 2003.

Grabski, Andrzej Feliks. *Orientacje polskiej myśli historycznej.* Warszawa: PWN, 1972.

Grabski, Andrzej F. "Warszawska szkoła historyczna: Próba charakterystyki." In *Polska myśl filozoficzna i społeczna*, volume 2, edited by Barbara Skarga, 456–534. Warszawa: Książka i Wiedza, 1975.

Grzybowski, Konstanty. "Szkoła historyczna krakowska." In *Polska myśl filozoficzna i społeczna*, volume 2, edited by Barbara Skarga, 535–92. Warszawa: Książka i Wiedza, 1975).

Hackmann, Jörg. "German East or Polish West? Historiographical Discourses on the German–Polish Overlap between Confrontation and Reconciliation, 1772–2000." In *Disputed Territories and Shared Pasts: Overlapping National Histories in Modern Europe*, edited by Tibor Frank and Frank Halder. Basingstoke: Palgrave Macmillan, 2011.

Hardtwig, Wolfgang, and Erhard Schütz, eds. *Geschichte für Leser: Populäre Geschichtsschreibung in Deutschland im 20. Jarhhundert.* Stuttgart: Franz Steiner, 2005.

Haupt Heinz-Gerhard, and Jürgen Kocka. "Historischer Vergleich: Methoden, Aufgaben, Probleme; Eine Einleitung." In *Geschichte und Vergleich*, edited by Haupt and Kocka, 9–46. New York: Campus, 1996.

Hertz-Eichenrode, Dieter. "Die 'Neuere Geschichte' an der Berliner Universität: Historiker und Geschichtsschreibung im 19./20. Jahrhundert." In *Geschichtswissenschaft in Berlin im 19. und 20. Jahrhundert*, edited by Reimer Hansen and Wolfgang Ribbe, 261–322. Berlin: Walter de Gruyter, 1992.

Hintze, Otto. "Johann Gustav Droysen." In Hintze, *Soziologie und Geschichte: Gesammelte Abhandlungen zur Soziologie, Politik und Theorie der Geschichte*, edited by Gerhard Oestreich, 453–99. Göttingen: Vandenhoeck & Ruprecht, 1964.

Hintze, Otto. *Staat und Verfassung: Gesammelte Abhandlungen zur allgemeinen Verfassungsgeschichte.* Göttingen: Vandenhoeck & Ruprecht, 1970.

Hostenkamp, Heinrich. *Die mittelalterliche Kaiserpolitik in der deutschen Historiographie seit v. Sybel und Ficker.* Berlin: Ebering, 1934.

Iggers, Georg G. *The German Conception of History.* Middletown, CT: Wesleyan University Press, 1968.

Iggers, Georg G. "The Intellectual Foundations of Nineteenth-Century 'Scientific' History: The German Model." In *The Oxford History of Historical Writing*, volume 4, edited by Stuart Macintyre, Juan Maiguashca, and Atilla Pók, 41–58. Oxford: Oxford University Press, 2011.

Jaeger, Friedrich, and Jörn Rüsen. *Geschichte des Historismus: Eine Einführung.* München: Beck, 1992.

Janion, Maria. *Niesamowita Słowiańszczyzna.* Kraków: Wyd. Literackie, 2006.

Janowski, Maciej. "Mirrors for the Nation: Imagining the National Past among the Poles and the Czechs in Nineteenth and Twentieth Centuries." In *The Contested Nation:*

Ethnicity, Class, Religion and Gender in National Histories, edited by Stefan Berger and Chris Lorenz, 442–62. Basingstoke: Palgrave Macmillan, 2011.

Jedin, Hubert. *Katholische Reformation oder Gegenreformation? Ein Versuch zur Klärung der Begriffe*. Luzern: Stocker, 1946.

Jedlicki, Jerzy. *Jakiej cywilizacji Polacy potrzebują*. Warszawa: PIW, 2002.

Julkowska, Violetta. *Retoryka w narracji historycznej Joachima Lelewela*. Poznań: Wyd. UAM, 1998.

Kaute, Wojciech. *Synteza dziejów Polski Michała Bobrzyńskiego*. Katowice: Wyd. UŚ, 1993.

Kipper, Reiner. *Der Germanenmythos im Deutschen Kaiserreich: Formen und Funktionen historischer Selbstthematisierung*. Göttingen: Vandenhoeck & Ruprecht, 2002.

Kirchner, Horst. *Das germanische Altertum in der deutschen Geschichtsschreibung des 18. Jahrhunderts*. Berlin: Ebering, 1938.

Klopp, Wiard von. *Onno Klopp: Leben und Wirken*. Edited by Franz von Schnabel. München: Schnell & Steiner, 1950.

Kobylińska, Ewa, Andreas Lawaty, and Rüdiger Stephan, eds. *Polacy i Niemcy: Sto kluczowych pojęć*. Warszawa: Więź, 1996.

Kolbuszewska, Jolanta. *Mutacja modernistyczna w historiografii polskiej (przełom XIX i XX wieku)*. Łódź: Ibidem, 2005.

Koselleck, Reinhart. *Futures Past: On the Semantics of Historical Time*. Translated by K. Tribe. Cambridge, MA: MIT Press, 1985.

Kożuchowski, Adam. "Contesting Conquests: Nineteenth-Century German and Polish Historiography of the Expansion of the Holy Roman Empire and the Polish-Lithuanian Commonwealth." *History of European Ideas* 41 (2015): 404–18.

Krapf, Ludwig. *Germanenmythos und Reichsideologie: Frühhumanistische Rezeptionsweisen der Taciteischen "Germania."* Tübingen: Niemeyer, 1979.

Krause, Hans. "Die alldeutsche Geschichtsschreibung vor dem Ersten Weltkrieg." In *Studien über die deutsche Geschichtswissenschaft von der Reichseinigung von oben bis zur Befreiung Deutschlands vom Faschismus*, edited by Joachim Streisand, 2:190–226. Berlin: Akademie Verlag, 1965.

Kraushar, Aleksander. *Rozwój dziejopisarstwa nowoczesnego polskiego*. Warszawa: Łazarski, 1928.

Lawaty, Andreas. "Zur romantischen Konzeption des Politischen: Polen und Deutsche unter fremder Herrschaft." In *Romantik und Geschichte: Polnisches Paradigma, europäischer Kontext, deutsch-polnische Perpektive*, edited by Alfred Gall, Thomas Grob, Andreas Lawaty, and German Ritz, 21–59. Wiesbaden: Harrassowitz, 2007.

Lenhard-Schramm, Niklas. *Konstrukteure der Nation: Geschichtsprofessoren als politische Akteure in Vormärz und Revolution 1848/49*. Münster: Waxmann, 2014.

List, Günther. "Historische Theorie und nationale Geschichte zwischen Frühliberalismus und Reichsgründung." In *Geschichtswissenschaft in Deutschland: Traditionelle Positio-*

nen und gegenwärtige Aufgaben, edited by Bernd Faulenbach, 35–53. München: Beck, 1974.

Malicki, Jan. *Mity narodowe: Lechiada*. Wrocław: Ossolineum, 1981.

Maślanka, Jan. *Słowiańskie mity historyczne w literaturze polskiego Oświecenia*. Wrocław: Ossolineum, 1968.

Maternicki, Jerzy. *Józef Szujski wobec tzw. idei jagiellońskiej*. In *Historia XIX i XX wieku: Studia i szkice*, edited by Andrzej Garlicki, Józef Ryszard Szaflik, and Marian Wojciechowski, 41–55. Wrocław: Ossolineum, 1979.

Maternicki, Jerzy. *Walerian Kalinka (1826–1886) i jego badania nad epoką porozbiorową*. Rzeszów: Wyd. URz, 2013.

Maternicki, Jerzy. *Warszawskie środowisko historyczne 1832–1869*. Warszawa: PWN, 1970.

Maternicki, Jerzy. *Wielokształtność historii: Rozważania o kulturze historycznej i badaniach historiograficznych*. Warszawa: PWN, 1990.

Meinecke, Friedrich. *Die Entstehung des Historismus*. 2 vols. München: Oldenbourg, 1936.

Meinecke, Friedrich. "Johann Gustav Droysen: Sein Briefwechsel und seine Geschichtsschreibung." In Meinecke, *Zur Geschichte der Geschichtsschreibung*, edited by Eberhard Kessel, 125–67. München: Oldenbourg, 1968.

Melman, Billie. "Claiming the Nation's Past: The Invention of an Anglo-Saxon Tradition." *Journal of Contemporary History* 26, no. 3–4 (1991): 575–95.

Momigliano, Arnaldo. "On Causes of War in Ancient Historiography." In Momigliano, *Studies in Historiography*, 112–26. London: Weidenfeld & Nicolson, 1966.

Mommsen, Wolfgang. "Deutsche Geschichtsschreibung im 19. Jahrhundert." In *Geschichte und Geschichtswissenschaft in der Kultur Italiens und Deutschlands*, edited by Arnold Esch and Jens Petersen, 70–107. Tübingen: Niemeyer, 1989.

Müller, Michael G. "Koniec dwu republik: Rozbiory Polski i rozpad dawnej Rzeszy." In *Polacy i Niemcy: Historia, kultura, polityka*, edited by Andreas Lawaty and Hubert Orłowski, 51–57. Poznań: Wyd. Poznańskie, 2003.

Müller, Michael G. "Republicanism versus Monarchy? Government by Estates in Poland-Lithuania and the Holy Roman Empire: Sixteenth to Eighteenth Centuries." In *Historical Concepts between Eastern and Western Europe*, edited by Manfred Hildemeier, 36–47. New York: Berghahn Books, 2007.

Nippel, Wilfried. *Droysen: Ein Leben zwischen Wissenschaft und Politik*. Munich: Beck, 2008.

Parker, Geoffrey, and Lesley M. Smith. *The General Crisis of the Seventeenth Century*. London: Routledge & Kegan Paul, 1978.

Poliakov, Léon. *Der Arische Mythos: Zu den Quellen von Rassismus und Nationalismus*. Hamburg: Junius, 1993.

Prüscher, Uwe. "Reichsromantik: Erinnerungen an das Alte Reich zwischen den Freiheitskriegen von 1813–14 und den Revolutionen von 1848–49." In *Heiliges Römisches Reich*

Deutscher Nation 962 bis 1806, edited by Hans Ottomeyer, Jutta Götzmann, Ansgar Reiss, Heinz Schilling, and Werner Heun, 319–27. Dresden: Sandstein Verlag, 2006.

Przybylski, Ryszard. *Klasycyzm czyli prawdziwy koniec Królestwa Polskiego*. Gdańsk: Marabut, 1996.

Raphael, Lutz, and Ilaria Porciani, eds. *Atlas of European Historiography: The Making of a Profession, 1800–2005*. London: Palgrave Macmillan, 2010.

Rutkowska, Neomisia. *Bishop Adam Naruszewicz and His "History of the Polish Nation": A Critical Study*. Washington, DC: Catholic University of America Press, 1941.

Rüsen, Jörn. "Johann Gustav Droysen." In *Deutsche Historiker*, edited by Hans-Ulrich Wehler, 2:7–23. Göttingen: Vandenhoeck & Ruprecht, 1971.

Samtleben, Wolfgang. *Die Idee einer altgermanischen Volksfreiheit im vormärzlichen deutschen Liberalismus*. Hamburg: Evert, 1935.

Schieblich, Walter. *Die Auffassung des mittelalterlichen Kaisertums in der deutschen Geschichtsschreibung von Leibniz bis Giesebrecht*. Berlin: Ebering, 1932.

Schilling, Heinz, and Wolfgang Reinhard, eds. *Die Katholische Konfessionalisierung*. Münster/Gütersloh: Aschendorf, Gütersloher Verl.-Haus, 1995.

Schivelbusch, Wolfgang. *Die Kultur der Niederlage*. Berlin: Alexander Fest, 2001.

Schleier, Hans. "Die Ranke Renaissance." In *Studien über die deutsche Geschichtswissenschaft von der Reichseinigung von oben bis zur Befreiung Deutschlands vom Faschismus*, edited by Joachim Streisand, 2:99–135. Berlin: Akademie Verlag, 1965.

Schleier, Hans. *Geschichte der deutschen Kulturgeschichtsschreibung*. Waltrop: Spenner, 2003.

Schulin, Ernst. "Universalgeschichte und Nationalgeschichte bei Leopold von Ranke." In *Leopold von Ranke und die moderne Geschichtswissenschaft*, edited by Wolfgang J. Mommsen, 37–71. Stuttgart: Klett-Cotta, 1988.

See, Klaus von. *Deutsche Germanen-Ideologie: Vom Humanismus bis zur Gegenwart*. Frankfurt: Athenäum-Verl., 1970.

Serczyk, Jerzy. *25 wieków historii: Historycy i ich dzieła*. Toruń: Wyd. UMK, 1994.

Serejski, Marian Henryk. *Naród a państwo w polskiej myśli historycznej*. Warszawa: PIW, 1977.

Serejski, Marian Henryk. *Zarys historii historiografii polskiej*. 2 vols. Warszawa: PWN, 1954–56.

Serejski, Marian Henryk. "Z zagadnień genezy państwa polskiego w historiografii (o tzw. teorii podboju)." *Kwartalnik Historyczny* 60, no. 3 (1953): 147–63.

Simon, Christian. *Historiographie*. Stuttgart: Ulmer, 1996.

Skurnowicz, Joan. *Romantic Nationalism and Liberalism: Joachim Lelewel and the Polish National Idea*. New York: Columbia University Press, 1981.

Słoczyński, Henryk Marek. *Światło w dziejarskiej ciemnicy: Koncepcja dziejów i interpretacja przeszłości Polski Joachima Lelewela*. Kraków: Wyd. Uniw. Jagiellońskiego, 2010.

Steinberg, Hans Josef. "Lamprecht." In *Deutsche Historiker*, volume 1, edited by Hans Ulrich Wehler, 58–68. Göttingen: Vandenhoeck & Ruprecht, 1971.

Stern, Fritz, ed. *The Varieties of History: From Voltaire to the Present*. London: Macmillan, 1970.

Stuchtey, Benedikt. "Literature, Liberty and the Life of the Nation: British Historiography from Macaulay to Trevelyan." In *Writing National Histories: Western Europe since 1800*, edited by Stefan Berger, Mark Donovan, and Kevin Passmore, 30–46. New York: Routledge, 1999.

Surynt, Izabela. *Postęp, kultura i kolonializm: Polska a niemiecki projekt europejskiego Wschodu w dyskursach publicznych XIX wieku*. Wrocław: Atut, 2006.

Thamer, Hans Ulrich. "Das Heilige Römische Reich als politisches Argument im 19. und 20. Jahrhundert." In *Heiliges Römisches Reich Deutscher Nation 962 bis 1806*, edited by Hans Ottomeyer, Jutta Götzmann, Ansgar Reiss, Heinz Schilling, and Werner Heun, 383–95. Dresden: Sandstein Verlag, 2006.

Tilly, Charles. *Big Structures, Large Processes, Huge Comparisons*. New York: Russell Sage Foundation, 1984.

Toynbee, Arnold J. *The Study of History*. Abridgement by D. C. Somervell. Oxford: Oxford University Press, 1947.

Troeltsch, Ernst. *Historismus und seine Probleme*. Tübingen: Mohr, 1922.

Ulewicz, Tadeusz. Świadomość słowiańska Jana Kochanowskiego: *Z zagadnień psychiki polskiego renesansu*. Kraków: Seminarium Historii Literatury Polskiej UJ, 1948.

Wagner, Jonathan F. *Germany's 19th Century Cassandra: The Liberal Federalist Georg Gottfried Gervinus*. New York: Peter Lang, 1995.

Walbank, Frank. "The Idea of Decline in Polybius." In *Niedergang: Studien zu einem historischen Thema*, edited by Reinhart Koselleck and Paul Widmer, 41–58. Stuttgart: Klein-Cotta, 1980.

Walicki, Ryszard. "Wacław Maciejowski i Zorian Dołęga Chodakowski: Studium z dziejów Słowianofilstwa polskiego." *Archiwum Historii Filozofii i Myśli Społecznej* 13 (1967): 271–301.

Whaley, Joachim. *Germany and the Holy Roman Empire*. 2 vols. Oxford: Oxford University Press, 2012.

Wiersing, Erhard. *Geschichte des historischen Denkens*. Paderborn: Schöningh, 2007.

Wierzbicka, Maria. *Dawne syntezy dziejów Polski: rozwój i przemiany koncepcji metodologicznych*. Wrocław: Ossolineum, 1974.

Wierzbicka, Maria. *Władysław Smoleński*. Warszawa: PWN, 1980.

Wierzbicki, Andrzej. *Historiografia polska doby romantyzmu*. Wrocław: Ossolineum, 1999.

Wierzbicki, Andrzej. *Spory o polską duszę: Z zagadnień charakterologii narodowej w historiografii polskiej XIX i XX wieku*. Warszawa: IH PAN, 1993.

Wierzbicki, Andrzej. *Wschód-Zachód w koncepcjach dziejów Polski. Z dziejów polskiej myśli historycznej w dobie porozbiorowej*. Warszawa: PIW, 1984.

Winkler, Heinrich August, ed. *Griff nach der Deutungsmacht. Zur Geschichte der Geschichtspolitik in Deutschland.* Göttingen: Wallstein, 2004.

Witkowska, Alina. *Sławianie, my lubim sielanki.* Warszawa: PIW, 1972.

Witkowski, Michał. *W kręgu "śpiewów historycznych" Niemcewicza.* Poznań: Wyd. UAM, 1979.

Wittkau, Annette. *Historismus: Zur Geschichte des Begriffs und des Problems.* Göttingen: Vandenhoeck & Ruprecht, 1992.

Zahorski, Andrzej. *Spór o Stanisława Augusta.* Warszawa: PIW, 1988.

Zernack, Klaus. *Niemcy–Polska: Z dziejów trudnego dialogu historiograficznego.* Edited by Henryk Olszewski. Translated by Łukasz Musiał. Poznań: Wyd. Poznańskie, 2006.

Ziffer, Bernard. *Poland: History and Historians; Three Bibliographical Essays.* New York: Mid-European Studies Center, 1952.

INDEX